# Slaves, Freedmen, and Indentured Laborers in Colonial Mauritius

In this ground-breaking social and economic history of Mauritius, Richard Allen highlights the important role of domestic capital in shaping the island's development between its settlement by French colonists in 1721 and the beginning of modern political life in 1936. He describes the relationship between the local sugar industry and different elements in colonial Mauritian society – slaves, free persons of color, ex-apprentices, and East Indian indentured laborers – and shows how demographic change, changing world markets, local institutions, and local dependence upon domestic capital reshaped these relationships during the nineteenth and early twentieth centuries. Based upon extensive archival research in Mauritius and elsewhere, and thoroughly attuned to current scholarship on colonial plantation systems, this book raises questions that will be of concern to anyone interested in the comparative study of slavery and plantation societies and economies.

RICHARD ALLEN received his doctorate from the University of Illinois at Urbana-Champaign. He has published articles in a number of scholarly journals and encyclopaedias.

*African Studies Series 99*

*A list of books in this series will be found at the end of this volume*

# Slaves, Freedmen, and Indentured Laborers in Colonial Mauritius

Richard B. Allen

**CAMBRIDGE**
UNIVERSITY PRESS

PUBLISHED BY THE PRESS SYNDICATE OF THE UNIVERSITY OF CAMBRIDGE
The Pitt Building, Trumpington Street, Cambridge, United Kingdom

CAMBRIDGE UNIVERSITY PRESS

The Edinburgh Building, Cambridge CB2 2RU, UK    http://www.cup.cam.ac.uk
40 West 20th Street, New York, NY 10011–4211, USA    http://www.cup.org
10 Stamford Road, Oakleigh, Melbourne 3166, Australia

First published 1999

Printed in the United Kingdom at the University Press, Cambridge

Typeset in Times [CE]

*A catalogue record for this book is available from the British Library*

ISBN 0 521 64125 X hardback

For my parents

# Contents

# Maps

# Tables

# Preface

The arrival in 1721 of a small group of French colonists on the Ile de France marks the beginning of the modern Mauritian experience. Various facets of that experience have been the subject of interest to British, French, Mauritian, and other historians. However, despite a substantial body of scholarship on topics such as the island's maritime history during the eighteenth century and Indian immigration during the nineteenth century, many aspects of Mauritius' social and economic history, and of the history of its Creole and Indo-Mauritian inhabitants in particular, have yet to be described in any detail, discussed within a comprehensive analytical framework, or assessed in light of the scholarship on plantation systems elsewhere in the colonial world. This study seeks to fill some of these historiographical lacunae.

This book is the product of a long-standing interest in the peoples, cultures, and history of the Indian Ocean basin, and was made possible by a Fulbright African Regional Research Award which permitted me to return to Mauritius in 1992–93 where I once again enjoyed the support of the Mahatma Gandhi Institute. Sections of the book are substantially revised and expanded versions of articles published originally in *Slavery and Abolition*, *The Journal of Imperial and Commonwealth History*, and *Itinerario*. Table 13 first appeared in *Slavery and Abolition* (vol. 10, no. 2, p. 139) and is reprinted here with the kind permission of Frank Cass & Co., Ltd.

Over the years, my research has been facilitated by the generous assistance of the staffs at the Mauritius Archives, the Mahatma Gandhi Institute, the Mauritius Chamber of Agriculture, the Carnegie Library in Curepipe, the Centre des Archives d'Outre-Mer, the Public Record Office, the British Library, the India Office Library, the United Society for the Propagation of the Gospel, the School of Oriental and African Studies, the Library of the London School of Economics, the Library of the University of Illinois at Urbana-Champaign, the Library of Congress, and the New York Public Library. A special note of thanks is due to Roland Chung and Vishwanaden Govinden for their unstinting help and good humor.

Thanks are also due to family, friends, and colleagues for their assistance, encouragement, and support over the years. Lynn Campbell, stalwart soul that he is, read the draft manuscript in its entirety and offered much appreciated comments and suggestions on matters of style, organization, and some of the finer points of my argument. Marina Carter not only shared the fruits of her own research on many occasions, but also provided me with a manuscript copy of her *Servants, Sirdars, and Settlers* well before it appeared in print. Bill Storey and Martha Keber both alerted me to important series of documents and passed along information and insights generated by their own work. In addition to offering me their warm hospitality, Raj and Mira Boodhoo and Prem and Vasanti Saddul helped me to savor more fully the richness of life on the Ile Maurice. I have long been privileged to count Huguette Ly-Tio-Fane Pineo and Madeleine Ly-Tio-Fane among my valued friends and colleagues, and their many kindnesses, both personal and professional, have helped to make this book possible. Besides offering me a place to hang my hat and write during the periodic dry spells that have been an integral part of life on the "gypsy circuit" in the modern academic world, Ken Strickler has been the source of much good company and moral support at times when both were needed. Lastly, I am deeply indebted to my parents. They know all the reasons why, and this book is dedicated to them as a small token of my appreciation for all they have done to make it possible.

# Abbreviations

| | |
|---|---|
| AIR | Colony of Mauritius – annual report of the Protector of Immigrants/Immigration Department |
| AR | Colony of Mauritius – annual report on the colony's condition |
| BB | Colony of Mauritius – Blue Book |
| BL | British Library |
| CAOM | Centre des Archives d'Outre-Mer |
| Census | Printed census of Mauritius and its dependencies |
| CL | Carnegie Library |
| CO | Colonial Office |
| CWM | Archives of the Council for World Mission |
| DBM | *Dictionnaire de biographie mauricien* |
| FSM | *Financial Situation of Mauritius. Report of a Commission Appointed by the Secretary of State for the Colonies, December, 1931* (PP 1931–32 VII [Cmd. 4034]) |
| GSB | Colony of Mauritius – annual report on the Government Savings Bank |
| IOL | India Office Library |
| MA | Mauritius Archives |
| MCA | Mauritius Chamber of Agriculture – annual report |
| MGI | Mahatma Gandhi Institute |
| MRC | *Report of the Mauritius Royal Commission, 1909* (PP 1910 XLII [Cd. 5194]) |
| PP | British Parliament Sessional Papers |
| RCETI | *Report of the Royal Commissioners Appointed to Enquire into the Treatment of Immigrants in Mauritius* (PP 1875 XXXIV) |
| RCETI-A | *Appendices to the Report of the Royal Commissioners Appointed to Enquire into the Treatment of Immigrants in Mauritius* (PP 1875 XXXV) |
| RMD | Colony of Mauritius – annual report of the Registration and Mortgage Department |

# Note on currencies

Several currencies circulated in colonial Mauritius. The French livre remained the official currency of account during the eighteenth century, but the Spanish piastre or dollar ($) was also used widely. The value of these two currencies fluctuated depending upon local and regional economic and political conditions. Between 1760 and 1767, for example, the piastre's value varied from almost eleven to more than thirty-three livres; from 1778 to 1786, by comparison, its value remained relatively steady, ranging only between eight to eleven livres. Inflation eroded the livre's value during the 1790s; an exchange rate of approximately 12 livres to the piastre at the beginning of 1792 fell to 34 livres by mid-1794, to 1,000 livres by late 1796, to more than 5,500 livres by mid-1797, and to 10,000 livres in late 1798.

The franc replaced the livre during the last years of French rule. The British pound sterling (£) became the official currency of account on January 1, 1826, but the piastre, valued at four shillings (£1 = $5) remained in widespread use until the mid-1870s. The rupee became the colony's official currency in 1876 with an initial value of 2 shillings (£1 = Rs. 10). From 1894 through 1898 the rupee fluctuated in value, from slightly more than 1s. 1d. to slightly less than 1s. 4d. Valued at 1s. 4d. from 1899 to 1918, the rupee rose to 2s. in 1919–21 before falling again to 1s. 4d. in 1922–23, and then to 1s. 6d., where it remained from 1924 until the end of the period under consideration.

# Introduction

On May 14, 1909, a royal warrant commissioned Sir Frank Swettenham, Sir Edward O'Malley, and Hubert B.D. Woodcock, Esq., to investigate the economic condition and resources of Mauritius in the wake of the severe financial crisis that had shaken this British Indian Ocean colony the year before. Although preoccupied with the details of administrative and fiscal reform, the Mauritius Royal Commission was not insensitive to the underlying causes of the colony's economic difficulties. In their final report, Swettenham, O'Malley, and Woodcock expressed their concern that the Mauritian economy depended almost exclusively upon sugar, and that this dependence left the colony at the mercy of the world market price for this commodity. They also noted the economic impact of the various natural disasters that had struck the island since the early 1890s, disasters which had reduced sugar production and destroyed or severely damaged important components of the colony's industrial infrastructure. Last, but far from least, the Royal Commissioners reported that the local sugar industry suffered from a severe lack of capital and observed that "until this disease is overcome the industry cannot be regarded as on a financially sound footing."[1]

The Royal Commissioners were not the first officials to comment upon the ills which plagued the Mauritian economy during the late nineteenth and early twentieth centuries. Annual reports on the colony's condition during the nineteenth century often discussed the impact which cyclones, drought, and epidemic disease had on sugar production. Beginning in the mid-1860s, these reports revealed a growing official awareness of the potentially disastrous consequences of Mauritian dependence upon sugar. In his report for 1868, Governor Sir Henry Barkly acknowledged that a severe agricultural crisis could easily bring the island to the brink of economic ruin.[2] The annual report for 1886 noted that the colony's financial woes during several preceding years could be traced to the low world market price of sugar, and recommended that no one should "trust too implicitly on sugar again fetching such prices as it has done in the past" and that "minor industries" should be encouraged to lessen

1

local dependence upon this one crop.[3] A decade later, another annual report succinctly described the market price of sugar as "the slender thread on which hang the life and future of the colony."[4] Where the Mauritius Royal Commission's report differed from these earlier accounts, however, was in its concern about capital investment or, more precisely, the lack thereof, in the island's sugar industry. Colonial authorities had taken occasional notice as early as the 1840s of the ways in which this industry was financed, but the Royal Commissioners were the first officials to discuss in any detail why the colony suffered from the effects of under-capitalization.

The nature and extent of capital investment in the Mauritian sugar industry bears directly upon our understanding of the island's past and present and how we view the development or underdevelopment of plantation societies and economies in other parts of the European colonial world. Sugar dominated the Mauritian economy for more than 160 years and, as events as recently as the early 1980s demonstrated yet again, the world market price for this commodity could have a marked influence upon the island's social, economic, and political life.[5] On a more general note, many of the financial problems which afflicted the Mauritian sugar industry during much of the nineteenth and early twentieth centuries – a scarcity of capital, high levels of domestic indebtedness, and reliance upon local financial agents for short-term operating capital – also plagued colonial sugar economies in the Caribbean, South America, and elsewhere.[6]

These problems may be traced in part to a series of profound changes in the world sugar market during the second half of the nineteenth century. This era witnessed an explosion in sugar production worldwide; between the 1860s and the end of the twentieth century's first decade, global production increased nearly sixfold, to almost 11,750,000 tons a year.[7] While production in many older sugar colonies also increased during this period, it did so only modestly, with the result that these colonies controlled an ever smaller percentage of the rapidly expanding world market. The dramatic increase in beet sugar production and the corresponding erosion of cane's share of the market compromised the position of the older sugar colonies still further, as did the steady decline in the world market price of sugar after the 1860s.[8]

The protracted nature of the financial problems associated with these changes suggests that we need to look more closely at the dynamics of capital formation in colonial sugar economies. The social and economic history of plantation colonies has frequently been described and analyzed in terms of metropolitan capital's penetration into the colonial world and the attendant consequences of incorporation into the modern capitalist world economy. Attempts to distinguish plantations from other large-scale agricultural production units have done so by emphasizing the dependence upon metropolitan capital as a defining criteria of these systems; attempts to develop a universal model of plantation economies have done likewise.[9] The importance of intrusive capital has also been stressed in discussions of these societies' underdevelopment and impoverishment in the post-colonial world.[10]

Since the 1970s, however, the assertion that metropolitan capital was the principal force shaping life in plantation systems has come under increasing scrutiny.[11] Research on plantations in Africa has highlighted the role which factors such as geography, ideology, domestic relations of production, and regional market forces can play in shaping the history of these societies and economies.[12] Other studies have recognized the need to pay closer attention to the particulars of capital accumulation and, in so doing, have considered some of the consequences that followed from the failure either to attract adequate metropolitan investment or to tap efficiently into locally generated funds.[13] The critique of the dominant, Marxian-inspired paradigm implicit in much of this work has become more explicit in recent years as scholars have challenged the ability of dependency theory and world-system theory to facilitate the kind of sophisticated analysis which the realities of the plantation experience demand.[14]

Despite this increasing sensitivity to the complexities of capital formation in plantation colonies, a number of problems continue to militate against a fuller understanding of these systems. In the first instance, little attention has been paid to domestic capital's role in shaping the plantation experience. On those rare occasions when studies of plantation colonies in the Americas mention domestic capital, local credit has been quickly dismissed as an unimportant element in patterns of investment.[15] Research on the Natal sugar industry indicates, however, that domestic capital's role in shaping the history of these societies cannot be underestimated.[16] Work on the centralized factory system in the Caribbean, the early British colonization of Jamaica, and the growth of South Carolina's low country plantation regime also demonstrates that any serious attempt to reconstruct the history of plantation societies and economies must consider the extent to which domestic capital influenced the course of colonial development.[17]

A second problem stems from the fact that important patterns of interaction between capital formations and local social and economic structures and institutions remain unexplored. Studies of free populations of color in the Caribbean basin, to cite one prominent example, have focused almost exclusively upon the legal and quasi-legal dimensions of their existence. Accounts of free colored economic activity usually do little more than list their occupations and report briefly upon the extent of their slave- and land-ownership. Far more importantly, little attention has been paid to the larger context within which these populations arose, and especially to the ways in which free persons of color exploited the opportunities afforded by the developing economic crisis in many older sugar islands during the late eighteenth century to enhance their status and standing in colonial life. Similar problems characterize much of the work on ex-apprentices during the post-emancipation era and Indian immigrants during the nineteenth and early twentieth centuries.

A third area of concern centers upon the common practice of drawing a sharp dividing line between pre- and post-emancipation developments in the slave-plantation world. In many sugar colonies, tens of thousands of Asian indentured laborers replaced slaves in the cane fields. Studies of the pre-emancipation period nevertheless frequently imply that forced labor came to an end with the abolition of slavery, and that the plantation complex subsequently declined and fell. Histories of post-emancipation labor relations and systems, in turn, often proceed from the premise that the life of these workers can be reconstructed without reference either to the slave-plantation experience or to the larger socio-economic realities of the day. Such conclusions are, at worst, ahistorical; at best, they leave us with an incomplete picture of the social and economic transformations which shook many plantation colonies during the mid- and late nineteenth century.

The relative paucity of empirical data on many aspects of colonial plantation life, the limitations of those data available to us, and the concomitant difficulties of engaging in the comparative study of these systems is a fourth source of concern. Only B.W. Higman and David Watts, for example, have compiled significant collections of quantitative data on plantation slaves in the Caribbean.[18] While these data are of undoubted importance to understanding slavery in this part of the world, they also ultimately remain of somewhat limited value to other historians because of their restricted chronological, geographical, or topical focus. Similar limitations characterize more specialized studies; among the many students of free populations of color in the Caribbean, only Jerome Handler has included a significant statistical dimension to his work.[19] Unfortunately, his work is also ultimately less valuable than it might otherwise be, since his figures on Barbadian freedmen are derived from a sample of only eighty-one wills and property inventories. Most research on Indian and other indentured laborers is marked by similar short-comings.[20]

A final problem is the continuing reluctance of many historians of plantation and forced labor systems to draw upon the insights which anthropology, sociology, and other disciplines can provide. Equally important has been the general failure to engage in the comparative study of these systems, a problem admittedly made more difficult by the relative dearth of reliable quantitative data on many aspects of plantation life. However, work on African and Asian systems of slavery, on worker resistance and accommodation in Australasia and Latin America, and on slave emancipation in Africa and Asia underscores the value of such undertakings, especially when they are focused upon issues or themes around which research and discussion can be consistently focused.[21]

The fragmented and often parochial nature of recent scholarship on colonial plantation systems is largely self-inflicted, and reflects an unwillingness to explore beyond the conceptual boundaries imposed by a heavy reliance upon official source materials or to use new methodologies to analyze the information contained in these sources.[22] The end result has been a continuing preoccupation with the issues that concerned abolitionists, colonial officials, imperial apologists, and anti-imperialists during the nineteenth century. The renewed debate over whether or not indentured laborers were really "free" and whether they benefited in any significant way from their time in the cane fields is a salient case in point. These are important issues but, as even a cursory survey of the secondary literature reveals, focusing upon them to the exclusion of other relevant questions can shed only so much light upon the quality of immigrant life and the reasons why the quality of that life did or did not change. As Marina Carter's recent work demonstrates, seeking out and making perceptive use of a wider range of primary source materials can pay handsome dividends, such as revealing important changes in the strategies used to recruit indentured laborers or exposing the role of women in immigrant society to the light of day.[23]

The obvious consequence of this general failure to expand research horizons is an incomplete understanding of what happened on the ground in many eighteenth- and nineteenth-century plantation colonies. As recent research on worker agency illustrates, the net effect has been to obscure the complex, nuanced, and changing nature of colonial and economic relationships. For example, while historians have long appreciated that slaves actively resisted oppression and exploitation, few attempts have been made to assess the degree to which maroon activity changed through time, to discuss why it did so, or to consider its long-term impact upon a colony's history. Slave resistance was, after all, not simply a matter of seeking to expand the bounds of personal freedom, but also of exercising control over labor, holding property, acquiring credit, and engaging in trade.[24] The extent to which slaves succeeded in these endeavors could have profound implications for a wide range of post-emancipation social and economic relationships.[25]

Mauritian historiography reflects this propensity toward highly compartmentalized studies, and underscores the need to raise a series of questions which bear directly upon our understanding of the island's history in particular and the dynamics of social and economic change in plantation colonies in general.

To what extent were eighteenth- and nineteenth-century plantation economies dependent upon domestic rather than metropolitan capital? If they were dependent upon both domestic and foreign capital, what was the relationship between these two kinds of capital? Did this relationship change through time and, if so, how and why did it change?

What were the sources of domestic capital? Were traditional elites such as merchants or planters the principal source of local capital, or did other groups in colonial society control significant amounts of this capital? If other groups were important players in this process of domestic capital formation, what are the social and economic foundations for their participation? When and how did they participate?

What role did domestic capital play in shaping the course of these societies' development? What were the patterns of interaction between domestic capital and local socio-economic institutions? To what extent did changes in the type and/or focus of this capital alter these patterns of interaction, and what were the effects of such changes?

The failure of previous studies of sugar colonies to consider these questions is the most obvious reason for posing them now. However, there are other reasons for doing so. More specifically, the dynamics of domestic capital formation go to the very heart of the Mauritian experience. If metropolitan capital played an important, if not paramount, role in the history of some plantation systems, domestic capital was the crucial factor which shaped the course of Mauritian development from the latter part of the eighteenth century onward. As we shall see, the consequences of this reliance upon locally generated capital became apparent as early as the 1840s and then again during the 1870s as the colony's planters struggled to come to grips with harsh new political and economic realities. The inability of Mauritian domestic capital to meet the demands made upon it, coupled with the colony's failure to attract significant long-term metropolitan investment, would precipitate two major sub-divisions of the island's sugar estates. The transformations produced by this interaction between the world market, domestic capital, and local social and economic institutions continue to color the fabric of Mauritian life.

The importance of domestic capital in Mauritian history raises the question of the extent to which locally generated and controlled capital shaped social and economic life of other plantation colonies. There are many similarities between the Mauritian experience and that of other sugar colonies, and it is not unreasonable to suspect that domestic capital was an important motor force in other plantation colonies during at least some periods in their history. If nothing else, developments in Mauritius underscore the need to reassess how these economies were financed, with particular attention being paid to the dynamics of capital formation over time.

A final reason for posing these questions is the growing awareness of the interpretative problems that the Eurocentric bias in plantation studies can entail. The following pages will reveal, for instance, that Indian capital figured prominently in late nineteenth- and early twentieth-century Mauritian economic life. While local entrepreneurs mobilized much of this capital from within the ranks of the Indian immigrant population, there are also indications that some of these funds came directly from India itself. Given the connections between the Indian Ocean and Atlantic worlds and the importance of Indian capital in Western Indian Ocean economic life during the nineteenth century,[26] common sense suggests that we would do well to keep an open mind about the extent to which non-Western capital, whether imported or locally generated, helped to shape social and economic developments in some New World plantation colonies.

This history of slaves, freedmen, and indentured laborers in colonial Mauritius is being undertaken with these problems, issues, and questions in mind. To better understand the role these populations played in shaping the Mauritian experience, chapter 1 will survey the island's social and economic history from 1721 to 1936, with particular attention to the dynamics of domestic capital formation during this period. The patterns of social and economic interaction outlined in this chapter are explored in greater detail in subsequent chapters, which are organized into two sections. The first of these sections examines Mauritian labor relations in light of relevant scholarship on Australian, Caribbean, Southeast Asian, and South Pacific plantations. Chapter 2 focuses specifically upon maroonage in the context of Mauritian slavery, while chapter 3 examines illegal absence, desertion, and vagrancy by indentured laborers in light of the maroon legacy. In addition to discussing how servile and indentured laborers responded to the demands of the plantation regime, these chapters will consider the extent to which and why local labor relations changed during the nineteenth century.

The second section, on land and the mobilization of capital, examines the ways in which the island's non-European residents acquired and made use of capital resources, and the impact of their doing so. Chapter 4 analyzes the rise of the local free population of color in light of what we know about these populations in the Caribbean basin. This population established the precedents which allowed some of their number to escape from the bonds of wage labor and become actors of some consequence on the colonial stage. As chapter 5 details, many ex-apprentices soon followed in the footsteps of their free colored brethren and, like their counterparts in the Americas, sought to establish themselves as independent smallholders. In so doing, this nascent peasantry helped to spur the importation of tens of thousands of indentured laborers to work the island's cane fields. The experience of these Indian immigrants is the subject of chapter 6. During the late nineteenth and early twentieth centuries some of these immigrants and their descendants would likewise become important players on the Mauritian stage because of their ability to become gardeners of sugar in their own right.

# 1 Creating a garden of sugar: land, labor, and capital, 1721–1936

> Cette ville [Port Louis] est très considérable, point fortifiée, les maisons presque toutes batie en bois, les rues tirées au cordeau, celle du rempart est la plus belle, c'est la résidence de tout ce qu'il y a de mieux dans cette ville, elle est peuplées de beaucoup de négoçiants qui ont des vaisseaux, et qui font un commerce très considerable aux indes, en chine, au cap de bonne ésperance, vont jusqu'au Suratte, Mascatte, Bassora, et moka ce qui enrichie considerablement cette isle, d'ailleurs Ses productions qui est le Sucre, l'araque, le caffée, le coton, ses mines de fer et de cuivres luy donne beaucoup d'influence dans le commerce.
>
> Maximillien Wiklinsky, circa 1770[1]

When Vasco da Gama rounded the Cape of Good Hope late in 1497 and sailed into the Indian Ocean, Mauritius and its sister Mascarene Islands of Réunion and Rodrigues were unknown to the world at large. Mauritius and Réunion were probably visited by Arab or Swahili sailors before 1500, but their permanent entry onto the historical stage dates to the Portuguese explorations of the early sixteenth century.[2] The islands remained uninhabited, however, until the early seventeenth century when the Dutch East India Company (VOC) began to take a serious interest in the Southwestern Indian Ocean. In 1638, the Dutch made the first of several attempts to colonize the island they named Mauritius in honor of Maurice of Nassau, the *stadthouder* of Holland. The VOC's interest in Mauritius was spurred largely by the desire to establish a refreshment station for its ships plying between Europe and East Asia, although exploitation of the island's forests of ebony also figured in these early attempts at colonization.[3] Despite the island's strategic location astride important trade routes in the Western Indian Ocean, Dutch interest in Mauritius remained lukewarm. Concerns elsewhere in Europe and the East Indies, coupled with the problems of maintaining the small and troublesome settlements on the island, finally led to the colony's abandonment in 1710.

Dusfresne d'Arsel claimed the island for France in 1715, but six years passed before a small party from the neighboring Ile de Bourbon

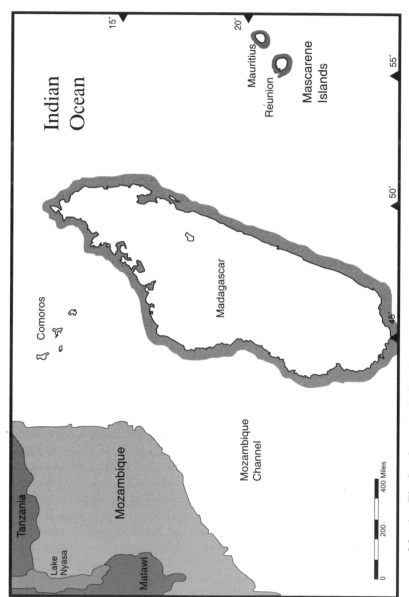

Map 1. The Southwestern Indian Ocean

(Réunion), colonized by the French Compagnie des Indes in 1670, settled on the island, now known as the Ile de France, in December, 1721. The fledgling colony struggled to survive during the 1720s and early 1730s, and it was not until the arrival of Bertrand François Mahé de La Bourdonnais that the French presence on the Ile de France was secured.[4] La Bourdonnais, governor from 1735 to 1746, envisioned the Mascarenes as a base from which French interests in India could be supported, and devoted most of his tenure in office to translating his vision into reality. As a result of his endeavors, the Ile de France soon became an important base from which French fleets attacked British possessions in India and French privateers preyed upon Anglo-Indian and allied shipping in the Indian Ocean during the War of Austrian Succession, the Seven Years War, the War of American Independence, and the revolutionary and Napoleonic eras. The island's strategic importance finally forced the British to muster an expeditionary force in 1810 to capture the Iles de France et de Bourbon. Concerned about the consequences of returning "the star and the key of the Indian Ocean" to her nemesis, Britain demanded permanent possession of Mauritius and its dependencies, a demand met by the Treaty of Paris in 1814. The Ile de Bourbon, bereft of good harbors, was restored to French control.

Inclusion in the British empire reset the stage for a series of profound transformations in Mauritian society and economy during the nineteenth and early twentieth centuries. Before 1810, Mascarene economic development had been governed by the strategic considerations enunciated by La Bourdonnais, with an emphasis upon producing the foodstuffs and naval stores needed to maintain French expeditionary forces in the Indian Ocean. In 1767, control of the Iles de France et de Bourbon passed from the bankrupt Compagnie des Indes to the French crown. The arrival of Pierre Poivre as the colony's first royal comptroller (1767–72) heralded a serious attempt to encourage the large-scale production of tropical commodities such as cotton, indigo, and spices.[5] These attempts to turn the island into a plantation colony failed. Competition from established producers of these commodities, periodic natural disasters which destroyed crops, and the lure of much more profitable maritime activities combined to undercut the island's potential development as a bastion of plantation agriculture.

The abrogation of the Compagnie's monopoly on France's Asian trade in 1769 and the subsequent ability of all French nationals to trade at Port Louis inaugurated a period of some four decades during which the island served as an increasingly important commercial entrepôt for the Western Indian Ocean. The grant of limited trading rights to American merchants in 1784 and Port Louis's designation as a free port open to all foreign nationals three years later accelerated this process, and the island was soon attracting shipping from as far away as northern Europe and the United States.[6] Port Louis's status as a free port, coupled with the island's tradition of privateering during the Anglo-French conflicts of the late eighteenth and early nineteenth centuries, created ideal conditions for the growth of local merchant capital. The number of merchants and traders residing in Port Louis, for example, soared from 103 in 1776 to 365 in 1808, while the number of vessels calling at the port each year rose from 78 in 1769 to a record high of 347 in 1803.[7] The scale of this activity and its impact upon the colonial economy is suggested by the fact that between 1793 and 1810, Mauritian privateers and French naval squadrons operating from the island captured more than 500 British and allied prizes estimated to be worth at least 80,000,000 gold francs.[8]

Mauritius' formal incorporation into the British empire brought an end to the island's role as an important regional entrepôt. The colony's subjection to the Navigation Acts in 1815, coupled with the rivalry of the British controlled Cape of Good Hope, undermined the local economy's commercial foundations. Left with few other viable options, Mauritian colonists turned to the production of agricultural commodities, especially sugar, for the imperial market. Sugar cane, first introduced by the Dutch during the seventeenth century, had been reintroduced following the French occupation in 1721.[9] However, despite the active encouragement of La Bourdonnais and his immediate successors, the cultivation of cane soon languished to the point where the industry was unable even to satisfy the local demand for sugar. A growing demand for the arrack needed by French naval expeditions spurred a modest increase in production late in the century.[10] The loss of St. Domingue in 1804 as France's principal source of sugar gave additional encouragement to the colony's fledgling sugar industry, and by 1810 the island had 9,000–10,000 arpents planted in cane. The arpentage devoted to cane continued to increase during the first years of British rule, but it was not until the late 1820s that sugar began to dominate the island's economy. The repeal in 1825 of the preferential tariff on West Indian sugar entering Britain revolutionized Mauritian agriculture. In only five years, the area planted in cane more than doubled, from 24,000 to 51,000 arpents, and the island's metamorphosis into a sugar colony was under way. By the mid-1850s, production exceeded 100,000 tons a year and Mauritius' fortunes were linked irrevocably to those of sugar.

As in other plantation colonies of the day, land, labor, and capital were the principal factors which shaped the Mauritian experience with sugar.

Throughout much of the period under consideration, land was the least problematic of these variables. Soon after colonizing the island, the Compagnie des Indes inaugurated a policy of making substantial land grants to attract settlers to the island and to encourage the production of the foodstuffs and other stores needed to maintain the French presence in the Indian Ocean. The royal government continued this policy after 1767. After the fall of the *ancien régime* in 1789, the colonial government ceased making such grants, opting instead to sell public lands at very reasonable prices. The properties granted or sold to colonists during the eighteenth century constituted the nucleus around which many nine-teenth-century sugar estates would be built.

If the government's decision to sell rather than to give away public land kept colonial residents from acquiring property at little or no cost to themselves, the Mauritian agricultural frontier nevertheless remained open for the better part of another century. Large tracts of privately owned land remained uncleared or undeveloped well into the mid-nineteenth century and, as the notarial record reveals, these properties (or portions thereof) were frequently available for sale to anyone with the purchase price in hand. The relative stability of land prices until the latter part of the century is additional evidence that the Mauritian agricultural frontier did not begin to close until the mid-1870s.

While access to land was not a serious impediment to agricultural development during much of the period under consideration, the same cannot be said of labor, especially after the sugar revolution took firm hold during the 1820s. Slaves had accompanied the first French settlers to the island in 1721, and the local slave population grew steadily in size during the eighteenth century, from 648 individuals in 1735, to 2,533 in 1746, to some 8,000 during the mid-1750s, to 15,027 in 1767, to 25,154 in 1777, to 33,832 in 1787, and to 49,080 in 1797. The first decade of the nineteenth century witnessed a continuation of this trend as the number of slaves on the island reached 60,646 in 1806 and 63,281 on the eve of the British conquest four years later.

Although slaves accounted for at least 75, and sometimes as much as 85, percent of the island's population between the 1730s and the 1820s, information about most aspects of slave life remains sketchy, especially during the eighteenth century. Bondsmen worked in various capacities – as artisans, fishermen, harbor- and shipyard-workers, household serv-ants, and sailors – but the great majority were used as laborers to produce foodstuffs, small quantities of export commodities, and naval stores.[11] Some slaves had access to provision grounds, while others were permitted to engage in petty trade.[12] The local slave regime was, by many accounts, a rigorous one marked by high rates of mortality; it was also a regime which apparently became even more oppressive as the cultivation of sugar spread. Governor Sir Lowry Cole, for one, reported in 1825 that the only object of Mauritian and Seychellois masters was "to extract from the slave the utmost possible amount of labor."[13] Cole also noted that male fieldhands usually wore only a piece of blue dungaree tied around their loins with a piece of string and that the daily ration of food for many slaves consisted of no more than 1.25 lb of maize or 3 lb of manioc.

The local demand for servile labor was not only a major factor in the dramatic expansion of the Malagasy and East African slave trades during the late eighteenth century,[14] but would also be the source of considerable friction between Mauritian colonists and the British government between 1811 and the formal abolition of slavery in 1835. Although slaves arriving in the Mascarenes came from as far away as Guinea, Malaya, and Indonesia, the great majority were imported from Madagascar and the comptoirs along the Mozambican and Swahili coasts. J.-M. Filliot estimates that 160,000 slaves reached Mauritius and Réunion between 1670 and 1810, with 45 percent of these bondsmen coming from Madagascar, 40 percent from Mozambique and East Africa, 13 percent from India, and 2 percent from West Africa.[15] The Compagnie des Indes oversaw the importation of some 45,000 slaves into the islands before 1769. Colonists and local merchants participated actively in the trade after Port Louis became a free port in 1769, and between 1769 and 1793 another 80,000 slaves reached the islands at an average rate of 3,000 a year, except for 1791–93 when imports climbed to 5,000 a year. The National Assembly's 1793 decree abolishing slavery throughout the French colonial empire was ignored in the Mascarenes and the slave trade continued unabated. Despite the disruptions caused by the almost continuous warfare between Britain and France after 1793, another 35,000 slaves were probably landed in the islands before British occupation brought an end to the legal slave trade in 1810.[16]

The abolition of the legal traffic in slaves did not, however, bring an end to slave-trading. The importance of servile labor to the island's economy, as well as the desire to placate a restive white population after the colony's capitulation, led Sir Robert Farquhar, the first British governor, to recommend that Mauritius be exempted from the 1807 ban on British subjects participating in the slave trade, a request which the Secretary of State for the Colonies promptly denied. Within months of the Colonial Secretary's decision, the island and its dependencies became notorious as the center of an illicit trade in slaves that lasted into the mid-1820s.

The number of slaves imported illegally into Mauritius and the

Seychelles after 1811 remains a subject of informed speculation. Various contemporary observers estimated that at least 30,000 slaves had been introduced surreptitiously into the colony by the early 1820s, despite governmental attempts to suppress the trade.[17] Census data from this era, although problematic, indicate that these estimates are not unreasonable and that the number of slaves who reached the island and its dependencies during these years was probably substantially higher. The magnitude of this clandestine trade soon led English abolitionists to charge that local officials had actively thwarted attempts to suppress it, charges that culminated in the appointment of the Commission of Eastern Inquiry to investigate the trade and other aspects of Mauritian social, economic, and political life.[18] The Commissioners would conclude in their report of March 12, 1828, that "nothing but a general disposition in the inhabitants in favor of the slave trade, and the negligence or connivance of the civil authorities in the districts, and great inefficiency, if not culpability in the police department, could have enabled bands of negroes to be landed and carried through so small an island and disposed of without detection . . ."[19]

Despite the clandestine importation of tens of thousands of slaves during the first years of British rule, it became increasingly apparent during the 1820s that the local slave population was inadequate to meet the labor needs of the colony's rapidly expanding sugar industry. As in other plantation colonies, this problem was not completely unexpected; the mortality rate among Mauritian slaves regularly exceeded the birth rate by a substantial margin, while the death of additional thousands of slaves during a severe cholera epidemic in late 1819 and early 1820 placed added strain on the colony's agricultural work force. Changes in the demographic structure of this population further compounded the problem, as the percentage of adult males capable of heavy field work declined during the 1820s and early 1830s. The impact of these trends is apparent from the limited information on slave occupations at our disposal. Whereas an 1823 census of 7,629 slaves on 206 estates described 58 percent of these bondsmen as field laborers, fieldhands accounted for only 45 percent of the 66,613 slaves for whom compensation was paid twelve years later.[20]

The labor crisis facing Mauritian planters by the early 1830s was exacerbated by other factors far beyond their immediate control. The Act of Abolition promised slave-owners continued access to the services of their former bondsmen, now transformed into "apprentices," but only for a maximum period of six years. The long-term viability of this work force was quickly brought into question, however, as many apprentices sought to emancipate themselves before the apprenticeship period came to an end. According to one local magistrate, some 9,000 apprentices purchased their liberty before the apprenticeship system in the colony collapsed on March 31, 1839, "amongst whom there has been no instance of a single individual having returned to the cultivation of the land."[21] Emancipation was followed, in turn, by the almost total withdrawal of the ex-apprentice population from the estates, a development which gave additional impetus to the importation of indentured labor from India.

The search for additional sources of labor had begun well before the abolition of slavery. As early as 1816, the colonial government decided to experiment with the use of Indian convict labor, and the following year some 500 convicts were being used to repair roads. By 1828, the number of convicts who had reached the island had climbed to at least 1,018.[22] At the same time, Mauritian planters dispatched their agents as far afield as China, Singapore, Ethiopia, and Madagascar in their search for additional sources of inexpensive agricultural labor. Their gaze returned inevitably, however, to the seemingly inexhaustible manpower of India.

Indian indentured labor was attractive to Mauritian planters and authorities for reasons other than just its proximity and apparent inexhaustibility. In the first instance, colonists already had extensive experience with Indian laborers. Perhaps 20,000 of the slaves imported into the Mascarenes prior to 1810 were of Indian origin, and the Ile de France had also become the home of a sizable population of free Indian craftsmen and artisans during the late eighteenth century.[23] Secondly, attempts to recruit indentured laborers in Madagascar or along the East African coast could easily leave colonists open to the charge that they were reviving the slave trade, a charge which, given their support of the illegal slave trade and opposition to the abolition of slavery,[24] could provoke additional unwanted Imperial intervention in the colony's affairs. The recruitment of free labor within the Empire carried fewer such risks. Recruitment from within the Empire likewise minimized the problems which dealing with foreign powers could entail. China, for example, either prohibited or severely restricted the emigration of its subjects to work as agricultural laborers during the first half of the nineteenth century. Finally, India's attractiveness was enhanced further by the existence of a British administration that regarded emigration as a means of relieving the country's overpopulation and allowing its inhabitants an opportunity to improve the quality of their lives.[25]

The 75 indentured laborers who arrived in Mauritius in 1834 proved to be the vanguard of more than 451,000 men, women, and children who reached the island before Indian immigration came formally to an end in 1910. More than 294,000 of these immigrants remained permanently on the island where their presence rapidly transformed the colony's social and economic landscape. By 1846, Indian immigrants comprised more than 35 percent of the colony's total population. The 1850s witnessed explosive growth in the size of the immigrant population, which soared from 77,996 in 1851 to 192,634 in 1861, or 62 percent of the colony's residents. Although the number of Indian immigrants reaching the island's shores began to decline during the 1860s, by 1871 they and their Indo-Mauritian descendants accounted for two-thirds of the island's population, a percentage which has remained relatively constant to the present day.

The process of capital formation is the most poorly understood of the factors which shaped the Mauritian experience with sugar. Among Mauritian historians, only Roland Lamusse has attempted to describe the colony's sources of capital and the local system of crop finance in a systematic, if somewhat limited, manner.[26] This reluctance to explore the history of Mauritian capital formation may be traced in part to the relative paucity of relevant data. Information on topics as straight-forward as the volume and value of the colony's trade during the French period is scarce, even in official sources. While figures on trade, specie flows, and other pertinent topics become more readily available during the nineteenth century, and especially after 1850, these data remain only general indicators of capital formation in the colony, and often problem-atic ones at that. Even the royal commissions of inquiry appointed to investigate the colony's condition during the nineteenth and early twentieth centuries tended to be reticent about colonial finances. However, despite these difficulties, the history of Mauritian capital can be reconstructed by a careful reading of the existing documentation.

Information on the local economy's condition during the Compagnie's tenure is sparse. Modern assessments of the Compagnie's agricultural policies echo those made during the eighteenth century that these policies had been "diametrically opposed to all kind of public prosperity."[27] Contemporary reports suggest that although individual colonists may have prospered, the colonial economy as a whole did not flourish under Compagnie rule. In 1756, for example, C.F. Noble reported that while many of the colony's planters had become rich because of the "great price given for all the productions of their plantations, many of which are become very extensive & valuable," the island could not feed itself and relied upon provisions from the Ile de Bourbon, Madagascar, and India to survive.[28] A 1766 census confirms that the colony's agricultural sector remained much less developed than it might otherwise have been. Fewer than 200,000 of 400,000 cultivable arpents had been distributed to colonists, and less than one-fourth of all granted land had been brought into production. Comments in the census reveal that colonial authorities

were aware that the island's full agricultural potential remained un-
tapped. According to one such notation, the Ile de France was deemed
capable of supporting 60,000 slaves and 30,000 head of livestock,
numbers far in excess of what the island actually housed at the time.[29]

The advent of royal administration did not bring about any immediate improvement in local agriculture. In 1772, the English naval
lieutenant John Colpoys reported that the colony was still unable to feed
itself, and that "were it not for the assistance which it gets from the
Cape of Good Hope and Madagascar, I am sure the number of souls
thats [*sic*] now in it would be sufficient to breed a famine."[30] Six years
later, an anonymous memorandum asserted that many estate-owners
were abandoning cultivation of their land or foregoing the establishment
of new plantations because of the local administration's fiscal woes and
its attendant refusal to purchase locally grown grain.[31] Little had
changed by late 1780, when John Buncle reported that "The Oppression
of a Military Government, the natural indolence of the Inhabitants &
their poverty, are the real reasons that so small a part of the Island is
cultivated."[32]

Buncle's observation underscores the extent to which government
policy contributed to the weakness of the colony's agricultural sector
throughout the eighteenth century. As in other colonies, especially those
far removed from close metropolitan supervision, the consequences of
these policies and practices were compounded by official venality.
Buncle, for one, reported that local officials did not encourage the
cultivation of maize despite the consequences of the colony's continuing
inability to feed itself, especially in times of war. The reason for their
refusal to do so was, he noted, simple and straightforward: they made
much more money for themselves when maize had to be imported.[33]

Despite these problems, government demand for foodstuffs and naval
supplies nevertheless helped to keep the colony's agricultural sector alive
during the eighteenth century, albeit often anemically so. The survival of
large numbers of contracts to supply royal warehouses, as well as the
records of the goods received in those storehouses, indicate that governmental spending was an important source of income for many colonists
throughout the French period. Various sources indicate that the purchase
of local grain and manufactures often accounted for at least 30 to 40
percent of colonial government expenditure during the 1780s and
1790s.[34] The extent to which other governmental monies in the form of
salaries, troop wages, etc., filtered into the island's economy cannot be
determined, but it is not unreasonable to assume that many of the Ile de
France's residents depended, at least indirectly, upon the public purse for
their livelihood.

If Mauritian agriculture had to struggle to hold its own during the latter part of the eighteenth century, the same cannot be said of the colony's commercial sector. The consequences of Port Louis's designation in 1769 as a port open to trade by all French nationals have already been noted. Contemporary observers appreciated the importance of this decision. In 1770, a British colonel, John Call, wrote that the Ile de France was a decided "national advantage" to France because of its capacity "To serve as a reposit or magazine for collecting the Merchandize of the several parts of India, and from thence shipping them to Europe, or as a place proper to fit out an Armament against our Settlements in another War, or to equip Vessels to cruize against our Trade in India and as far as S$^{t.}$ Helena ..."[35] The wars which France and England were to fight during the coming decades would confirm the probity of his observations.

The incentives to engage in commerce and trade rather than agriculture were substantial. During the early 1790s, according to one report, the manipulation of bills of exchange returned profits of 25 to 33 percent compared to the 5 or 6 percent realized by successful planters.[36] The low level of commodity production at this time underscores the colonial propensity to pursue commercial and maritime rather than agricultural interests. According to William Milburn, the annual produce of the Ile de France (probably during the 1790s or early 1800s) amounted to no more than 6,000 bags of coffee, 2,000 bales of cotton, 300,000 lb of indigo in a good year, 20,000 lb of cloves, 5 million lb of raw sugar, and an undetermined quantity of several kinds of woods.[37] The value of these items is difficult to ascertain, but there can be no doubt that it was small compared to the value of the trade in manufactured goods from Asia. Between 1771 and 1778, for example, the value of the goods arriving at Lorient from the Mascarenes averaged 882,747 livres each year, while those imported from the East Indies and China each year were valued at 10,763,956 and 7,012,370 livres respectively.[38]

If the Mascarenes were not a place where merchants went looking for merchandise to sell in Europe or Asia during the late eighteenth century, the islands were a potentially lucrative market for goods imported from elsewhere. The Abbé Raynal reported that the Compagnie des Indes realized a 100 percent return on the goods it imported into the islands from Europe, and a 50 percent return on goods it imported from India.[39] Maximillien Wiklinsky claimed *circa* 1770 that merchants could expect a 400–500 percent return on the imported goods they sold locally.[40] The colony's trade with Africa and India was also profitable, so much so that local investors were often guaranteed a 25 to 35 percent return on their investment. Such was the case in January, 1781, when the Port Louis firm of Pitot Frères et C$^{ie}$ guaranteed M. de Courcy a 35 percent return on his investment in the snow *La Baptistine* which was about to sail to the African coast and the Cape of Good Hope before returning to the colony.[41] Several months later, the firm informed M. de Maurville that his 15,000 livres investment in five ships, guaranteed variously at 25, 30, and 35 percent, had yielded a net profit of 31 percent.[42] A report which probably dates from the early 1790s indicates that returns of 25 to 30 percent were also common in the colony's trade with India.[43]

While the profits from local and regional trade were an important inducement for merchants to establish themselves on the Ile de France, the greatest spur to commercial activity came from the island's status as a base from which corsairs preyed upon British and allied shipping in times of war. The fact that one merchant from Nantes had realized a net profit of 1,300,000 livres on his investment in four Mascarene-based privateers at the end of the War of Austrian Succession demonstrated how lucrative such ventures could be.[44] Privateering during the War of American Independence proved to be equally remunerative. On March 26, 1781, for example, Pitot Frères informed the Comte de St. Maurice that his 2,400-livres investment in the privateer *La Philippine* had yielded a return of more than 440 percent.[45] Five months later, after the sale of three English prizes taken by *La Philippine*, the firm reported that a share in the privateer was now worth 7,481 livres, or 523 percent more than the original purchase price of 1,200 livres.[46]

The total value of the prizes taken by corsairs operating from the Mascarenes is difficult to determine. In September, 1781, the Pitots reported that the prizes taken by local privateers since 1778 had sold for 12,000,000 livres.[47] The firm also noted that losses to the enemy were actually double this figure because of the unreported depredations committed on board ships at the time of their capture. Following the resumption of hostilities between Britain and France in 1793, privateers based in the Mascarenes once again inflicted heavy losses upon enemy commerce. One contemporary estimate put the value of the shipping captured by these privateers between 1793 and mid-1804 at £2,500,000.[48] Auguste Toussaint estimated the value of some 200 prizes taken by Mauritian corsairs between 1793 and 1802 at 30 to 40 million francs, and perhaps more. He put the value of corsair prizes between 1803 and 1810 at approximately 17,700,000 francs, and concluded that French frigates operating in the Indian Ocean during the same period captured additional prizes worth approximately 32 million francs.[49]

It is impossible to ascertain how much of the proceeds from this activity and the trade associated with it remained in the Mascarenes. While some privateers returned to France with fortunes,[50] substantial amounts of prize money and other merchant capital also remained in the colony. Partnership agreements from the early 1780s reveal that local merchants could mobilize significant financial resources. Fulerand Dejean and Emmanuel Touche du Poujol, for instance, each contributed 100,000 livres to capitalize the commercial house they established in Port Louis on October 12, 1780.[51] Two years later Louis Joseph Pigeot de Carey, his brother Isidore Pigeot de St. Vallery, and Paul Trebillard de la Relandière contributed 200,000, 120,000, and 80,000 livres respectively toward the capitalization of a partnership they were establishing for three years.[52] Amounts such as these pale in comparison, however, to those at the command of Paul de la Bauve d'Arifat, who declared on July 31, 1780 before two notaries that he had cash assets totaling 1,000,000 livres.[53] Among d'Arifat's other assets were the 400 slaves, worth at least 660,000 livres, that he put at the king's service during the War of American Independence.[54]

The extent to which this merchant capital found its way into the colony's agricultural sector during the eighteenth and early nineteenth centuries cannot be determined with any degree of precision. It is clear nevertheless that some merchants and seamen invested directly in landed property and that increasing numbers of them did so over time. Evidence of this trend comes from Savanne where, in 1788, at least four of the district's thirteen landed proprietors had a commercial or maritime background. By 1795, the number of such persons had increased to five, four of whom were new landowners who had acquired their estates between 1788 and 1795. Twenty years later, the district's fifty-three proprietors included four merchants, three ship's lieutenants, a commercial agent, and two seamen.[55] There can also be no doubt that merchant capital flowed into the colony's agricultural sector in other less visible ways. Many of the merchants who established themselves on the island married local women,[56] and it is reasonable to assume that significant sums of merchant capital subsequently found its way into the colony's agricultural sector via familial connections. The growing demand for the provisions needed by the navy from the 1780s onward provided additional incentives for persons with mercantile or maritime interests to invest some of their money in landed property.

The blockade inaugurated by the British in 1806 spelled the beginning of the end of the Ile de France's prominence as a commercial entrepôt. Following the island's capture in December, 1810, some of its wealthier inhabitants returned to France, one consequence of which was "an unusual scarcity of bullion" in the colony.[57] The island's formal cession to Britain in 1814 and its subjection to the Navigation Acts in 1815 caused considerable economic hardship and further eroded the commercial foundations upon which local social and economic life had rested. With few other viable alternatives open to them, colonists turned their attention to the development of the island's fledgling sugar industry.

As was noted earlier, the origins of this industry date to the early 1740s when La Bourdonnais actively encouraged the cultivation of sugar cane. Despite this encouragement, the industry languished during much of the eighteenth century. In 1789, only 1,000 arpents were planted in cane and the colony contained from just eight to ten sugar mills, which produced a mere 300 tons of sugar a year. The growing demand for arrack and the interruption in sugar supplies caused by the Haitian revolution encouraged planters on the Ile de France to expand their production. By 1806–10, some 9,000–10,000 arpents were planted in cane, and sugar production had climbed to 3,000–4,000 tons a year.[58] Access to the London market, which came with inclusion in the British Empire, together with the high price of sugar near the end of the Napoleonic wars (see table 1), encouraged estate-owners to expand their arpentage in sugar even further.

The industry's development during the nineteenth and early twentieth centuries was shaped in no small measure by its organizational structure and the local system of crop finance. Throughout the nineteenth century the sugar industry was composed largely of individually or family owned and managed estates, and its structure remained highly personalized even after more advanced forms of industrial organization such as limited liability companies began to be introduced during the 1880s.[59] This reliance upon personalized forms of industrial organization limited the capital resources available to planters and made many dependent upon short-term credit for their operating expenses, even in boom times. The fragility of estate finances would be a source of constant concern to the Mauritius Chamber of Agriculture, founded in 1853 by the colony's more prominent planters in the midst of a period of relative prosperity. As early as 1856, the Chamber was studying the possibilities of creating mortgage loan societies to provide planters with much-needed long-term capital at moderate rates of interest.[60] Three such societies came into existence in 1864, but proved to be inadequate to the industry's needs, especially in the wake of a financial crisis in 1865 and the natural disasters of 1866–68. As a result, by 1868 the Chamber was expressing its interest in the establishment of an agricultural bank.[61] The passage of time did little, however, to alleviate this problem. In 1902, the Chamber's annual report noted the serious threat which a lack of operating capital posed to the colony's future.[62] Seven years later, Governor Sir Cavendish Boyle reported that "for some considerable time the lack of capital and the want of money obtainable at reasonable rates" had left their mark on

Table 1. *Mauritian sugar and the world market, 1812–1934*

| Period | Annual average per quinquenium | | | |
| | Exports (tons) | % World cane production | % Total world production | Average price (£/ton)[a] |
|---|---|---|---|---|
| 1812–14 | 426 | — | — | 61.3 |
| 1815–19 | 3,097 | — | — | 52.8 |
| 1820–24 | 11,107 | — | — | 32.5 |
| 1825–29 | 20,407 | — | — | 33.6 |
| 1830–34 | 33,784 | — | — | 27.0 |
| 1835–39 | 32,502 | — | — | 37.4 |
| 1840–44 | 34,707 | 4.0 | 3.8 | 39.2 |
| 1845–49 | 56,069 | 5.4 | 5.0 | 28.2 |
| 1850–54 | 71,388 | 6.0 | 5.2 | 21.6 |
| 1855–59 | 111,522 | 8.6 | 6.8 | 26.6 |
| 1860–64 | 123,609 | 9.0 | 6.8 | 22.6 |
| 1865–69 | 113,311 | 7.0 | 4.9 | 22.2 |
| 1870–74 | 111,445 | 6.3 | 3.9 | 23.6 |
| 1875–79 | 115,844 | 6.3 | 3.6 | 21.0 |
| 1880–84 | 116,019 | 5.7 | 2.8 | 18.8 |
| 1885–89 | 119,815 | 5.1 | 2.3 | 13.2 |
| 1890–94 | 113,219 | 3.5 | 1.6 | 13.1 |
| 1895–99 | 143,641 | 5.0 | 1.9 | 10.0 |
| 1900–04 | 167,380 | 2.9 | 1.4 | 9.3 |
| 1905–09 | 181,636 | 2.5 | 1.3 | 9.8 |
| 1910–14 | 223,746 | 2.5 | 1.3 | 11.0 |
| 1915–19 | 223,139 | 2.0 | 1.4 | 28.3 |
| 1920–24 | 218,682 | 1.7 | 1.1 | 27.8 |
| 1925–29 | 216,359 | 1.3 | 0.9 | 11.9 |
| 1930–34 | 191,820 | 1.2 | 0.8 | 5.7 |

*Note:* [a] In London (cost, insurance, and freight).
*Sources:* BB 1840 42, 1845 48, 1850.
       Deerr 1949–50, vol. II, pp. 490–91, 531.
       *Mauritius Almanac for 1889*, p. 70.
       MCA 1859, attached appendix.
       PP 1826–27 XVIII [283]; 1835 XLIX [53]; 1836 XLVI [55]; 1837 XLIX [100]; 1837–38 XLVII [151]; 1839 XLV [213]; 1840 XLIII [281]; 1865 LV [3508]; 1866 LXXIII [3709]; 1878 LXVIII [C. 2093]; 1886 LXVIII [C. 4825]; 1890 LXXVIII [C. 6160]; 1899 CIV [C. 9459]; 1900 C [Cd. 307]; 1910 CVI [Cd. 4984]; 1914–16 LXXIX [Cd. 7786]; 1924 XXIV [Cmd. 2247]; 1929–30 XXX [Cmd. 3434]; 1937–38 XXVIII [Cmd. 5582)].

the colony.[63] That same year, the Mauritius Royal Commission likewise noted that "the great majority of owners have practically no working capital and run their estates on borrowed money."[64]

The Chamber of Agriculture's call for the establishment of financial institutions capable of making low-interest loans to planters reflected the weaknesses inherent in the local system of crop finance which rested upon individuals known as *bailleurs de fonds*. Like the Caribbean agent or *commissionnaire* and the Brazilian *correspondente*, *bailleurs de fonds* were usually local merchants or produce-brokers who possessed substantial liquid capital resources of their own as well as good credit with local banks. Their activities focused upon providing planters with the short-term operating capital they did not have or could not raise elsewhere. The financial relationship between a planter and a *bailleur de fonds* often led to the latter functioning as an estate's business manager with responsibility for providing the plantation with needed supplies and money, as well as selling the annual crop.[65]

The legacy of this personalized system of crop finance was to foster a "special psychology of credit" among planters who took advantage of periods of relative prosperity to borrow large sums to pay off their creditors and to finance capital improvements.[66] However, the steady decline in the world market price of sugar that began during the 1860s, together with the fluctuation of these prices from year to year, and sometimes even from month to month, made large-scale borrowing a risky undertaking which resulted in many estates accumulating ever larger amounts of debt. In 1902, according to the Chamber of Agriculture, the cost of financing capital improvements and paying mortgage interest charges was approximately 25,000,000 rupees.[67] By 1909, only eleven of the sixty-six estates with factories were reported to be free of encumbrances; the other fifty-five estates carried debts estimated at Rs. 12,000,000.[68] By the early 1930s, the consequences of the industry's dependence upon domestic capital in an era of declining sugar prices were apparent even to uninformed observers of colonial life. *Bailleurs de fonds* had become caught up in a vicious cycle of refinancing ever larger estate debts, which were also their own personal debts, in a desperate effort to stave off financial ruin. According to the commissioners who investigated the state of colonial finances in 1931, this situation had developed because nothing – neither high interest rates nor insufficient security – limited further borrowing by planters:

So far from being harsh and unconscionable the traditional policy of the *bailleurs de fonds* towards their clients' difficulties is that of forbearance carried beyond the extreme limit of prudence. In the small white community of Mauritius, closely bound together by the ties of inter-marriage and of long-standing family relationships, the influence of public opinion makes for lenient and sympathetic treatment of debtors, whose insolvency is concealed and assisted by further credit often beyond the creditor's own capacity to allow without endangering his own security. As a result of this tendency and of the weakness of the *bailleur de fonds'* own position under an arrangement which makes him personally liable for his client's default, arrears in indebtedness have been allowed to accumulate on many estates to an extent which in some cases exceeds the whole amount of the realizable assets, including the land itself.[69]

The commissioners noted that a "very considerable" number of estates were reported to be in just such a condition.

The best way to alleviate this growing financial distress remained a subject of vigorous debate. The colony's chambers of agriculture and commerce, keenly aware that local financial institutions lacked the resources to effect a long-term solution, saw government loans as the only viable alternative, and regularly pressed a reluctant administration to make loans to the sugar industry. There were precedents for doing so. In 1816, the colonial government had extended a $100,000 line of credit to the Mauritius Bank in the wake of a fire which devastated Port Louis's commercial district, while in 1829 and again in 1830 the government had advanced sums totalling $500,000 "in aid of the agricultural and commercial interests of the Colony, suffering under the pressure of great and unexpected embarrassment."[70] Additional loans, however, came only in the wake of the devastating cyclone of 1892, when the government advanced Rs. 5,868,450 to planters. Other government loans were subsequently made in 1898 (for Rs. 1,491,000) and in 1903 (for £382,917) to finance capital improvements and underwrite the costs of cultivation. The Royal Commission of 1909 reported that these loans had been or were being repaid on schedule, and concluded that there was little risk that the colonial government would lose any appreciable portion of the monies lent. The Commissioners even recommended the advance of another £115,000 to the colony's planters for additional capital improvements.[71]

Within several decades, however, the colony's financial situation had deteriorated to the point where the Financial Commission of 1931 vigorously opposed any additional government loans to the sugar industry on the grounds that the "history of such loans in recent years has been a singularly unfortunate one ..."[72] In addition to its enormous indebtedness to mortgagees and *bailleurs de fonds*, the Commissioners noted that the industry was carrying five successive government loans totaling some Rs. 20,000,000 on which it was unable to pay either interest or principal. This mountain of debt convinced the Commission that the colony's estates could be restored to profitable cultivation only by an increase in the export price of sugar, either as a result of the operation of market forces or through an increase in the imperial subsidy.

The repeated calls for government loans during the late nineteenth and early twentieth centuries attest to the increasing inability of local financial institutions to meet the demand for operating capital. The colony housed only two banks in 1909 and while one of these banks was financed by British capital, both it and its locally owned and managed rival possessed only limited resources. The 1909 Royal Commissioners appreciated this fact, and noted that what the colony really needed was a branch office of a large banking company capable of adapting to local exigencies and weathering periods of depression.[73] The colony continued to be dependent upon domestic capital, however, for the simple reason that it failed to attract and keep significant metropolitan investment after 1848.

Mauritius remained of little long-term interest to British or other foreign investors for several reasons. Prior to 1825, Mauritian sugar was subject to a substantially higher tariff than was West Indian sugar entering Britain, an economic fact of life that discouraged potential British investment in the colony. The abolition in 1825 of the preferential West Indian tariff was accordingly an event of major consequence to Mauritian planters. The industry's dramatic expansion after 1825, coupled with the higher prices that Mauritian sugar now fetched on the London market, encouraged English speculators to invest.[74] The resulting boom was short-lived, however, and collapsed in response to the termination of the apprenticeship system and the suspension of Indian immigration in 1839.

British investors returned to the colony following the resumption of Indian immigration late in 1842, drawn by the expectation of high rates of return on their investment. In February, 1848, Edward Chapman, a co-owner of seven estates and the commercial agent for ten to twelve other estates, estimated the value of this investment since 1843 at £500,000.[75] The collapse that same year of four of the five London commercial houses that had financed a substantial portion of the Mauritian crop sent the colony's economy into what Governor Sir G.W. Anderson readily characterized as a "considerable depression."[76] Hopes during the early 1850s that a reviving economy would attract new British capital remained unfulfilled, and for the rest of the century the colony was not the object of significant metropolitan investment. In 1909, only 19 of the colony's 145 sugar estates were reported to be foreign owned: 13 by three companies based in London, 4 by French interests, and 1 each by interests based in Bombay and Pondichéry.[77] The Financial Commission of 1931 subsequently observed that the falling price of sugar continued to discourage metropolitan investment in a colony where "the existence of a foreign [i.e., French] and in some respects antiquated system of law and procedure in matters relating to property and business naturally tend to deter English businessmen from interesting themselves in its affairs."[78]

Under such circumstances, the sugar industry's fortunes, as well as those of the colony as a whole, rose and fell upon the ability of local capital to meet the demands being made upon it. Two principal factors governed domestic capital formation in Mauritius after 1810: the world market price for sugar and the industry's profitability. Despite the colony's importance as a producer during the mid-nineteenth century, Mauritian planters exercised no control over the market price of sugar, and the colony was accordingly forced to cope with repeated cycles of economic boom and bust as the price of sugar rose and fell from year to year, sometimes dramatically so. The impact of these price fluctuations was compounded by the fact that while local sugar production increased during the nineteenth and early twentieth centuries, it did so in fits and starts with production levels remaining relatively constant over extended periods of time (see table 1, p. 23).

The quality of estate management, the availability and cost of labor, and the willingness to adopt new agricultural and manufacturing techniques to increase cane production and factory efficiency also influenced profit margins. The cost of labor was the most important of these variables. Edward Chapman reported that labor regularly accounted for 50 percent of production costs during the 1840s.[79] Projections based upon the size of the contractual work force and average monthly wages suggest that labor costs continued to account for approximately one-half of direct operating expenses throughout the mid-nineteenth century. During the 1860s, for example, the minimum wage bill for estate-owners was probably £625,000–670,000 a year, a sum equal to 28 to 31 percent of the sugar crop's export value. It should be noted that this estimate covers only wages, and does not include the cost of the rations, clothing, housing, and medical care planters were legally required to provide for their workers.

The profitability of Mauritian sugar estates, like that of Caribbean plantations, is a problematic topic.[80] Reports of rates of return are scarce, and even the various commissions charged with investigating conditions in the colony were often reticent about the industry's profitability or lack thereof. The earliest available information on this topic dates to 1828 when the Commission of Eastern Enquiry was informed that the average net profit from an arpent of cane on the best estates ranged from $28 to about $100.[81] Twenty years later, Sir George Larpent, Bart., who had 1,500 of his 3,787 acres planted in cane, declared that he had lost £95,000 between 1834 and 1844–45.[82] Edward Chapman claimed in turn that local planters lost £195,000 on the 1847–48 crop, a figure which climbed to £480,000 if interest charges were included in the calculations.[83] The extent to which these two reports accurately represent local conditions, however, must remain open to question. Sir George, for one, implied that some of his losses since 1844–45 (and probably before 1844 as well) were the result of declining property values rather than unprofitable sugar crops *per se*.[84]

More precise data about the industry's profitability are available for only three years between 1812 and 1936. Figures reported by A. Walter and Noël Deerr indicate that the market price of Mauritian sugar exceeded production costs by 12.3 percent in 1853 and by 20.4 percent in 1893, while costs exceeded income by 9.7 percent in 1906.[85] These figures must be viewed with some care, since it is unclear whether the reported production costs included all relevant charges. The Royal Commission of 1909 revealed that four unnamed estates showed a profit on twelve of fifteen sugar crops between 1893 and 1907, with an average return of 16 percent over costs.[86] Profits ranged from 17 cents to Rs. 3.50 for 50 kilograms of sugar produced, while losses varied from 5 to 89 cents for 50 kilograms. Unfortunately, the Commissioners made no attempt to indicate the extent to which these rates of return were representative of the industry as a whole.[87]

Although many features of its financial condition remain hidden from view, a sense of the Mauritian sugar industry's financial condition may be gauged by reviewing the general state of the colony's economy between the 1810s and the mid-1930s. Sugar accounted for 85 percent of the value of Mauritian exports as early as 1833–34, and over the next 100 years at least 85, and often 90, percent or more of local export earnings came from sugar. Because the island's economic fortunes were bound so inextricably with those of the sugar industry, reports on the value of sugar exports, the colony's balance of trade, the movement of specie to and from the island, and other indices of economic activity afford an opportunity to chart the industry's fortunes in some detail.

The first decades of British rule were clearly ones of diminished prosperity for the island. Colonists had complained bitterly about the economic hardships they had to endure after the island's capture, complaints which the negative balance of trade between 1812 and 1814 reveals were not unfounded (see table 2). The colony's continuing inability to cover the cost of its imports before the mid-1840s, despite the sugar industry's explosive growth between 1825 and 1830, underscores the extent of the economic difficulties which many planters had to face in the wake of the abolition of slavery, emancipation of the apprentices, and the suspension of Indian immigration.

The 1850s and early 1860s have commonly been regarded as the heyday of the Mauritian sugar industry, and the increasing value of sugar exports and incoming specie flows, as well as the increasingly favorable balance of trade, confirm that this era was one of considerable

Table 2. *Condition of the Mauritian economy, 1812–1934*

| Period | Value of sugar exported | Net balance of trade[a] | Net specie flow | Per capita value of imports[b] |
|---|---|---|---|---|
| | Annual average per quinquenium (£ sterling) | | | |
| 1812–14 | (19,586)[c] | −206,529[d] | — | 8.22[d] |
| 1815–19 | (122,642)[c] | — | — | — |
| 1820–24 | (270,734)[c,e] | −98,835[f] | — | 6.47[f] |
| 1825–29 | (514,256)[c,g] | −188,561[b] | — | 7.63 |
| 1830–34 | (684,126)[c,h] | +5,915[b] | — | 6.68 |
| 1835–39 | (911,681)[c] | −129,948[b] | — | 9.00 |
| 1840–44 | (1,020,386)[c] | +5,634 | +143,662 | 7.09 |
| 1845–49 | (1,185,860)[c] | +363,069 | +191,258 | 6.70 |
| 1850–54 | 1,110,164 | +195,313 | +203,544 | 6.08 |
| 1855–59 | 1,929,847 | +378,543 | +454,921 | 8.84 |
| 1860–64 | 2,147,047 | +132,504 | +385,953 | 7.93 |
| 1865–69 | 2,234,454 | +528,588 | +150,845 | 6.02 |
| 1870–74 | 2,550,997 | +686,294 | +85,223 | 7.26 |
| 1875–79 | 2,923,108 | +1,240,030 | +125,247 | 6.60 |
| 1880–84 | 3,369,634 | +1,223,215 | +81,326 | 7.40 |
| 1885–89 | 2,832,363 | +786,436 | +62,388 | 6.91 |
| 1890–94 | 1,913,630 | −397,159 | +72,763 | 7.54 |
| 1895–99 | 1,517,848 | +256 | +50,432 | 4.99 |
| 1900–04 | 2,064,593 | +107,767 | +18,479 | 6.06 |
| 1905–09 | 2,315,990 | +506,061 | +23,038 | 5.33 |
| 1910–14 | 2,630,593 | +378,757 | +41,623 | 6.59 |
| 1915–19 | 5,596,360 | +2,466,624 | +18,923 | 9.30 |
| 1920–24 | 7,380,983 | +1,147,676 | +181,941 | 17.78 |
| 1925–29 | 3,403,079 | −504,023 | −81,908 | 10.18 |
| 1930–34 | 1,931,400 | −436,600 | −50,600 | 6.23 |

*Notes:* [a] Exclusive of specie unless otherwise indicated.     [b] Inclusive of specie.
[c] Official figures either do not exist or exist for only some years of the quinquenium in question. This figure has been calculated using the average price of raw sugar (cost plus insurance and freight) in London by Deerr 1949–50, vol. II, p. 531, minus 25 percent for freight and other charges. N.B. Deerr reports a sometimes substantial range of prices within any given year between 1814 and 1838. These figures should therefore be regarded only as a relative indication of export values, especially when they are compared with the few official figures that are available (see below).
[d] For the period 1812–16.
[e] The official value of the sugar exported in 1824 was £170,342.
[f] For 1822–24 only.
[g] Official figures put the average annual value of sugar exports between 1825 and 1828 at £368,743.
[h] Official figures put the average annual value of sugar exports between 1833 and 1834 at £558,134.
*Sources:* See table 1.

economic growth. However, if these data point to the relative strength of the Mauritian economy at this time, the sometimes substantial fluctuations in the balance of trade and the per capita value of imports indicate that this economy remained vulnerable to forces far beyond its control. Between 1845 and 1849 and 1850 and 1854, for example, the average price of sugar declined by 23.4 percent, only to rebound to earlier levels again during the second half of the 1850s.

While the increasing value of sugar exports underwrote a steady expansion of the local economy during the mid-nineteenth century, signs of long-term difficulties began to manifest themselves during the second half of the 1860s when the amount of specie entering the colony declined precipitously, a development which heralded the beginnings of a growing capital liquidity problem. By the mid-1880s, patterns of decline are discernible in other indices of economic well-being, such as the value of sugar exports and the balance of trade. These difficulties were mirrored by trends within the sugar industry itself. Between 1860 and 1885, the number of sugar factories declined by more than 40 percent as the manufacturing process became increasingly centralized; by 1900, the number of factories would be reduced by an additional 37 percent.[88] The subdivision of large properties that began *circa* 1875 likewise became more pronounced as the 1880s came to an end. The growing weakness of the colonial economy would become readily apparent during the 1890s, a decade which proved to be another watershed period in the island's social and economic history.

While the advent of the twentieth century witnessed a recovery from the various natural and economic disasters of the 1890s, the problems facing the Mauritian economy remained fundamentally unchanged. The outbreak of World War I in 1914 spurred a short-lived recovery in sugar prices which soared to astronomical levels by 1920 before beginning an equally precipitous decline to pre-war levels by 1925. The impact of this price decline was such that in March, 1928, the Chamber of Agriculture called for a new government loan in the amount of £1,500,000 on the grounds that the sugar industry had operated at a loss over the preceding four years.[89] The global depression that began in late 1929 delivered another punishing blow to the industry as the price of sugar plummeted still further. By 1933, the Chamber of Agriculture was reporting that "The resources in locally-owned liquid capital, on which the industry is dependent for financing its working requirements, have been severely contracted in consequence of a success of adverse trade years from 1923–31..." Only a series of profitable harvests, the Chamber continued, would ensure the "possibility of reconstructing an adequacy of working capital."[90]

The Great Depression revealed that neither the colonial nor the imperial government could cope with the conditions created by Mauritius' dependence upon a monocultural economy, a fickle world market, and the resources of domestic capital. The social and economic distress created by this reliance helped to light the fuse of widespread political protest which contributed to the rise in 1936 of the Mauritius Labor Party, the first political organization devoted to representing the interests of the colony's agricultural workers. Within a year, the colony's small planters were also being drawn into the political arena as they too sought to redress grievances and secure relief from the disabilities under which they had to live and work.[91] The forces unleashed at this time would help to set the stage for the movement toward independence which came on March 12, 1968. However, even as they moved along the path toward self-government, Mauritians would find themselves still bound by the slender, sweet thread that their fathers and grandfathers had known so well.

*Part 1*

# Labor and labor relations

# 2     A state of continual disquietude and hostility: maroonage and slave labor, 1721–1835

> Considerant que le maintien de l'ordre & l'éxecution des lois qui l'ont établi, sont le fondement de la prospérité des sociétés & singulièrement des Colonies, & qu'il est de notre devoir de travailler avec une continuelle application à maintenir l'Ordre public, & à rétablir les parties qui sont les plus negligées; nous avons jugé que nos premiers soins devoient régarder la Police des nègres esclaves ...
>
> Ordonnance concernant la police des noirs (29 septembre 1767)[1]

Like their counterparts in other slave-plantation societies, colonists on the Ile de France were plagued by the problem of maroonage, or the flight of slaves from their masters. Even the earliest settlers had to contend with this problem; in 1725, less than four years after the French occupation of the island, the missionary Ducros reported that maroon slaves were the principal danger feared by colonists.[2] Two years later, the decree establishing an administrative council for the Iles de France et de Bourbon noted that the "solid settlement of the Isle de France" required the destruction of the fugitive slaves inhabiting the island.[3] Governor La Bourdonnais claimed to have eradicated most of these maroons,[4] but any such success was, at best, only temporary. Admiral Kempenfelt observed in 1758 that maroons were still numerous despite the fact that fugitive slave patrols, or *détachements*, had captured or killed many of them.[5] The advent of British rule in 1810 did little to change the situation. In 1821, the Rev. Henry Shepherd wrote that the "numerous herds of Maroons, or runaway Slaves, in the interior, are notorious to all who have visited that Island."[6] Eleven years later, eighteen estate-owners in Pamplemousses district complained to their civil commissioner that "the number of maroons ... is increasing every day in a frightening manner."[7]

Fugitive slaves on the Ile de France elicited the same feelings of fear, anxiety, and revulsion they inspired elsewhere in the slave-owning world. These feelings stemmed in part from their ability to pose a serious threat to life, limb, and property. In June, 1749, Baron Grant reported that while the colony's fugitives generally contented themselves "with pillaging what they want for their support ... they will sometimes accompany their plunder with fire and sword."[8] C.F. Noble noted in the mid-1750s that maroons had "descended in the nights, on the neigh-bouring plantations and Villages, burnt & destroyed them, killed many of the Inhabitants & most trusty slaves, carried off their Women, and committed great depradations."[9] Fifty years later, Jacques Milbert reported that maroon slaves continued to couple murder and arson with theft and pillage.[10]

This fear of fugitive slaves was not conditioned simply by the threat they could pose to an individual's life or property. Authorities on the Ile de France, like colonial officials elsewhere, were equally concerned about the threat that maroon slaves could pose to the colony as a whole if they managed to create and maintain their own communities. They had only to look to the Caribbean and parts of South America for examples of what could happen if maroonage was not controlled.[11] Developments in Jamaica were particularly instructive; in that colony, the establishment and successful maintenance of fugitive slave communities in the Cockpit country eventually left colonial authorities with no other option but to recognize the Maroons as a separate community within the local body politic and to negotiate formal treaties in 1739 clarifying their status and position in Jamaican society.[12]

As was the case elsewhere, the Mauritian response to maroon activity was one of harsh repression. In addition to forming *détachements* of armed slaves to hunt down fugitives, the colonial administration vigor-ously enforced the laws that pertained to escaped slaves and those who aided them. The Code Noir of 1723 decreed that first-time fugitives were to lose both ears and be branded on the shoulder with a *fleur de lis*; the penalty for a third escape was death. The residents of the Ile de France did not hesitate to apply the full force of the law. The Bureau de Police recorded, for example, that at least eighty-three captured maroons lost one or both ears and were branded and/or whipped between July 29, 1767, and May 11, 1769.[13] Colonists also did not hesitate to shoot first and ask questions later. Baron Grant noted that fugitive slaves were "treated as wild animals: they are shot whenever the opportunity affords."[14] Some sixty years later, Milbert reported that fugitives con-tinued to be shot at will.[15]

The suppression of maroonage on the Ile de France was, as both the Baron and Milbert attest, driven by colonists' fears of the consequences if they lost control of the large servile population in their midst.[16] Studies of slave-plantation societies in the Americas have long acknowledged that such fears played an important role in shaping white attitudes in settings where, as in Mauritius, slaves often outnumbered whites by a margin of eight or nine to one, if not more. The violence directed against maroon slaves has accordingly been regarded as yet another manifestation of colonial paranoia and racism, an important aspect of class exploitation, or additional evidence that coercion was the cement that held these societies together.[17] What these studies have not done, however, is to ask basic questions about the act of maroonage itself: how many slaves marooned each year? What percentage of the slave population did they constitute? How long did most desertions last? What were the demographic and occupational characteristics of fugitive slaves? To what extent did maroon activity change with the passage of time, and why did it do so?

Answers to these questions are crucial not only to understanding how public order was maintained in these plantation societies, but also to assessing the long-term impact of slave resistance on colonial life. There can be no doubt, for example, that the maroon legacy influenced social and economic relationships on Mauritius long after the abolition of slavery in 1835 and the emancipation of the apprentices in 1839. The Royal Commissioners who investigated the treatment of Indian immigrants in the colony in 1872 reported that the "traditions of slavery" still persisted, and that the local police force continued to engage in periodic "maroon hunts."[18] These operations, directed against the tens of thousands of indentured Indian laborers in the colony, were conducted under the authority of desertion and vagrancy ordinances modeled upon the old fugitive slave laws. The persistence of these attitudes and practices in Mauritius and elsewhere is, in turn, often cited as evidence that the conditions under which indentured laborers worked and lived was nothing less than a "new system of slavery."

Early studies of maroon activity largely ignored these questions, concentrating instead upon the reasons why slaves ran away from their masters or upon the structure, organization, and history of individual maroon communities. More recent work on fugitive slaves in the Caribbean and elsewhere has begun to correct this oversight,[19] but the results of this scholarship remain problematic, partly because of the limited nature and restricted scope of the sources upon which it was based, and partly because of an often unquestioning acceptance of the resulting data. The exceptionally low maroonage rate (often less than 1 percent a year) reported in many of these slave societies is the most obvious case in point.[20] Figures such as these must invariably raise the question of whether we can reasonably expect the well-documented concern about maroonage to have been driven by such small numbers of fugitive slaves. The extent of our knowledge about slavery, and especially about slave resistance, in various parts of the colonial plantation world

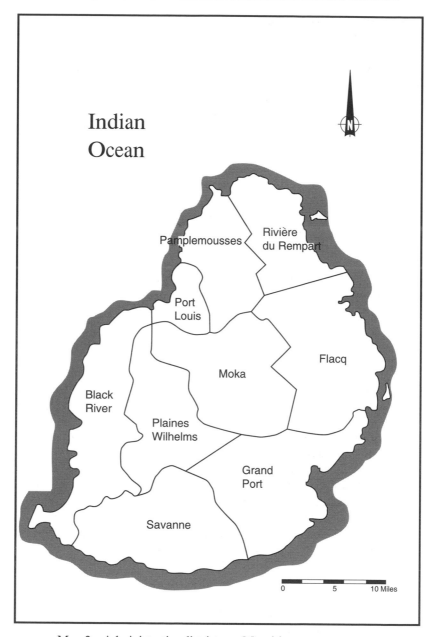

Map 2    Administrative districts on Mauritius

suggest that these data and the conclusions drawn from them must be viewed with care, if not outright skepticism.

In the case of Mauritius, the preservation of a number of maroon registers from the late eighteenth and early nineteenth centuries affords a unique opportunity to examine the nature and dynamics of maroonage on the island and, by implication, in other colonial plantation societies as well. These registers often contain a substantial amount of information about the island's fugitive slaves: name, sex, ethnicity or place of origin, owner, date of desertion and capture or return, and place and circumstances of capture. A total of five such registers exist: those for the districts of Rivière du Rempart (1772–94), Plaines Wilhems (1799–1805), and Moka (1825–33); the 1772–75 maroon capture book for the entire island; and the 1799–1812 register of the Bureau du Marronage. Other important sources of information about maroon activity include the record of punishments carried out by the police between 1767–69, many of which were inflicted upon maroon slaves, police ledgers which frequently contain entries about fugitive slaves, and the reports on maroon activity submitted to the Commission of Eastern Enquiry in 1828 by John Finniss, the colony's chief of police.

Although Mauritian colonists complained incessantly about the number of fugitive slaves on the island, the archival record is largely silent about the incidence of maroonage before the 1770s. One of the first such references concerns *Le Rubis*, a ship which arrived at the Ile de France on December 8, 1722, with a cargo that included sixty-five slaves, nineteen of whom quickly became maroons.[21] Other slaves joined these fugitives until their number totaled some fifty individuals.[22] According to La Bourdonnais, no more than 45 of the island's 2,616 slaves were fugitives in 1740.[23] Thirty-seven years later, Pierre Poivre estimated the number of maroons on the island to be about 600, or 3.2 percent of the local slave population.[24] Various contemporary sources indicate that the ranks of the maroon population swelled still further during the early 1770s. John Colpoys, an English naval lieutenant, reported in 1772 that he had been "well assured" that the island's woods concealed between 3,000 and 4,000 fugitive slaves, while Etienne de Bompar, the French navy's comptroller on the Ile de France, put the number of maroons in 1775 at 1,200.[25] At the same time, the capture book for the island recorded the apprehension of a total of 1,375 fugitive slaves from 1773 through 1775, a figure which may represent from 40 to 50 percent of all declared desertions during this period.[26]

Bompar's figure, together with estimates that can be derived from the capture book, indicate that from 4 to 5 percent of the island's slave population marooned each year during the early 1770s. Colpoy's figure for 1772 is obviously inflated beyond reasonable limits and must be dismissed; not even during the 1820s, when figures on the colony-wide incidence of maroonage again become available, did the equivalent of 15 to 20 percent of the local slave population desert in any given year. The only district register to survive from the eighteenth century – that for Rivière du Rempart – confirms that the local maroonage rate averaged between 4 and 5 percent a year during the 1770s. The register recorded seventy-four desertions between December 3, 1775, and December 3, 1776, a figure equal to 4.25 percent of the district's slave population during the second half of 1776. Another eighty-eight cases of maroonage were reported between December 4, 1776, and November 16, 1777, a figure equal to 5.05 percent of the district's slave population in 1776.[27]

Although information on the colony-wide incidence of maroonage does not become available again until the 1820s, the Rivière du Rempart and Plaines Wilhems registers reveal something of the nature, extent, and dynamics of maroon activity throughout the island during the inter-vening decades. These registers indicate, among other things, that the number of fugitive slaves increased steadily during the late eighteenth and early nineteenth centuries. The average number of desertions in Rivière du Rempart, for example, rose from 7.2 a month between 1773 and 1782 to 11.6 a month between 1783 and 1793. The Plaines Wilhems register, which recorded an average of almost thirty-four desertions each month between September 23, 1799, and September 22, 1805, confirms this general trend.[28]

Such increases are not unexpected; the local slave population doubled in size during the last quarter of the eighteenth century, from 25,154 in 1776 to 49,080 in 1797, and its ranks continued to swell after 1800, climbing to at least 60,646 in 1806. Compared to these figures, the increased incidence of maroonage in Rivière du Rempart by the early 1790s is actually somewhat lower than might otherwise be expected under such circumstances. However, if the Rivière du Rempart and Plaines Wilhems registers attest that ever-greater numbers of slaves fled from their masters after mid-1770s, the Plaines Wilhems data also suggest that the overall rate of maroon activity remained relatively constant throughout the late eighteenth and early nineteenth centuries. An average of 407 desertions occurred in the district each year between September 23, 1799, and September 22, 1805, a figure which represents about 5.5 percent of the district's slave population during each of these six years.[29]

The level of maroon activity, which had remained relatively constant at approximately 5 percent a year during the last years of French rule, increased dramatically following the island's cession to Britain at the end of the Napoleonic wars. John Finniss informed the Commission of Eastern Enquiry in 1828 that more than 52,000 declarations of maroonage had been filed with colonial authorities from 1820 through 1826, figures which point to an average desertion rate of 11.2 to 11.7 percent over this seven-year period.[30] The Moka register confirms that a significantly larger percentage of the colony's slave population was engaging in maroon activity by the 1820s; the 257 cases of desertion reported in the district during 1825 equaled 9.4 percent of the district's slave population that year.[31] Desertion rates remained elevated even as it became increasingly apparent during the early 1830s that the abolition of slavery was looming on the horizon. B.H. de Froberville, for one, estimated that 3,000 slaves had fled from their masters between September, 1831, and April, 1832, a figure which points to an annual maroonage rate of not less than 7.1 percent.[32]

The depth of colonial concern about maroon activity becomes more comprehensible in light of these data. The intensity of the local reaction to maroonage cannot be explained, however, only in terms of the existence of a large, and expanding, fugitive slave population. A closer reading of the available documentation reveals that the impact that these high rates of maroon activity had on the colonial psyche was compounded by the demographic characteristics of these fugitive slaves.

Although the kind of detailed information that exists for some Caribbean colonies is unavailable for the Ile de France, the general outlines of the Mauritian population's age and sex structure can be discerned without much difficulty. As in most other colonial plantation societies of the day, the death rate among Mauritian slaves exceeded the birth rate by a substantial margin,[33] and the colony had to rely accordingly upon the continual importation of new slaves to maintain a viable servile work force. The archival record is silent about the sexual composition of the slave cargoes that reached the Mascarenes before 1810, but Mauritian census data indicate that the general pattern of imports was consistent with the ratio of approximately two males to every female that characterized European slave-trading, and French slave-trading in particular, at this time.[34] These data also reveal that the local slave population was composed largely of adults (i.e., individuals of fifteen years of age and older), and that adult males accounted for at least 50 percent, and often a substantially higher percentage, of the colony's bondsmen during much of the period under consideration.

Although the Rivière du Rempart, Plaines Wilhems, and Moka registers did not record the age of fugitive slaves, there is every reason to believe that the overwhelming majority of maroons were adults. The rigors of life on the run, which often severely tested even the most hardened and experienced of escapees, effectively precluded the involvement of large numbers of children. On those few occasions when children are mentioned explicitly in the district registers, they are invariably reported as having fled in company with their mothers. The registers reveal that males regularly accounted for 80 to 90 percent of all fugitives, despite comprising less than two-thirds of the colony's servile population. The problematic nature of some of the data on female fugitives suggests that the percentage of female maroons was somewhat higher than the figures in table 3 indicate.[35] It should be noted, however, that even if women accounted for a slightly higher percentage of the colony's maroons, the sexual composition of the Mauritian fugitive population was comparable to those in many parts of the Americas.[36]

Mauritian slaves originated from throughout the Indian Ocean world as well as beyond its bounds, and the district registers illustrate the ethnic diversity of this population, recording as they do the presence of Abyssinians, Bambaras, Bengalis, Cafres, Guineans, Lascars, Malabars, Malambous, Malays, Talingas, and Timorians among the colony's fugitives.[37] However, most of the island's slaves were classified as belonging to one of four principal ethnic categories: Creole, Indian, Malagasy, and Mozambican. As elsewhere in the European colonial world, Mauritian slave-owners assigned stereotypical qualities and attributes to each of these groups. Mozambican slaves, for example, were widely regarded as being suited physically to plantation labor but lacking in intelligence; Indian slaves, on the other hand, tended to be praised for their docility and grace while being deemed unfit for hard physical labor. Creole, or locally born, slaves were generally castigated for their laziness and fondness of sensual pleasures, and there was almost unanimous agreement that slaves from Madagascar were the most prone to desert.[38] Given their preconceptions about the aptitudes and abilities of each of these groups, colonists often employed Indian and Malay slaves as domestic servants and artisans, while those of African or Malagasy origin more commonly served as agricultural laborers.

However, as the district registers reveal, these ethnic stereotypes were, at best, an imprecise indicator of which slaves were most likely to desert their masters. Although Malagasies accounted for an estimated 45 percent of all slaves imported into the Mascarenes before 1810, table 3 suggests that Malagasy slaves marooned less frequently during the late eighteenth century than either their reputation or their numbers might otherwise suggest. The Rivière du Rempart and Plaines Wilhems registers likewise demonstrate that Indian slaves were not nearly as docile as colonists liked to believe, deserting as they did in numbers generally

Table 3. *Sex and ethnicity of maroon slaves, 1772–1833*

| | (Percent) | | | | | |
| District | Moz.[a] | Malg.[a] | Ind.[a] | Creole | Other[a] | No. |
|---|---|---|---|---|---|---|
| Rivière du Rempart, 1772–94: | | | | | | |
| All maroons | 47.4 | 30.9 | 7.5 | 5.5 | 8.7 | 2,487 |
| Male maroons | 49.9 | 31.2 | 6.1 | 4.7 | 8.1 | 2,227 |
| Female maroons | 26.2 | 28.1 | 19.6 | 12.3 | 13.8 | 260 |
| Plaines Wilhems, 1799–1805: | | | | | | |
| All maroons | 54.8 | 19.6 | 10.3 | 8.2 | 7.1 | 2,586[a] |
| Male maroons | 52.6 | 19.4 | 12.3 | 9.0 | 6.7 | 1,515 |
| Female maroons | 46.3 | 13.6 | 17.9 | 16.3 | 5.9 | 324 |
| Moka, 1825–33: | | | | | | |
| All maroons | 41.5 | 19.2 | 1.1 | 36.5 | 1.7 | 1,524 |
| Male maroons | 45.4 | 20.0 | 1.1 | 31.9 | 1.6 | 1,256 |
| Female maroons | 23.5 | 15.7 | 0.8 | 57.8 | 2.2 | 268 |
| Slave ethnicity, | | | | | | |
| 1806: | 44.0 | 18.2 | 10.2 | 27.6 | — | 60,646 |
| 1827: | 27.7 | 18.3 | 3.4 | 50.3 | 0.3 | 69,201 |

*Notes:*
[a] Ind.   Indian
   Malg.   Malagasy
   Moz.   Mozambican
   Other   Cafre, Guinean, Malay, Timorian, and ethnicity not specified.
[b] The sex of 747 maroons could not be determined.
*Sources:* CO 167/141 – Return of Slaves Registered in Mauritius between the 16th of
         October 1826 and the 16th of January 1827 ...
         MA: A 76 – Municipalité des Plaines Wilhems, Registre de déclarations de
         marronage, 16 germinal An VII–30 brumaire An XIV (5 avril 1799–1 novembre
         1805); IA 40 – Registre des marronages, Moka (1 janvier 1825–15 mai 1833);
         OA 70 – Registre pour l'enregistrement des déclarations de noirs fugitifs
         envoyées du quartier de la Rivière Basse du Rempart (14 novembre 1772–31
         mai 1794).
         Milbert 1812, vol. II, p. 233 bis.

proportional to their representation in the slave population as a whole. Finally, these data reveal that the ethnic composition of the fugitive population varied depending upon the gender of the slaves in question. In Rivière du Rempart, a disproportionately large percentage of female fugitives were Creoles or of Indian origin; Creoles likewise accounted for a disproportionately large number of the women who fled from their masters in Moka.

The harshness of the Mauritian response to maroonage becomes more understandable in light of these data. At a psychological level, there can be little doubt that this response was driven by fear of a servile population that not only outnumbered white colonists by a margin of as much as ten to one, but also demonstrated on a daily basis that it was anything but docile and obedient. These realities, together with the ability of fugitive slaves to destroy crops, livestock, and buildings, to kidnap other slaves, and to threaten life and limb, contributed to a sense of paranoia about which John Le Brun, an English missionary with several years of experience living in the colony, wrote tellingly in 1817: "One evening ... [a district civil commissioner] ... saw in his dreams a number of black people assembled upon the mountain with Colours &c. He sends immediately a message to the officers of police that the blacks by hundreds were preparing to revolt. They ran with all speed armed to the spot, but find only a few Malgaches, performing their funeral rites over one of their nation, as they always do."[39] The fact that the majority of fugitive slaves were not only adult males, but also often Mozambicans renowned in colonial minds for their physical prowess, only compounded this sense of fear and paranoia.

Fear and paranoia were not the only factors, however, which helped to foster the well-developed sense of antipathy toward fugitive slaves that characterized eighteenth-century Mauritian life. As contemporary observers of colonial life readily appreciated, this hatred of maroon slaves was also driven by economic considerations. In addition to the immediate monetary losses which estate-owners might suffer as a result of a maroon incursion, maroon activity also threatened slave-owners with the permanent loss of a substantial capital investment. The price of an adult slave during the 1770s and 1780s, for example, ranged from 1,200 to 1,500 livres, while the services of a skilled artisan could easily cost 1,800 livres or more, a sum large enough to purchase at least forty or fifty arpents of good agricultural land. The act of maroonage could similarly imperil an individual's capital liquidity, a potentially serious problem in a colony that frequently had to cope with periodic shortages of specie. As the notarial record attests, it was not uncommon for slaves to be used in lieu of cash to purchase land or shares in privateers and to settle outstanding debts.

The economic impact of maroonage manifested itself in other ways. The connection between slave ethnicity and occupational status outlined above suggests that 75 percent or more of all fugitive slaves were involved directly in productive enterprises.[40] High rates of maroonage could accordingly have a significant impact upon estate operations or, in the case of small slave-owners who depended upon the income generated from renting out their slaves, upon their very livelihood. Although the correlation between occupational status and maroon activity becomes more difficult to document as the slave population became increasingly creolized during the nineteenth century, there is reason to believe that this relationship remained intact. Of the 56,699 "effective" bondsmen for whom compensation was paid after slavery was abolished in 1835, some 34,400 were reported to be praedial or agricultural slaves. More than four-fifths of these praedial slaves were described specifically as field laborers.[41]

The propensity for fugitives to be agricultural workers raises the question of the extent to which maroonage coincided with plantation labor cycles. Scholarship on the Americas has revealed that maroon activity could be closely linked to these cycles.[42] The Rivière du Rempart register, however, points to no particular correlation on the Ile de France between estate activities and when slaves marooned, at least during the latter part of the eighteenth century. During the 1820s, as the cultivation of sugar cane became increasingly widespread, some colonists thought they could discern a distinct pattern to maroon activity. In testimony before the Commission of Eastern Enquiry, John Finniss suggested that the increase in the number of desertions earlier in the decade was due to "the greater degree of labour performed during the Sugar Season,"[43] but the figures he submitted to the Commissioners do not substantiate his claim. The Moka register likewise reveals that the number of desertions in any given month could fluctuate widely from year to year. In some years, maroon activity in the district remained very low during the months when the cane harvest, a particularly grueling time for estate workers, took place. It was at precisely such times that the incentives to maroon could be particularly strong; on the other hand, these were also the months when the supervision of slaves could be especially close. In other years, maroonage was more or less evenly spread throughout the year.

Mauritian maroons, like fugitive slaves elsewhere, were often highly mobile while at liberty. The capture book for 1772–75 and the register of the Bureau du Marronage contain numerous references to fugitive slaves who were captured or killed in districts at the opposite end of the island from where they had originally marooned. Unfortunately, more detailed information about the geographical distribution of maroon activity does not exist. However, a sense of the spatial dynamics of this activity, at least during the 1820s, can be inferred from another of John Finniss' returns which reports the number of fugitives captured in 1826 by local *détachements*. This return reveals that significant disparities existed between a district's percentage of the total slave population and its percentage of maroon captures. Port Louis, which housed less than 20 percent of the colony's slaves, accounted for almost 40 percent of all captures that year.[44] In six of the island's eight rural districts, by way of comparison, the percentage of captures was often markedly lower than the district's percentage of the total slave population.

These disparities could be, of course, nothing more than an index of the effectiveness of local *détachements*; in some districts, only one or two out of six or seven such patrols seem to have actively pursued fugitive slaves. Other sources suggest, however, that the pattern noted above is neither unusual nor unexpected. Port Louis housed the bulk of the colony's rapidly growing free population of color, the presence of which clearly afforded fugitives, such as the Indian slave Camille, an opportunity to pass themselves off as free persons of color.[45] Contemporary legislation and numerous entries in police registers also confirm that Port Louis remained a powerful magnet for many escapees.

The length of time fugitive slaves remained at liberty ranged from just a day or two to several years or more. District registers and police records contain a fair number of references to desertions that lasted for extended periods of time. On June 19, 1767, for example, the Bureau de Police recorded the capture of Sylvestre, La Rose, and Thérèse, all Malagasy slaves who had each been free for at least a year and a half.[46] Thirty-seven years later, the Bureau du Marronage recorded the capture of Philippe, another Malagasy slave, who had fled from his master six years earlier.[47] The following year, the Bureau reported that Jupiter, a Mozambican slave, had been killed after having reportedly been free for twelve to fifteen years.[48]

Cases such as these gave credence to the perception among many colonists that acts of maroonage often deprived them of the services of their slaves for extended periods of time. John Finniss seemed to give substance to such beliefs when he informed the Commission of Eastern Enquiry that 57 percent of the fugitive slaves captured between 1823 and 1827 had been *grand* maroons, that is, fugitive for more than thirty days. However, the police chief also admitted implicitly that these figures did not accurately reflect the length of many desertions when he acknowledged that the individuals who led fugitive slave patrols often kept the slaves they had apprehended "not only with a view to have the Slaves labor, but by the delay to increase the amount of the reward."[49] The reward for *grand* maroons was substantially higher than that for *petit* maroons who had been absent for only three to thirty days. The district registers cast additional doubt on the police chief's assertions about the prevalence of *grand* maroonage. More specifically, the registers recorded a capture or return date for 40 to 50 percent of all reported cases of maroonage and, as the figures in table 4 indicate, at least one-half, if not two-thirds or three-fourths, of such desertions lasted less than one month, and often only a week or two.

Table 4. *Characteristics of maroon activity, 1772–1833*

| | (Percent) | | |
| --- | --- | --- | --- |
| Nature of Activity | Rivière du Rempart, 1772–94 | Plaines Wilhems, 1799–1805 | Moka, 1825–33 |
| Length of desertions: | | | |
| 7 days or less | 12.0 | 25.7 | 22.5 |
| 8–31 days | 42.7 | 49.0 | 45.5 |
| 1–3 months | 29.7 | 18.4 | 22.4 |
| 3–6 months | 10.3 | 4.3 | 6.6 |
| 6–12 months | 4.0 | 2.2 | 2.9 |
| 1 year or more | 1.3 | 0.4 | 0.1 |
| No. = | 1,170 | 1,129 | 773 |
| Group desertions: | | | |
| % of all desertions made by groups: | 39.8 | 31.5 | 22.0 |
| Size of group: | | | |
| 2 | 63.2 | 68.2 | 82.9 |
| 3 | 20.2 | 21.0 | 8.1 |
| 4 | 8.6 | 5.7 | 1.8 |
| 5 + | 8.0 | 5.1 | 7.2 |
| No. = | 361 | 314 | 111 |

*Sources:* MA: A 76; IA 40; OA 70.

The tendency for maroon registers to record the name of a slave's master as well as the date of his or her desertion makes it possible to determine the extent to which maroonage was an individual or group act. The figures in table 4 are based upon the assumption that whenever two or more slaves fled from the same master on the same day, they probably did so in concert. These data reveal that a substantial majority of desertions involved slaves acting alone; they also indicate that the percentage of group desertions declined over time. While mass escapes of ten, twelve, seventeen, eighteen, and twenty-three slaves occurred, the overwhelming majority of these desertions involved only two or three individuals. While the extent to which the members of these groups stayed together is unclear, the district registers suggest that it was not uncommon for at least some of the participants in a group desertion to remain together throughout their period of freedom.

These data help to explain why viable maroon communities failed to develop on the island. Eighteenth-century observers such as C.F. Noble reported that fugitive slaves often formed "very strong bodys,"[50] while *détachements* frequently reported encountering maroon bands and camps during their sweeps through the countryside. Most of these bands, however, seem to have been little more than *ad hoc* groups that stayed together for relatively short periods of time. This is not to say that maroon communities could not or did not exist, especially during the eighteenth century when large parts of the island's central plateau and southern coast remained largely unsettled. During his visit to the island in 1769–70, Maximillien Wiklinsky reported the existence of a maroon village at Le Morne Brabant in the far southwestern corner of the island. According to Wiklinsky, the maroons in this community, prior to its destruction by a local planter, had constructed cabins, planted crops, elected a chief, and were increasing in number as a result of natural reproduction.[51] The existence of such a community undoubtedly provided the basis of the folk tales that tell of a small band of maroons that hid out near Le Morne for many years.[52] Police and other records indicate, however, that maroon communities were never able to establish themselves on Mauritius as they managed to do on the Ile de Bourbon[53] and in various parts of the Caribbean and Central and South America.

This absence of viable maroon communities on the Ile de France is not unexpected given the factors which worked against their establishment and ability to maintain themselves. The small size of the groups that were formed is the most obvious case in point. The Bureau du Marronage noted occasionally how many fugitives were in the bands or camps attacked by district *détachements*; the largest such band consisted of sixteen persons.[54] In the five other bands for which information is available, the number of members ranged from as few as four to as many as twelve individuals. Such small groups clearly could not hope to stand up to the colony's well-armed police and military forces. Secondly, the increasing settlement of the island's interior during the eighteenth and early nineteenth centuries deprived maroon slaves of secure places where they could hide. Last, and perhaps most importantly, the island's small size and the relative absence of the kind of rugged terrain found on the Ile de Bourbon deprived Mauritian fugitives of the kind of geographical isolation that was an absolute prerequisite to the establishment and maintenance of maroon communities.

If Mauritian authorities did not have to deal with some of the problems that confronted their colleagues elsewhere in the colonial world, the extent of maroon activity suggests nevertheless that the local government's ability to control fugitive slaves remained limited. Colonists complained repeatedly about the ineffectiveness of local police forces. As late as 1832, eighteen residents of Pamplemousses district wrote pointedly to their civil commissioner that the gendarmes attached to his office seemed to do nothing except deliver messages.[55] The large number of desertions in Rivière du Rempart that lasted for a month or more indicates that at least during the late eighteenth century such complaints were not unfounded. While the percentage of these longer-term desertions subsequently declined, John Finniss still had to inform the Commission of Eastern Enquiry that an average of 23 percent of all fugitives remained unaccounted for at the end of each year from 1820 through 1826.[56] The Plaines Wilhems and Moka registers likewise confirm that maroon slaves remained active and resourceful protagonists.

The reasons for the colonial preoccupation with the suppression of maroonage and the maintenance of public order become readily apparent in light of these data. In the first instance, this concern was clearly driven by the scale of maroon activity. Large numbers of slaves ran away from their masters every month of the year. During the late eighteenth and early nineteenth centuries approximately 5 percent of the island's slave population could be expected to maroon each year. By the early 1820s, the annual incidence of maroonage frequently ranged from 11 to 13 percent or more of the colony's servile population. Secondly, most of these fugitives were adult males, a source of additional concern to a white population worried not only about its small numbers *vis-à-vis* the local slave population, but also by its stereotypical images of the non-white males in its midst. As Baron Grant observed, the threat posed by these fugitives was "increased by the perfect knowledge they possess of the plantation they have deserted ... their old comrades and mistresses will frequently give them information of the most convenient opportunities to descend on their pillaging parties; so that they may be said to keep us in a state of continual disquietude and hostility."[57] Lastly, the great majority of maroons were praedial slaves whose absence not only deprived their owners of valuable labor, but also threatened them with a substantial capital loss.

The dramatic increase in maroonage by the early 1820s, together with the significant numbers of fugitive slaves who remained unaccounted for at the end of the year or who enjoyed a month or more at liberty, suggest that colonial authorities were increasingly hard-pressed to control maroon activity during the early nineteenth century. As was noted earlier, many colonists were quick to blame their police force, and not without reason. The impact that determined policing could have on maroon activity had been demonstrated on the Ile de Bourbon, where a desertion rate that ran as high as 6 percent in 1741 fell to less than 1 percent by 1768 in response to the measures taken by local *détachements*.[58] However, a similar sense of determination appears to have been absent on Mauritius by the 1820s; in 1826, only eleven of forty-two rural *détachements* seem to have actively pursued fugitive slaves, accounting as they did for more than three-fifths of all captures that year.[59]

While figures such as these confirm that police inaction facilitated maroonage in Mauritius, it is important to put this lack of effectiveness in perspective. In the first place, we must note that the island's slave population quadrupled in size between the 1770s and the early 1820s without a corresponding increase in the size of the local police force.[60] Secondly, and more importantly, the marked increase in maroon activity that was being reported by the early 1820s occurred within the larger context of significant changes in the colony's social, economic, and political life. Under these circumstances, it is clear that considerations other than just police inefficiency contributed to the growing willingness and ability of Mauritian slaves to desert their masters.

The amelioration of the penalties for maroonage was one such factor. The death penalty for third-time maroons had been commuted to less severe forms of punishment as early as 1775, with the result that the chaining of captured fugitives for extended periods of time became the established practice. The advent of British rule in 1810 brought a continued lessening of the punishments inflicted upon fugitive slaves. In January, 1813, Governor Sir Robert Farquhar abolished the reward paid for dead maroons, together with the practice of presenting a severed hand as proof of death, and the number of fugitives killed by *détachements* declined dramatically. John Finniss reported in due course that local *détachements* had killed only sixteen fugitives between January, 1813 and June, 1828, compared to the 102 such deaths recorded by the Bureau du Marronage between 1799–1812.[61] The growing movement during the 1820s to ameliorate the conditions of slave life further reinforced this trend toward milder forms of punishment for maroon activity.

If Mauritian slaves deserted in greater numbers during the early nineteenth century because the penalties for maroonage became less severe, they were also encouraged to do so because of the growing possibilities of shelter and aid from their free or emancipated brethren; between 1806 and 1825, the local free population of color doubled in size to more than 14,000 persons, or 17 percent of the island's total population. Such assistance was important because the steady clearance and settlement of the island's heavily wooded interior reduced the number of places where fugitive slaves could hide. According to some accounts of colonial life, the relationship between slaves and free persons of color, or *gens de couleur*, was one of mutual antagonism,[62] but police records indicate that many free persons of color were more than willing to help maroons avoid detection and capture. On November 7, 1799, for example, the Port Louis police discovered Camille, an Indian slave belonging to Citizen Dagot, in a house in the *Camp des citoyens de couleur* owned by Agathe, a free woman of color.[63] Agathe's association with several Indian seamen at the time of the raid suggests that she may have been trying to arrange for Camille's escape from the island. An Indian and three Mozambican sailors were similarly involved in a plot, uncovered on September 6, 1790, to steal a ship and return as many as fifty-four slaves (forty-two men and twelve women) belonging to forty-three masters to Madagascar.[64]

The Code Noir of 1723 recognized that the bond between slaves and *gens de couleur* could be a strong one, and stipulated accordingly that freedmen or free persons of color were subject to a fine of 10 piastres for every day of shelter they gave to a fugitive slave; whites, on the other hand, were to be fined only 3 piastres a day for the same offense. However, such provisions seem to have had little impact upon relations between slaves and freedmen. Eugène Bernard reported in 1834 that most of the bondsmen who had been emancipated since 1827 survived on what they received from friends and relatives still enslaved on local estates.[65] The close ties that existed between some *gens de couleur* and slaves would be further attested to during the post-emancipation era.

Contemporary sources also indicate that the higher rates of maroonage reported during the 1820s reflected subtle, but important, changes in the ideology of desertion. Eighteenth-century observers of Mauritian life readily ascribed the propensity of slaves to run away to their continuing "love of liberty," a sentiment subsequently articulated by individuals such as Narcisse, one of the slaves arrested during the attempted mass escape of September 6, 1790. The fact that fugitives would endure difficult living conditions while they were at liberty, or would attempt to sail the 500 miles to Madagascar in small, open canoes, is additional evidence of the intense desire of some slaves to escape completely from the bonds of servitude.[66] As entries in the Bureau du Marronage register confirm, the desire to be free continued to impel slaves to maroon during the early nineteenth century.

However, the desire to be free was not the only reason slaves ran away from their masters. Mauritian slaves, like those in other plantation colonies, had to endure harsh living and working conditions as well as the constant threat of physical and psychological abuse. According to some accounts, the slave regime in Mauritius was a particularly brutal one, even by contemporary standards.[67] John Finniss acknowledged as much when he noted that, for many slaves, imprisonment for maroonage was preferable to working on their master's estate. The reason for this preference, wrote the chief of police, was simple and straightforward:

prisoners in the Bagne Prison were fed better than they were on many plantations.[68]

On those occasions when Mauritian slaves speak to us themselves, it is clear that desertion was one of the ways they coped with the hardships of daily life.[69] As this population became increasingly creolized during the early nineteenth century, there are also indications that slaves who knew no other home came to view maroonage less as a way of escaping from servitude *per se* and more as a way of preserving "a species of freedom within slavery."[70] A notation in the Plaines Wilhems register suggests, for instance, that one of the largest group desertions reported in the district was actually a temporary work stoppage to protest poor working and/or living conditions rather than a classic act of maroonage.[71]

Entries in the Moka register likewise indicate that maroonage became an increasingly valuable tactic during the early nineteenth century, as slaves sought to expand control over various aspects of their personal lives, and especially to maintain family and other important social ties. The career of Azoline, a Creole slave, is an instructive case in point. Azoline deserted from her master no less than twenty-one times between January 11, 1825, and April 1, 1832.[72] While we do not know where Azoline went when she marooned, the frequency of her desertions, their relatively short duration, and the fact that she took her child with her on at least four occasions suggests that the purpose of her desertions was to visit a husband, family members, or friends on nearby estates. The increasingly individualistic nature of maroon activity at this time, as well as the growing number of desertions that lasted for a week or less (see table 4, p. 47), also point to the development of a more complex maroon ethos as the island's slaves, like their American counterparts, defined freedom in variable terms.[73]

It is tempting to argue in light of these data that the higher rates of maroonage found in Mauritius by the early 1820s were due largely to the initiative taken by individual slaves like Azoline. Recent scholarship has emphasized that slaves played an active role in shaping the plantation experience in the New World, and the archival record confirms that Mauritian slaves, like their American counterparts, were anything but passive actors on the colonial stage. What is much less clear, however, is exactly how and why these men and women managed to "empower" themselves, if only in limited ways. That personal talent, courage, and perseverance allowed some slaves to do so cannot be doubted. The depth of our knowledge about plantation systems nevertheless suggests that the actions of resolute individuals, no matter how inspiring, cannot adequately explain this increased incidence of maroon activity on Mauritius.

The key to a more comprehensive understanding of these developments is to be found in the various socio-economic changes that
characterize the first decades of British rule. More specifically, we may
note that a slave population of some 61,000 persons in 1810 soared to
approximately 80,000 between 1817 and early 1819, only to decline to
perhaps as few as 63,000 souls by 1822 in the wake of a vigorous
campaign from mid-1818 to mid-1820 to suppress the clandestine slave
trade and a cholera epidemic during late 1819 and early 1820 that may
have killed as many as 7,000 bondsmen. At the same time, this population became not only increasingly Creole, but also one in which
children under sixteen years of age accounted for an ever-larger percentage of all bondsmen.[74]

These demographic trends accentuated the growing labor crisis faced
by the colony's rapidly expanding sugar industry. Although the illicit
slave trade resumed late in 1820 and probably continued until *circa* 1826,
the level of imports during this period remained substantially lower than
in the years before 1819. The impact of this shortage of servile field
hands was compounded by the sugar industry's shaky financial condition
which precluded the importation of costly indentured laborers. In
circumstances such as these, where many estate-owners were preoccupied
with the need to maintain an available work force, maroon activity, or
even the threat of maroonage, provided many slaves with a powerful
weapon that could be used to renegotiate some of the conditions under
which they lived and worked. As Azoline's remarkable career suggests,
one aspect of this revised system of colonial labor relations may even
have been a tacit understanding between some masters and slaves that
occasional, circumscribed acts of desertion would be more or less
tolerated.

The abolition of slavery in Mauritius on February 1, 1835, did not bring
an end to maroonage or to attempts to suppress it. On the eve of
abolition, Governor Sir William Nicolay sent a dispatch to London that
included a copy of an ordinance that amended, rather than abolished, the
laws relating to runaway slaves. The need for this legislation stemmed
from the expectation that the colony's new "apprentices" would continue
to run away from their masters, as indeed they did. During 1835, 1836,
and 1837 an average of 7.7 percent of the apprentice population was
apprehended each year for desertion.[75] Even the impending final emancipation of the apprentices did not bring an end to the local preoccupation
with desertion. On August 20, 1838, police chief Finniss declared that he
was not prepared to dispense entirely with the services of the *chasseurs de
police* because,

something of this kind must be kept up either under their present designation or as an "Auxiliary Police" to be employed in hunting fugitives and vagabonds who take refuge in the Forests and upon the Mountains from whence they descend at night and commit all kinds of depredations upon the adjoining Estates. This has become a Serious and alarming evil daily increasing since the introduction of Indian Labourers.[76]

The implication of his remarks was clear and unequivocal. The indentured Indian immigrants who had begun to arrive on the island in 1834 to work in the cane fields were rapidly becoming the focus of the colonial concern about desertion, illegal absence, and vagrancy. As the coming years would reveal, the maroon legacy was alive and well and ready to flourish for at least another half century.

## 3    Indentured labor and the legacy of maroonage: illegal absence, desertion, and vagrancy, 1835–1900

> The Governor has seen with the deepest regret that the influx of Indian labourers from the Country Districts to the general Police with complaints continues without intermission. And His Excellency has in consequence directed me to draw the attention of the Civil commissioners to this great evil, and to point out to them the necessity of exerting themselves to prevent these men from quitting the districts in which they are employed for the purpose of prefering complaints before the Police of Port Louis.
>
> ... His Excellency cannot help thinking that the local Magistracy have hitherto failed in impressing the Indians with a due reverence for their proceedings and judgments; and, generally speaking, that they have not secured that confidence on the part of the Indian Labourers which would lead them to bring their complaints before the District Magistrates and to rest satisfied with their decisions.
>
> Geo. Dick, Colonial Secretary, to Civil Commissioners, March 15, 1837[1]

Even before the abolition of slavery in 1835, Mauritian planters had begun the search for supplies of free labor to work their estates. The local slave population's inability to supply the labor needed by a rapidly expanding sugar industry had become apparent by the early 1830s, while the availability of this work force over the long term was also increasingly open to question. The act of abolition promised planters the services of their former slaves, now transformed into "apprentices," as praedial laborers, but only for a period of six years. Some estate-owners no doubt suspected that the apprenticeship system might come to an end earlier than scheduled, as indeed was to happen in 1839. Others may have suspected that many apprentices would leave the plantations upon their final emancipation, as indeed most of them subsequently did. The colony's planters accordingly dispatched their agents as far afield as China, Singapore, Ethiopia, and Madagascar to search out possible supplies of inexpensive free labor. Their gaze returned repeatedly, however, to the readily accessible and seemingly inexhaustible manpower of India.

Almost 24,000 privately recruited indentured Indian laborers stepped ashore at Port Louis between 1834 and late 1838. Upon their arrival, many of these workers fell victim to the abuses of what abolitionist and humanitarian groups characterized as a "new system of slavery."[2] The public outcry in both Britain and India over the crass exploitation to which these earliest immigrants were subjected forced the Government of India to suspend emigration to Mauritius late in 1838. Immigration resumed late in 1842 only after repeated appeals from the colony's governor and the local sugar industry that the continued suspension of the so-called "coolie trade" would spell economic disaster for the island. However, to prevent the kind of abuses that had prompted its suspension in 1838, immigration resumed under governmental, rather than private, auspices.[3]

Despite their obvious relief over the resumption of Indian immigration, Mauritian planters and colonial officials often remained rather ambivalent about the indentured work force in their midst. On the one hand, there was widespread agreement that the massive influx of Indian laborers after 1842 had saved the island's sugar industry – and the colony itself – from economic ruin. In his annual report for 1851, Governor J.M. Higginson stated categorically that immigration was "the corner-stone of Mauritian prosperity,"[4] a sentiment that would be echoed by other occupants of Government House. On the other hand, there was also considerable annoyance over the problems spawned by this system of contractual labor, not the least of which were those associated with worker absenteeism and desertion. In 1845, Governor Sir William Gomm wrote pointedly about the "extreme licentiousness with regard to absenteeism among the labouring population."[5] By 1854, Major General Charles Hay was castigating Indian vagrancy as a "monster evil," the suppression of which required the "most strenuous efforts of the Government."[6] Six years later, even the Protector of Immigrants would chime in that desertion was not only one of the most serious evils facing local agriculture, but also one of the most difficult to remedy.[7]

As other contemporary observers of Mauritian life acknowledged, the often harsh treatment of indentured workers was conditioned by the colony's prior experience with slave labor and maroonage. The Royal Commissioners who investigated the treatment of Indian immigrants on the island in 1872 did not hesitate to state that the "traditions of slavery" still survived in the colony.[8] Faced with the need to control a huge alien work force, planters and their allies in the colonial government relied upon the same kinds of measures they had used to control the island's slave population. For their part, the colony's newest inhabitants resorted just as quickly to the same tactics slaves had used to resist exploitation and oppression. Flight from their employers was the most public of these tactics and, until the late nineteenth century, the struggle between Mauritian "masters" and "servants" would be epitomized by the local preoccupation with illegal absence, desertion, and vagrancy.

Compared to the pre-emancipation era, the dynamics of labor control and resistance in post-emancipation plantation societies have not been the subject of serious scholarly interest, at least until quite recently.[9] Most histories of Mauritius, for instance, do little more than discuss labor relations after 1835 in the same terms used by nineteenth-century commissions of inquiry which devoted most of their reports to describing master–servant ordinances and cataloguing the sufferings of the Indian immigrant population.[10] This emphasis upon the legal and quasi-legal dimensions of labor control and the sometimes gruesome details of workers' daily lives also characterizes much of the scholarship on post-emancipation plantation societies in Africa, the Caribbean, Southeast Asia, and the South Pacific.[11] At the heart of many of these studies is the belief, enunciated originally by nineteenth-century abolitionists and since elaborated upon, that indentured laborers were the victims of a "new system of slavery" that arose in the wake of slave emancipation.[12]

This approach has yielded some important insights into the nature of nineteenth-century colonial plantation life and the dynamics of post-emancipation labor relations. In so doing, this historiographical tradition has served as something of a counterweight to the assertion that the classic plantation systems of the eighteenth and early nineteenth centuries declined and fell after the abolition of slavery. In addition to describing the superficial similarities between the experiences of some slaves and indentured laborers, this tradition has highlighted some of the structural connections between the pre- and post-emancipation worlds. The tendency for many of the ordinances which were designed to control indentured worker absenteeism to be little more than slightly disguised versions of the old fugitive slave laws is perhaps the most obvious example of the continuities between these two eras.

Unfortunately, this preoccupation with the most visible and sensational aspects of the indentured experience has also left us with an incomplete, if not somewhat distorted, picture of labor relations in many parts of the colonial plantation world during the nineteenth and early twentieth centuries.[13] As in maroon studies, basic questions about the dynamics of indentured labor control and resistance have remained largely unasked and unanswered: how many workers engaged in what kinds of acts of resistance? What percentage of the contractual work force did they constitute? What were the demographic characteristics of these deserter and vagrant populations? To what extent did "master–

servant" relations change with the passage of time? When and why did they do so? Answers to these questions are crucial to reconstructing the Indian immigrant experience in Mauritius; they are also central to understanding labor control and resistance in other nineteenth-century plantation colonies and, by implication, the dynamics of social, economic, and political change in the larger post-emancipation world.

Illegal absence, desertion, and vagrancy in post-emancipation Mauritius must be examined against a backdrop of rapid demographic change, a shift in local attitudes toward Indians, the policies of the colonial state, and the fortunes of the island's sugar industry. The origins of the demographic revolution that shook the colony during the mid-nineteenth century have already been noted. Despite the suspension of immigration between 1838 and 1842, Indians comprised more than one-third of the colony's population only twelve years after immigration began in 1834 and more than two-thirds of the island's permanent residents by 1871, a figure that would remain relatively constant during the remainder of the period under consideration.

A salient feature of this demographic revolution was a marked disparity between the sexes. Females accounted for less than 2 percent of Indian immigrants in 1838, and thirteen years later, despite growing official concern about the consequences of such a sexual imbalance, the immigrant population remained overwhelmingly male. Beginning in 1855, government regulations sought to ensure that at least 30 percent of all immigrants reaching the island were women, a proportion subsequently increased to 35 percent in 1857, to 40 percent in 1858, and to 50 percent from 1859 to 1865.[14] Despite such measures, the sex ratio within the immigrant population remained seriously unbalanced throughout the nineteenth century. The census of 1901 found that females comprised less than 45 percent of an Indian population that numbered 259,086 persons. Equally important was the fact that the great majority of the men who arrived in the colony during the mid-nineteenth century were young and unmarried. In 1871, one-half of all Indian males were between fifteen and thirty-nine years of age, while less than 10 percent of 135,587 adult males were reported to be married.[15]

This demographic revolution was accompanied by a significant change in colonial attitudes toward Indians. The Indian slaves and *gens de couleur* who resided on the island during the eighteenth and early nineteenth centuries had generally been praised for their industry, sobriety, intelligence, grace, and docility, qualities which, in the eyes of most colonists, more than compensated for their alleged physical frailty.[16] Such positive, albeit paternalistic, views of Indian character did not long survive the advent of Indian immigration. Witnesses who appeared before the Rawson Committee in 1845 emphasized the purported Indian propensity toward idleness, thievery, petty commerce, and financial irresponsibility as important reasons for desertion and absenteeism.[17] This characterization of immigrants as lazy, unreliable, and prone toward criminal behavior did not diminish with the passage of time. The 1872 Royal Commission of Inquiry reported without hesitation that "as a class, the Indians are regarded with fear and distrust, as dangerous and lawless vagabonds; or at least, with pitying contempt, as ill-regulated children, fit only to be treated accordingly."[18] The argument that immigrants needed to be protected against themselves was, the Commissioners noted, a common justification for the colonial legislation "which has pressed so heavily upon the Indian population."[19]

The impact of this demographic revolution was magnified by economic uncertainty and an unsettled labor market. As has already been noted, the local sugar industry's financial condition remained shaky throughout much of the nineteenth century. The industry's dependence upon domestic capital, especially after 1848, placed a premium upon controlling expenses, and especially labor costs, if sugar estates were to remain solvent, much less profitable. Well-informed sources such as Edward Chapman reported that labor costs consumed 50 percent or more of a plantation's annual operating expenses during the mid-1840s.[20] Reliable figures on the cost of labor are unavailable for most of the period under consideration, but projections based upon the size of the contractual work force and average monthly wages suggest that such costs accounted regularly for one-half or more of the industry's operating expenses well into the late nineteenth century (see below, pp. 69–70).

The ex-apprentice withdrawal from plantation life during 1839–40 meant that Indians quickly monopolized this sector of the local labor market. By 1846, immigrants comprised almost 85 percent of all agricultural laborers and more than 96 percent of the sugar industry's work force.[21] Immigrant domination of the agricultural work force did not lead, however, to the creation of a stable labor market, in part because the number of indentured laborers reaching the colony varied widely from year to year. In 1844, for example, only 11,549 immigrants landed on the island compared to 34,525 the previous year; in 1848, fewer than 5,400 Indians would step ashore at Port Louis.

Although planters informed colonial authorities of their projected labor needs each year, the number of laborers actually sent to Mauritius depended to a considerable extent upon conditions in India,[22] and the number of immigrants arriving in the colony continued to fluctuate from year to year during the 1850s and early 1860s, sometimes dramatically so. The irregular distribution of the men who reached the island further aggravated the problems created by this erratic supply of laborers. No consistent policy for allocating new immigrants among estates ever seems to have been formulated or implemented and many planters reacted accordingly, competing openly against each other for allocations of new immigrants, raiding one another for laborers already under contract, and dispatching their own agents to India to recruit workers.[23]

Detailed information on this work force during the first twenty-five years of Indian immigration is rather sparse, and it is not until 1859, when the Protector of Immigrants began to file his annual reports, that many aspects of nineteenth-century immigrant life become visible for the first time. Although the information contained in these reports reflects official interests and concerns, they provide us with an important vantage point from which to chart the changing structure and composition of the contractual work force during the mid-nineteenth century and to discern the forces that shaped local labor relations from 1860 to 1900. In so doing, these reports also shed light on the restructuring of Mauritian social and economic relationships that began during the late 1860s and early 1870s, and the role Indians played in these transformations.

Immigration had resumed in 1842 with the proviso that contracts between masters and servants could be made for no more than one year at a time. By limiting the length of contracts, the Government of India hoped to prevent the egregious abuses to which the earliest indentured laborers had fallen victim. Before very long, however, the Mauritian government began to whittle away at these restrictions at the behest of the local planter class. In 1849, only seven years after the resumption of Indian immigration, a local ordinance legalized contracts of three years duration. Ordinance No. 16 of 1862, in turn, would reauthorize the five-year contracts that had prevailed between 1834 and 1838.

Despite these various attempts to stabilize it, the local labor market remained unsettled. In 1860, Acting Protector H.N.D. Betys reported that only one-third of all Indian laborers had agreed to work for more than one year for the same employer, and that just one-third of those signing contracts that year had re-engaged with the same employer.[24] Subsequent attempts to encourage, if not force, indentured workers to sign longer contracts likewise came to naught. Contracts of a year or less not only remained an integral part of Mauritian agricultural life, but also became increasingly prevalent. By the late 1870s, such short-term agreements regularly accounted for 85 percent or more of all written contracts of service.

Instability in the local labor market was also fostered by the tendency for the number of persons working under written contracts to vary widely from year to year. During the early 1860s, for example, the contractual work force climbed from 60,748 in 1860 to 70,215 in 1861 and then to 80,962 in 1862 before dropping to 71,050 in 1863, after which it rose again to 81,824 in 1864.[25] With the advent of the 1870s, the size of this work force began a marked decline, falling from a yearly average of 70,500 between 1870 and 1874 to 50,000 during the early 1880s, and then to less than 40,000 by the mid-1890s. This era also witnessed a major geographical redistribution of this work force, as districts such as Port Louis and Pamplemousses experienced a steady decline in the number of contractual laborers employed within their borders, while those working in Flacq, Moka, Grand Port, and Savanne increased by 75 to 100 percent.

These trends attest to the unsettled character of the Mauritian labor market during the first several decades of Indian immigration. During the late 1860s and early 1870s, however, there are indications that colonial labor relations were becoming somewhat less tumultuous. The steadily increasing percentage of laborers who re-engaged with the same employer is the most obvious evidence of this change. Between 1860 and 1864, an average of less than 45 percent of the contractual work force had agreed to re-engage with the same employer each year. By 1880–84, this figure had climbed to 71 percent.

Some colonial officials viewed this trend as the logical outcome of their vigorous enforcement of Ordinance No. 31 of 1867, the so-called Labour Law of 1867, which rationalized earlier labor legislation and strengthened police and judicial powers to deal with recalcitrant workers. However, others, such as Protector Beyts, argued that the increasing number of re-engagements reflected, at least in part, a growing awareness among immigrants themselves that continued service in the colony was preferable to returning to India.[26] The changing structure of the indentured work force at this time suggests that the Protector had a better understanding of the situation than did many of his colleagues. More specifically, the 1860s witnessed a dramatic decline in the number of New Immigrants in indentured service and a corresponding increase in the number of Old Immigrants working under contract. In 1861, the first year for which such figures are available, New Immigrants accounted for almost 40 percent of all contractual workers. Just four years later, New Immigrants comprised only one-quarter of all such workers, and within a decade they would constitute 15 percent or less of the sugar estate work force. By the mid-1870s, the composition of this work force was changing yet again as Indo-Mauritians (i.e., Mauritian-born Indians) became an ever larger component of both the Indian population as a whole and the sugar industry's labor force.

The distinction between "Old" and "New" immigrants was first articulated in Ordinance No. 22 of 1847, enacted as the first of the thousands of laborers who had arrived in 1843 stood on the verge of completing their mandatory five years of "industrial residence." New Immigrants were defined as laborers who had not completed their industrial residence, that is, who had not worked under a written contract of service for five years or freed themselves of this obligation by payment of a specified tax. Successful completion of such a residence usually entailed working on a sugar estate. Upon having done so, immigrants could return to India (at government expense until 1852) or remain in the colony as Old Immigrants. Although Old Immigrants were theoretically free to earn their living in a manner of their own choosing, the freedom of action conferred by this status was actually less than it seemed to be. Indians who remained in the colony were compelled under threat of the vagrancy laws to work and support themselves. Many did so, as these laws intended, by hiring themselves out as agricultural laborers.

During the first decades of Indian immigration, Mauritian planters complained repeatedly about the inadequacy of the labor supply at their disposal. This problem stemmed in part from their inability to legally compel indentured laborers to remain on their estates once they had completed their five years of industrial residence. As a result, increasing numbers of time-expired immigrants left the estates to pursue other livelihoods. By the mid-1840s, planters were complaining vigorously to colonial authorities that the island housed far too many Indian shop-keepers and petty traders and not enough agricultural laborers.[27] The creation of the distinction between "Old" and "New" immigrants and the attendant application of the colony's vagrancy laws to Old Immigrants provided planters with the legal tool they needed to try to force Old Immigrants back onto their estates.

The ineffectiveness of existing legislation underscored the need for such a tool. During the 1830s and early 1840s, indentured laborers had been subject to the laws designed to control the colony's apprentice and ex-apprentice populations. Ordinance No. 16 of 1835, subsequently vetoed by the Secretary of State for the Colonies because of its blatantly repressive nature, was one such law. This ordinance had stipulated that all persons of sixty years of age or under who were able to work but had no occupation, employment, or known means of subsistence could be punished as vagabonds. The ordinance also required that any person over twenty-one years of age who wanted to hire himself out for a period of more than one month had to register with the police and obtain a "ticket" which recorded his name, birthplace, marital status, occupation, and employer's name. Aimed primarily at apprentices who managed to emancipate themselves before the end of the apprenticeship period, the ordinance contained many of the features found in later legislation that sought to control Indian immigrants.

Labor legislation directed specifically against these immigrants first appeared on the colony's law books in 1842. The tenor and tone of these earliest laws is suggested by the provisions of the disallowed Ordinance No. 21 of 1843 which prohibited any person introduced into the colony from Africa or Asia as an agricultural laborer from working in a shop or warehouse without governmental approval. In addition to distinguishing between Old and New Immigrants, Ordinance No. 22 of 1847 required Old Immigrants to carry a ticket as proof of their status. The net effect of this and subsequent ordinances in 1848 and 1852 was to subject Indian immigrants to a number of restrictions and penalties from which non-Indians were exempt. For example, any immigrant who could not prove that he was either an Old Immigrant or working under a written contract of service could be arrested without a warrant if he was found in a district in which he did not reside or on any premises without the owner's consent. Employers were also empowered to withhold laborers' certificates of discharge if they had not worked the full amount of time specified in their contracts.

This legislation became increasingly repressive during the 1860s and 1870s. Ordinance No. 65 of 1860 allowed for the tacit renewal of three year contracts if, three months prior to the termination of the original contract, Indian workers failed to apply to an Immigration Agent to commute their contracts to a cash payment or to re-indenture with a different master. The infamous "double cut," which fined workers two days' salary for every day of illegal absence, was sanctioned repeatedly until it was finally abolished on January 1, 1910. The Labour Law of 1867 consolidated and reaffirmed police and judicial powers dating to the 1830s. Among its many provisions, the ordinance stipulated that the passes carried by Old Immigrants must henceforth include the bearer's photograph to facilitate identification. Later regulations impinged even further upon the lives of Old Immigrants. Those of August 25, 1869, for instance, specified that immigrants had only eight days following the completion of their industrial residence, or any other engagement, to arrange the future course of their life; failure to do so could result in a £2 fine or seven days in prison, as well as any other punishment that might be imposed for vagrancy. The last significant piece of nineteenth century labor legislation, Ordinance No. 12 of 1878, continued this process of refining the disabilities under which Indian immigrants had to live and work.

The purpose of this legislation, as many contemporary observers of Mauritian life readily acknowledged, was clear and unequivocal: to ensure the continued presence of a large pool of inexpensive agricultural labor for the colony's sugar estates. Adolphe de Plevitz, a planter himself, succinctly summarized the rationale for ordinances such as the Labour Law of 1867 when he noted that local planters realized that "if Old immigrants could be compelled to re-engage on the old terms, it would be the immediate means of diminishing their expenses and putting money in their pockets."[28] However, as many colonial officials knew all too well, enacting a body of labor legislation was one thing; controlling the Indian immigrant population, and especially the incidence of illegal absence, desertion, and vagrancy, was something else entirely.

Throughout the mid-nineteenth century, colonial authorities frequently described desertion as not only a serious plague afflicting Mauritian agriculture, but also one for which there appeared to be no sovereign remedy. Many colonists were quick to explain desertion and its attendant evils of absenteeism and vagrancy in terms of the various physical, moral, and psychological imperfections which, in their eyes, character-ized the Indian constitution. Others argued that these alleged deficiencies were compounded by serious shortcomings in the existing system of labor control: the short duration of most engagements, the ease with which immigrants could work by the week or the month, the willingness of planters to abduct laborers already under contract, and the rigid discipline and ill-treatment found on many estates. The passage of time did little to alter the substance of these explanations. Protector J.F. Trotter, commenting upon the state of labor conditions in 1881, readily attributed the continuing incidence of illegal absence to Indian dislike of the manner in which they were treated and managed by estate autho-rities.[29] When immigrants themselves speak to us, it is clear that they deserted for the same reasons that had induced slaves to maroon: physical and psychological ill-treatment, a desire to visit family and friends on other estates, and the need to get away, if only temporarily, from harsh living and working conditions.[30]

For colonial authorities, the problems of illegal absence, desertion, and vagrancy were made all that much more serious because of the seemingly unscrupulous methods deserters and vagrants used to avoid capture. Acting Protector A. Chastelneuf noted, for example, that a decline in the number of arrests for vagrancy between 1861 and 1862 did not reflect a decrease in the number of vagrants, but rather the ability of these individuals to escape detection by using forged tickets or making fraudulent use of genuine tickets. To give substance to his assertion, Chastelneuf reported that immigrants had made 30,075 applications for duplicate tickets and passes during 1862.[31] To diminish the fraudulent use of genuine tickets and the manufacture of counterfeit ones, the Protector announced in 1864 that new tickets would henceforth include the bearer's photograph, a measure subsequently incorporated into the Labour Law of 1867.[32] Such measures nevertheless failed to stop deserters and vagrants from avoiding capture. In 1875, Acting Protector Thomas Elliott would complain vigorously about the willful deceptions captured deserters were practicing upon local magistrates. To illustrate the severity of this problem, Elliott cited the case of one deserter who had deceived magistrates no fewer than twenty-four times about who his employer was.[33]

In theory, illegal absence, desertion, and vagrancy were separate and distinct offenses, with illegal absence and desertion involving a breach of contract while vagrancy entailed a more serious offense against society as a whole.[34] As a general rule of thumb, desertion ordinances dealt with New Immigrants and other contractual laborers, while vagrancy laws covered Old Immigrants who had left the sugar estates to earn their living. In the eyes of many colonists and local officials, however, these offenses were often indistinguishable from one another.[35] Reports about the colony's prison population during the 1850s and early 1860s, for instance, did not distinguish between committals for desertion and those for vagrancy. The "vagrant" or "maroon hunts" organized by the police were directed at all immigrants without proper documentation, regardless of their legal status. Even on those occasions when an ordinance distinguished between these offenses, it was not unusual for another ordinance to blur the line between them again, as was the case with Ordinance No. 4 of 1864 which considered desertion to be an act of vagrancy.

Information on the incidence of illegal absence and desertion during the first quarter-century of Indian immigration is sparse and often problematic. The earliest available figures date to late 1838 and early 1839, when a local committee investigated the living and working conditions of the colony's indentured Indian laborers. According to the returns provided to the committee by local planters, just 2.4 percent of this work force was absent without leave, a figure which must be viewed with a certain skepticism since planters in four of the island's eight rural districts did not furnish the committee with the information it had requested.[36]

Subsequent reports indicate that illegal absence and desertion were much more common by the mid-1840s. In 1845, the Rawson Committee estimated that 6 percent of the 35,000 Indian estate laborers in the colony were deserters, while another 11 percent were temporarily absent without leave, 8 percent could not work because of illness, and 2 percent were in

Table 5. *Complaints against Indian immigrants by employers and overseers, 1860–1899*

| | | | Annual average per quinquenium | | | |
|---|---|---|---|---|---|---|
| | | | Type of complaint (percent) | | | |
| Period | No. of contract laborers | No. of complaints | Illegal absence/ desertion | Refusal of labor[a] | Other[b] | Conviction rate (%) |
| 1860–64 | 72,960 | 15,491 | 87.3 | 6.1 | 6.6 | 77.6 |
| 1865–69 | 69,165 | 12,903 | 69.8 | 3.9 | 26.3 | 73.9 |
| 1870–74 | 70,499 | 4,831 | 80.5 | 8.1 | 11.4 | 84.8 |
| 1875–79 | 61,322 | 4,457 | 76.9 | 14.8 | 8.3 | 85.3 |
| 1880–84 | 50,323 | 3,398 | 30.5 | 54.2 | 15.3 | 66.2 |
| 1885–89 | 42,632[c] | 3,194 | 44.5 | 45.2 | 10.3 | 68.9 |
| 1890–94 | 39,951 | 3,317 | 47.6 | 45.3 | 7.1 | 69.9 |
| 1895–99 | 35,716[d] | 2,339 | 35.6 | 56.7 | 7.7 | 70.8 |

*Notes:*
[a] Habitual idleness, refusing to work, neglect of work.
[b] Assault, false papers, insubordination, malicious injury of property, and other unspecified charges.
[c] For 1885 and 1889 only.
[d] For 1895–98 only.
*Sources:* AIR 1860–99.

the midst of changing masters.[37] Of the 33,651 estate laborers enumerated on 31 March the following year, 7.7 percent were reported to be deserters, 6.2 percent had been absent from work for less than two weeks, and another 5.1 percent were ill and unable to work.[38] Other data from this period indicate that the propensity of laborers to run away could vary significantly depending upon the kind of estate on which they worked; absenteeism and desertion on sugar plantations averaged 11.9 percent a year between 1845 and 1850 compared to 7.9 percent on other kinds of estates.[39] Unfortunately, the archival record is silent about the extent of this activity during the 1850s, but the large number of committals to prison for desertion and vagrancy during this decade – an average of 3,463 a year from 1852 through 1859 – indicates that illegal absence and desertion remained a prominent feature of colonial life throughout the decade.[40]

A fuller picture of local master–servant relations can be discerned after the Protector of Immigrants began to file his annual reports in 1859. Despite the uneven and occasionally problematic quality of the information in these reports,[41] there can be little doubt that colonial labor relations remained tumultuous, and perhaps became even more so, during the 1860s. The number of committals to prison for desertion and vagrancy, for instance, rose dramatically between 1860 and the end of 1863, to an average of 5,824 each year.[42] On any given day between mid-1865 and late 1871 from 8 to 10 percent, and sometimes more, of the colony's agricultural labor force was temporarily absent from work.[43]

The Protector's reports also provide us with an opportunity to examine the nature of resistance to the plantation regime after 1860 in greater detail. Planters and overseers lodged numerous formal complaints against their contractual laborers, charging them with a wide array of offenses including assault, destruction of property, habitual idleness, refusing to work, and the possession of false papers. During the 1860s, a staggering 18 to 22 percent of Indian workers had formal complaints lodged against them and, as table 5 reveals, unlawful absence dominated local master–servant relations, as it would also subsequently do in Fiji.[44] Of the 209,001 complaints lodged against Indian immigrants from 1860 through 1885, more than 34 percent were for illegal absence, while more than 38 percent were for desertion. These data, coupled with those from the 1840s, point to an average desertion/absenteeism rate of 12 to 15 percent each year between the mid-1840s and the mid-1880s. This rate is comparable not only to the incidence of maroonage among Mauritian slaves during the 1820s, but also to those reported for indentured workers in other parts of the plantation world during the late nineteenth century.[45]

Unfortunately, it is impossible to determine to what extent Indian desertion and absenteeism paralleled maroon slave activity in other respects. The Protector's annual reports are silent about how long these desertions lasted, from whence deserters fled and where they were apprehended, and whether they tended to act alone or in groups. Although the demographic characteristics of this population also remain hidden from view, census data indicate that deserters were overwhelmingly male. In 1846, only 657 of the 38,096 Indians employed in agriculture were women, and women continued to comprise less than 2 percent of all agricultural laborers under contract throughout the remainder of the nineteenth century.

Vagrancy was another prominent feature of the Mauritian social and economic landscape during the mid-nineteenth century. Figures on the incidence of vagrancy do not exist before 1861, in part because of the already noted propensity of colonial authorities to blur the distinction between vagrants and deserters. The few figures at our disposal reveal that an average of 8.8 percent of the Indian immigrant population was arrested for vagrancy each year from 1861 through 1871.[46] The large

Table 6. *Indian immigrant complaints against employers and overseers, 1860–1899*

| | | Annual average per quinquenium | | | | |
| | | | Type of complaint (percent) | | | |
| Period | % Contract laborers involved | No. of complaints | Non-payment of wages | Rations[a] | Other[b] | Conviction rate (%) |
|---|---|---|---|---|---|---|
| 1860–64 | 11.4 | 8,346 | 76.4 | 8.4 | 15.2 | 76.2 |
| 1865–69 | 9.7 | 6,690 | 75.0 | 6.0 | 19.0 | 72.8 |
| 1870–74 | 5.0 | 3,541 | 57.2 | 11.4 | 31.4 | 55.2 |
| 1875–79 | 4.5 | 2,737 | 70.1 | 10.1 | 19.8 | 59.2 |
| 1880–84 | 1.5 | 756 | 70.1 | 11.3 | 18.6 | 44.7 |
| 1885–89 | 1.2 | 531 | 87.5 | 1.0 | 11.5 | 53.5 |
| 1890–94 | 0.4 | 157 | 75.8 | 4.7 | 19.5 | 52.7 |
| 1895–99 | 0.3 | 92 | 83.1 | 2.4 | 14.5 | 41.8 |

*Notes:*
[a] Non-delivery or irregular delivery of rations.
[b] Assault, ill-usage, ill-treatment, non-delivery of tickets and discharges, lack of medical care, and other unspecified charges.
*Sources:* AIR 1860–99.

number of arrests for this offense (an average of more than 18,800 a year during this period) and the surprisingly low conviction rate in such cases (only 44.5 percent on average) led the 1872 Royal Commissioners to characterize enforcement of the vagrancy and labor laws as nothing less than the unbridled harassment of the Indian population.[47] Arrests for vagrancy, like those for illegal absence and desertion, declined dramatically during the latter part of the century; between 1889 and 1893, an average of only 617 Indians were charged with this offense each year.[48] Entries in the few vagrant registers that survive indicate that it was not uncommon for the same individual to be arrested for vagrancy several times a year. The number of such repeat offenders is, regrettably, impossible to determine.

The willingness of large numbers of Indian laborers to lodge formal complaints against their employers and overseers not only highlights the dynamic nature of nineteenth-century Mauritian labor relations, but also throws the economic dimension of these relationships into sharp relief. Although immigrants charged their employers with assault, the irregular delivery of rations, the late or non-delivery of tickets and discharge papers, and lack of adequate medical care, the great majority of their complaints concerned the non-payment of wages (see table 6). Once again, a lack of documentation makes it impossible to determine the extent of this practice before 1860. However, the fact that 72 percent of the 110,940 complaints filed by immigrants from 1860 through 1885 centered on their failure to receive their wages either on time or in full, together with a conviction rate of almost 71 percent in such cases, suggests that this problem was probably a serious one for indentured laborers before, as well as after, 1860.

More detailed reports on the deductions made from laborers' wages sheds additional light on this problem. A survey by the 1872 Royal Commission of the practices on sixteen estates revealed that deductions for illness and absenteeism work cost workers from 12.1 to 38.5 percent of their wages, and that wages were not paid for 3.9 to 19.4 percent of all days worked.[49] A better sense of the prevailing norm is indicated by the fact that on twelve estates deductions for illness and absence consumed 20 percent or more of labourers' wages, while on eleven estates laborers were not paid for 10 percent or more of all days worked. The Protector of Immigrants reported occasionally on the amounts of money involved. According to one such report, contract laborers had $442,700.69 deducted from their wages during the first six months of 1873, a sum equal to at least 28 percent of the total wage bill for this period.[50] Two years later, planters and job contractors withheld $359,528.57 over another six-month period, a sum equal to at least 23 percent of all wages due during the same period.[51] Workers continued to endure such practices well into the 1880s, losing an average of 24.4 percent of their wages for various reasons between 1880 and 1884.[52] On some estates, deductions for illegal absence diminished wages by more than 45 percent.[53]

It is tempting to regard these practices as simply another manifestation of the well-documented *mentalité esclavagiste* that pervaded the Mauritian planter class throughout the nineteenth century. However, as observers such as Adolphe de Plevitz appreciated, there were other powerful incentives for planters to resort to such measures. Labor, which could account for one-half or more of an estate's operating expenses, was the one variable over which they could hope to exercise some measure of direct control. Unfortunately, the archival record is silent about the actual amount of the sugar industry's wage bill each year during the nineteenth century. The first indication of that bill's size comes from the annual report for 1856, which suggests that the services of some 73,000 contract laborers cost planters at least £600,000, a sum equal to 35.6 percent of the export value of that year's sugar crop.[54]

Beginning in 1860, the Protector of Immigrants reported frequently on both the size of the sugar estate work force and the average rate of pay for contract labor, information which makes it possible to estimate the

Table 7. *Projected Mauritian sugar industry labor costs, 1860–1899*

| | Annual average per quinquenium | | | |
| | Contract labor[a] | | Sugar estate labor[b] | |
| Period | Projected minimum wage bill (£) | % Value of sugar exports | Projected minimum wage bill (£) | % Value of sugar exports |
|---|---|---|---|---|
| 1860–64 | 668,936 | 31.2 | — | — |
| 1865–69 | 625,938 | 28.0 | — | — |
| 1870–74 | 572,116 | 22.4 | 585,942[c] | 21.8[c] |
| 1875–79 | 550,224 | 18.8 | 640,694 | 21.9 |
| 1880–84 | 420,474 | 12.8 | 531,258 | 15.8 |
| 1885–89 | 309,462 | 10.9 | 395,039 | 13.9 |
| 1890–94 | 291,560 | 15.2 | 383,341 | 20.0 |
| 1895–99 | 183,113 | 12.1 | 233,595[d] | 15.5[d] |

*Notes:*
[a] Only laborers working under written contracts of service.
[b] Total sugar estate work force including persons working under written and verbal contracts.
[c] For 1872–74 only.
[d] For 1895–96 only.
*Sources:* AIR 1860–99.

sugar industry's minimum wage bill during the last four decades of the century. As table 7 reveals, this bill was a substantial one during the 1860s and early 1870s, equaling 22–30 percent or more of the export value of the colony's sugar crop. We must remember that these figures are for wages only, and do not include the cost of the housing, rations, clothing, and medical care that planters were also legally required to provide for their workers. Furthermore, we must remember that these costs had to be borne by an industry whose financial condition was often shaky, even in the best of times, and that the mid- and late 1860s marked the beginning of an era during which industry finances became increasingly uncertain. Under such circumstances, the willingness of estate-owners to exploit local labor ordinances so as to reduce their wage bill by an average of 20 percent or more each year comes as no great surprise.

If the first decades of Indian immigration constituted an era of unbridled harassment and exploitation in colonial labor relations, by the late 1860s there is evidence that the nature of these relations was beginning to change. As early as 1866, Protector Beyts pointed to a gradual decline in the number of immigrant complaints against employers and overseers as proof of the "healthier tone" of local master–servant relations.[55] The early 1870s witnessed a dramatic decline in the number of complaints employers and laborers were lodging against one another (see tables 5 and 6). This trend was so well established by 1881 that Protector Trotter described the relationship between Indian immigrants and their employers as being "most satisfactory."[56] The early 1880s also witnessed a significant change in the nature of the complaints being made against Indian immigrants. The charge of "habitual idleness" began to be levied against contractual laborers in 1879, and the number of such complaints quickly outstripped those for desertion and illegal absence combined. Implicit in this growing concern about "idleness" was an acknowledgement that the agricultural work force had become much more settled than had been the case earlier in the century.

Other signal changes during this era include a substantial reduction in the size of the agricultural work force, a growing preference for verbal rather than written contracts, and the emergence of Indian job contractors as players of some consequence in the local labor market. The number of persons working under written contracts of service started to decline during the late 1860s, and by the early 1880s the number of such workers had fallen by almost one-third. This trend continued through the 1880s and into the 1890s, in part because planters increasingly preferred to enter into verbal contracts with their workers in order to avoid having to provide certain services required by law. The extent of this practice is suggested by reports that 13 percent of all contracts in 1897–98 were verbal rather than written.[57] During this era, Indian job contractors, who controlled and hired out their own gangs of workers for short periods of time or by the task, also became increasingly prominent. Protector Beyts reported not only that the number of job contractors increased noticeably during the mid-1860s, but also that these individuals were expanding their operations. According to the Protector, job contractors employed 6,364 persons in 1864 and 7,173 individuals in 1865, numbers equal to about 8 percent of the total contractual work force in each of these years.[58]

The nature and extent of these changes point to the late 1860s and early 1870s as being a watershed period in Mauritian social and economic history. Many observers of colonial life traced the origins of this new era in labor relations to the passage of the Labour Law of 1867. Protector Beyts, for one, attributed the "marked improvement" he discerned in the social and moral condition of the colony's work force at this time to the decrease in vagrancy made possible by this new law.[59] Nicholas Pike, the United States consul at Port Louis, agreed that vagrancy had ceased to be a serious problem in the colony now that the vagrancy laws were "working satisfactorily."[60] Others, however, were less sanguine about this legislation's effectiveness. The 1872 Royal Commissioners argued that any such success was very much in the eye of the beholder.[61] To illustrate their point, the Commissioners noted that, an increase in the number of persons working under contract notwithstanding, the number of laborers actually employed on sugar estates had declined since the Labour Law's passage. Its impact upon vagrancy was reportedly a subject of debate even among the officers of the colony's police force.[62]

Unlike most of their contemporaries and many modern students of indentured labor systems, the Royal Commissioners understood, at least implicitly, that focusing exclusively upon the legal or quasi-legal aspects of illegal absence, desertion, and vagrancy can shed only so much light on the nature and dynamics of post-emancipation labor relations. Mauritian authorities tinkered continuously with local labor and vagrancy laws in an attempt to exercise more effective control over the island's Indian population in general and its contractual work force in particular. Nevertheless, as their own reports revealed only too clearly, their efforts to do so did not meet with the success they had anticipated; large numbers of Indian indentured workers refused to play by these elaborate colonial rules. Given these realities, it becomes apparent that colonial labor relations need to be examined in light of other considerations, not the least of which is the larger socio-economic context within which this labor legislation was enacted and enforced.[63]

The 1860s and 1870s witnessed the beginning of several developments that would have a marked impact upon the course of late nineteenth-century Mauritian labor relations. The domestic labor market became much less unsettled as the percentage of the contractual workers re-engaging with the same employer rose steadily, from less than 40 percent in 1861 to more than 71 percent by the early 1880s. Demographic change contributed to this trend as Old Immigrants replaced New Immigrants as the largest single component of this labor force during the late 1850s and early 1860s. The structure of this work force started to change yet again during the mid-1870s, as increasing numbers of Mauritian-born Indians entered the work force. By 1885, for instance, Indo-Mauritians accounted for 28 percent of all contractual workers compared to less than 8.5 percent just twelve years earlier.

These changes occurred in tandem with a major restructuring of the domestic economy during the late nineteenth century, the details of which will be discussed in chapter 6. We may note for the time being that planters had complained as early as the mid-1840s that the colony housed too many Indian shopkeepers and petty traders and too few agricultural workers. Protector Beyts confirmed in 1860 that large numbers of Indians were leaving the sugar estates and earning their living as small landowners, shopkeepers, peddlers, and craftsmen once they were free of their engagements.[64] A little more than a decade later, the Royal Commission of Inquiry reported that the greater part of the colony's petty trade was now in Indian hands, that the Indian community included 11 planters and 314 "independent proprietors" among its numbers, and that 3,100 immigrants had invested £87,568 in real property between 1860 and 1871.[65] Early in the following decade, Protector Trotter confirmed not only that Indians worked as carters, domestic servants, gardeners, messengers, porters, policemen, railwaymen, shoemakers, and silversmiths, but also that many immigrants owned land and other property.[66]

Census data reveal the magnitude of these socio-economic transformations. In 1851, for example, Indians accounted for less than 3 percent of all professional people; by 1881, that figure had climbed to more than 25 percent. Indian representation among the colony's independent proprietors increased in a like manner, from less than 5 percent in 1851 to almost 27 percent three decades later. The immigrant presence had an even more pronounced impact upon other sectors of the colonial economy. Whereas only 14 percent of all persons employed in commerce, trade, and industry in 1851 were Indians, by 1871 that figure had soared to 80 percent. One consequence of this dramatic expansion of immigrant economic activity was to provide some of the colony's Indian residents with the resources that would allow them to exploit the opportunities created by the long-term economic crisis that began to take shape during the 1860s and early 1870s.

The falling world market price of sugar, the higher cost of imported goods, and the various natural catastrophes that struck the island during the 1860s were heavy blows to an economy dependent upon the resources of local capital. Planters responded to this developing economic crisis by beginning a process of retrenchment. Their calls for the continued importation of large numbers of indentured laborers became less frequent and, like their counterparts in the Americas, they began to rationalize and upgrade their operations to increase efficiency and cut costs. The number of sugar factories declined 60 percent between 1860 and 1900 as cane milling became more centralized. Sharecropping became increasingly common during the 1880s, and by the late 1890s, one-fourth of the colony's sugar estates were engaging in this practice. At the same time, many plantation-owners also started to subdivide their holdings and sell off small plots of land to Indian laborers, most of whom became cane farmers in their own right.

This process of subdivision, or *morcellement*, began during the mid-1870s and steadily gained momentum through the 1880s and 1890s and into the early twentieth century. As a result, Indians accounted for almost one-half of the island's independent proprietors as early as 1891. By 1909, Indians would be cultivating 30 percent of all land planted in cane, a figure that would subsequently climb to 45 percent by the early 1920s. As the notarial record attests, the subdivision of these estates was a carefully planned operation in which Old Immigrant and other Indian entrepreneurs played an active role. The regularity with which the colony's new smallholders paid the full purchase price for their land at the time of a sale's formal completion underscores the economic rationale for the *morcellement* process: to extract the substantial sums of ready cash in Indian hands needed by an industry with increasing capital liquidity problems. By the late 1880s, Indian immigrants and their descendants were spending more than 1,200,000 rupees a year on real estate, a figure which subsequently climbed to more than Rs. 1,700,000 a year between 1895 and 1900.

The nature and dynamics of nineteenth-century Mauritian labor relations become clearer in the context of these social and economic transformations. On the one hand, the experience of Indian laborers in the decades after 1834 illustrates the continuities between the pre- and post-emancipation eras in many plantation colonies. Earlier concerns about maroonage were quickly translated into a continuing preoccupation about illegal absence, desertion, and vagrancy. Ordinances designed to control the local slave population in general and maroon activity in particular disappeared from the law books, only to reappear in new guises that did nothing to conceal their intent. Over the long term, however, this legislation proved to be as ineffective at controlling the colony's indentured work force as the old slave and maroon ordinances had been. Increasing numbers of slaves had fled from their masters during the late eighteenth and early nineteenth centuries, driven by the threat of physical and psychological violence, the desire to maintain familial ties and other important social relationships, and the need to escape, if only temporarily, from harsh living and working conditions. Equally large numbers of Indian laborers deserted their employers for the same reasons.

If Mauritian slaves and indentured "servants" shared certain experiences in common, the relationship between indentured laborers and their employers nevertheless differed from that between slaves and their masters in several important respects. While it is abundantly clear that many Indian immigrants fell victim to the same kind of abuses to which slaves had been subjected, they were never chattel. In the eyes of the law indentured laborers were free persons capable of exercising certain rights:

to enter into contracts and to negotiate the length and conditions of those contracts, to leave an estate upon completion of their contractual obligations and pursue other livelihoods, and to seek legal redress of their grievances. As the historical record reveals, many indentured workers exercised these rights, albeit often not to the full extent that the law allowed or that many of them would have wished. Lastly, Indian immigrants, unlike slaves, could return to their homeland if they chose to do so, and it is important to remember that one-third of the immigrants who arrived in Mauritius eventually returned to India.

The incidence of illegal absence, desertion, and vagrancy in nineteenth century Mauritius highlights the desire of indentured laborers to control their own lives as much as possible. Their continued attempts to do so, coupled with the unsettled state of colonial labor relations that resulted from their actions, lend support to recent arguments that the characteriztion of nineteenth-century indentured labor systems as little more than "new systems of slavery" is something of a misnomer.[67] The dramatic decline in the number of these offenses after the 1860s illustrates, moreover, the speed with which the social relations of production in post-emancipation colonies could be transformed. Work on late nineteenth- and early twentieth-century plantations in the South Pacific and Latin America has revealed that the restructuring of these relationships was also often a complex process.[68] The history of unlawful absence in post-emancipation Mauritius underscores not only the extent to which local conditions and circumstances shaped these processes, but also the role which regional or global developments, such as changes in the world sugar market, played in framing the context within which these transformations took place. On Mauritius, the constraints imposed by their dependence upon domestic capital left planters with no other option but to participate in, if not facilitate, a restructuring of the island's social relations of production, one result of which would be the demise of a fraying system of labor control that they could no longer afford to maintain.

*Part 2*

Land and the mobilization of domestic capital

# 4    Becoming an appropriated people: the rise of the free population of color, 1729–1830

Il est parmi les Colons, une Classe très nombreuse, c'est la classe indigente des hommes de couleur libres, qui ne possedent point de terre et qui, sur les grandes routes, les chemins de traverse, le bord de la mer, sont établis dans des cases délabrées qui leur servent d'abri. Ces individus sans industrie traînent une existence misérable qu'ils ne soutiennent, les un que par la chasse & la pêche, les autres par le *brocantage* des effets, denrées & vivres qu'ils reçoivent des noirs volant leur maîtres, et à très-vil prix: heureux encore quand ils ne se livrent pas, pour vivre, à des pratiques coupables, qui les exposent à des punitions flétrissantes: ce dont on a de fréquens exemples, ainsi que le constatent les registres concernant les affairs de police correctionelle dans lesquelles on voit presque toujours figurer des individus de cette classe.

"Exposé" of Mr. Marcenay, October 12, 1827[1]

On June 22, 1829, an Order-in-Council directed that any law, statute, ordinance, or proclamation that subjected free persons of African or Indian birth in Mauritius to "any disability, civil or military, to which persons of European birth and descent are not subject, shall be ... hereby repealed, abolished and annulled."[2] The issuance of this directive was a signal event in the history of the island's free population of color, and came in response to the Commission of Eastern Enquiry's call in 1828 for the immediate repeal of all legislation which discriminated against *gens de couleur libre*. The Commissioner's recommendation had been prompted by several considerations: their sensitivity to the arbitrary manner in which white or colored status was assigned to persons of mixed European and non-European descent, their acknowledgment that "although the property of the coloured class is far inferior to that of the Whites, it is still considerable in Lands and Slaves," and their awareness that a distinct sense of corporate social identity existed among many *gens de couleur*.[3] This sense of social consciousness had manifested itself during the early 1820s when *gens de couleur* pressed actively for the removal of the local color bar. Their agitation had focused upon three symbolically important aspects of that bar: the illegality of marriages between whites and free persons of color, their inability to gain

79

admittance to the Royal College of Mauritius, and the prohibition against their being buried in the same cemeteries as whites.

The Commission's preparation of a separate report on the condition of local free population of color, coupled with its recommendation for an end to all legal discrimination against *gens de couleur*, attest that this community had achieved a certain standing in Mauritian life by the mid-1820s. This prominence was newly found; at the beginning of the century, free persons of color accounted for a mere 7 percent of the island's total population and played only a limited role in the colonial economy. By the late 1830s, however, *gens de couleur* wielded sufficient social and economic power that they would be able to help thwart attempts to drive the colony's ex-apprentices back onto the sugar estates. Their willingness to do so stemmed in no small measure from their ability to capitalize upon the opportunities created by the island's transformation into a sugar colony during the first decades of the nineteenth century.

Like their counterparts in the New World, free persons of color in eighteenth- and early nineteenth-century Mauritius were an "unappropriated" people, neither slave nor free. As in the Americas, the marginal status of Mauritian *gens de couleur* in colonial life may be traced in part to the racism endemic to slave-plantation societies of the day.[4] Studies of these societies in the Caribbean basin have emphasized the role legal mechanisms and white social conventions played in defining and maintaining the parameters of free colored social and economic organization and activities.[5] Mauritian whites likewise used their control over manumission, the legal and social distinctions between whites and non-whites, and possible avenues of socio-economic mobility to relegate local free persons of color to the margins of colonial life.

Approaching the history of free colored populations in these terms has provided important insights into the means by which white colonists sought to control the *gens de couleur* in their midst. However, the tendency to concentrate upon the legal and quasi-legal dimensions of the free colored life to the exclusion of other facets of that experience also suggests that we may have a somewhat distorted picture of these populations and the reasons for their marginal status. The failure of previous studies to examine free colored social and economic organization and activity in greater detail has, at a minimum, left us with an incomplete understanding of how and why these populations developed the way they did. The attendant lack of information about the important details of free colored life has, in turn, sharply limited opportunities for the comparative study of these populations.

This emphasis upon the legal and quasi-legal aspect of free colored history poses other problems as well. For example, the argument (explicit or otherwise) that the fate of these populations rested largely, if not exclusively, in the hands of colonial whites is potentially ahistorical on at least two counts. In the first instance, it denies or minimizes the complexity of the interactions that characterize all human social and economic relations. Sidney Mintz and Richard Price noted more than two decades ago that the history of free populations of color must be examined in terms of the interaction between the slave and free sectors of slave societies.[6] This point, however, may be taken one step further: we must also view the history of these populations in terms of their ability to influence their own destiny and that of the societies of which they were an integral part. Secondly, such an argument implies not only that free colored social and economic institutions were static rather than dynamic entities, but also that local conditions were of paramount importance in shaping their development. Such a conclusion ignores the larger context within which these populations arose and, more specifically, the extent to which free colored life was shaped by the interaction between local social and economic structures and the processes of capital formation.

Developments in early nineteenth-century Mauritius highlight the need to examine the history of free colored populations in terms of such interactive processes. While we know a great deal about the socio-legal conventions that governed the lives of these individuals, we know much less about their social organization and economic activities. Previous accounts of free colored economic activity, for instance, have done little more than list their occupations, report how much land they possessed, and note the number of slaves they owned. As a result, many fundamental questions about free colored economic life remain unanswered: what kind of role did *gens de couleur* play in colonial economies? To what extent and why did free persons of color remain marginal to colonial economic life? If free colored economic life changed over time, when and why did these changes occur? How and in what ways did free colored social structure influence free colored economic life, or vice versa? Answers to these questions are important not only to reconstructing the history of the Mauritian free population of color, but also to understanding the ways in which slave plantation systems worked.

Research on late eighteenth- and early nineteenth-century colonial sugar economies in the Americas underscores the need to examine the free colored experience in terms of the relationship between capital and local socio-economic structures. This scholarship reveals that many free populations of color in the Caribbean arose during an era of growing economic distress caused by stagnant or declining levels of sugar production, competition from new producers, reduced metropolitan investment, and a widely fluctuating world market for this commodity.[7] Estate-owners and managers responded by cutting costs, rationalizing production, and relying upon the increasingly inadequate resources of domestic capital to survive. One consequence of this retrenchment process was to deprive many West Indian *gens de couleur* of opportunities they might otherwise have had to improve the quality of their lives. Under these circumstances, it comes as no surprise that many free persons of color in the Americas seemingly remained confined to the margins of colonial social and economic life.

The Mauritian free population of color also came into its own during a period of economic change, but the experience of these *gens de couleur* differed from that of their American counterparts in several respects. More specifically, this population emerged onto the local scene during a period of relative prosperity. While the development of a mercantile economy during the late eighteenth century limited the ability of a small and non-commercial population to improve its overall economic condition, *gens de couleur* nevertheless shared in the prosperity of the times and began to acquire the resources that would allow them to exploit the opportunities created by the island's transformation into a sugar colony after 1810. Their acquisition and control of increasingly significant economic resources would, in due course, provide them with the means to step away from the wings and onto the stage of nineteenth-century Mauritian history as actors in their own right.

Free persons of color numbered among the Ile de France's residents no later than 1729, but *gens de couleur* as a group did not figure prominently in the island's social and economic life until the latter part of the eighteenth century. As in other slave colonies, the Mauritian free population of color was initially too small to be of consequence; in 1767, the colony housed 3,163 whites and 15,027 slaves but only 587 free persons of color. This community grew steadily in size, however, and in 1806 the island sheltered 7,154 *gens de couleur* compared to 6,798 whites and 60,646 slaves. This population doubled again in size in less than two decades, climbing to 14,133 in 1825, while five years later the island's 18,109 *gens de couleur* accounted for two-thirds of its non-slave inhabitants and one-fifth of its total population.

The Mauritian free colored population drew its members from various sources, including the ranks of the colony's manumitted slaves. Baron d'Unienville, the colonial archivist during much of the first two decades of British rule, reported that 4,836 slaves were manumitted between 1767 and 1824,[8] but the reliability of his data remains open to

question. While the Baron asserted that 1,126 bondsmen were freed
between 1768 and 1789, Musleem Jumeer has uncovered formal acts of
manumission for only 785 slaves during this same period.[9] Discrep-
ancies also exist in the number of manumissions reported for 1808
through 1822; according to Governor Sir Robert Farquhar, only 1,704
slaves were freed during this period compared to d'Unienville's figure of
2,039.[10] The exact number of slaves manumitted in the colony may
never be known, but the fact that none of these figures is particularly
large suggests that the manumission rate remained low and relatively
constant over time. Even if we accept the Baron's higher figures at face
value, it is clear that no more than 0.2 percent of the Mauritian slave
population could expect to be freed each year during the late eighteenth
and early nineteenth centuries.[11]

Mauritian slaves came from all over the Indian Ocean world, as well as
far beyond it, and the colony's new freedmen came from correspondingly
diverse backgrounds. Among the slaves manumitted between 1768 and
1789 were Guineans, Lascars, Malabars, Malagasies, Malays, Mozambicans, and even a Canary Islander. The relevant acts also reveal that
slaves with certain ethnic or cultural backgrounds tended to be freed
more often than those from other places of origin. Indians, for example,
comprised less than one-tenth of the island's bondsmen between 1768
and 1789, but accounted for more than one-third of those freed during
this period; disproportionately large numbers of Creole (i.e., locally
born) slaves also acquired their freedom at this time. While similar data
have yet to be developed for the period after 1789, it is reasonable to
assume that slaves from selected ethnic or cultural backgrounds continued to be manumitted in disproportionately large numbers well into
the early nineteenth century.

Like bondsmen elsewhere, slaves on the Ile de France were manumitted for various reasons: as compensation for years of loyal service, as
a reward for heroic acts such as saving a master's life, as a token of a
master's affection, or as an act of religious piety. The demographic
structure of this emancipated population makes it clear, however, that
many of these manumissions were an act of indemnity for women who
had borne their masters' children.[12] The basic pattern to manumissions –
high percentages of women and children and low numbers of adult men –
was well established by the late eighteenth century. The 785 freedmen for
whom Jumeer uncovered formal *actes de liberté* included 347 women, 173
men, 133 boys, and 132 girls.[13] Governor Farquhar's report reveals that
the tendency for three females to be liberated for every two males
remained unchanged during the first decades of the nineteenth century,
while other sources indicate that the proportion of adult women, adult

men, and children (i.e., individuals under fifteen years of age) being freed remained relatively constant into the 1820s.[14]

While many slaves were manumitted for sentimental or altruistic reasons, a significant number also acquired their freedom, at least in part, because their masters wanted to avoid the cost of caring for unproductive workers. One-fifth of the 418 slaves manumitted between 1821 and 1826 were reported to be forty years of age or older, a figure which suggests that it was not uncommon for older bondsmen to be viewed as an economic liability rather than as an asset. Freeing such a slave could save his or her owner a substantial sum, despite the legal requirement that masters had to provide new freedmen with enough money or property to ensure that they did not become a public charge. Children, like the aged and the infirm, could also be a financial liability, and the high percentages of children manumitted between 1768 and 1789 and 1821 and 1826 may likewise reflect the economic considerations that could dictate which slaves received their freedom.

A second component of the local free population of color were those persons who came to the colony either of their own accord or to work under contract. Indian and Malay sailors serving on Compagnie and other vessels numbered among these *gens de couleur*, as did carpenters, masons, and other skilled workmen from the French possessions in India. These artisans, who were recruited to work in the colony because their services were less expensive and more readily available than those of European craftsmen, first reached the Ile de France in 1729 and continued to arrive until the mid-1780s, if not later.[15] Immigrants from other parts of the French colonial empire also found their way to the island's shores. During 1787, for example, Jean Perouel, a mulatto from Saint Domingue, signed a contract in Port Louis to work as a cooper in the king's service for one year while Dorothée, a mulatress from Grenada, received a grant of land in the city's *Camp des noirs libres*.[16]

The number of these freedmen and immigrants was much too small, however, to account for this population's rapid growth during the late eighteenth and early nineteenth centuries. The magnitude of these increases, together with the large number of children reported in colonial censuses, indicate that high rates of natural reproduction were largely responsible for this dramatic population growth. D'Unienville's survey of civil status records from 1804 to 1825 indicated that the free colored birth rate was never less than 35 per 1,000 each year in the island's rural districts and ran at a staggering 60 per 1,000 each year in Port Louis,[17] figures which point to a birth rate of 45 per 1,000 for the colony as a whole. The free colored death rate during this same period reportedly averaged only 11.5 per 1,000, a figure which suggests that the free colored population grew at a very healthy rate of 3.35 percent a year during the first decades of the nineteenth century. Similar data are unavailable for the late eighteenth century, but it is not unreasonable to assume that comparable rates of increase may have prevailed during the 1780s and 1790s.

An important consequence of these trends was the creation and maintenance of an unbalanced sex and age structure. Free women of color outnumbered free men of color by a significant margin no later than the early 1780s, and by 1806 *femmes de couleur* outnumbered *hommes de couleur* by more than two to one in the colony as a whole and by almost three to one in Port Louis. While this sexual imbalance began to lessen during the 1810s, women continued to outnumber men by a significant margin well into the nineteenth century. At the same time, children constituted an ever larger percentage of this population, accounting for more than one-half of all *gens de couleur* as early as 1780, and a staggering 62 percent of the free colored community by 1819.

In addition to revealing these structural features of free colored society, censuses from this era shed considerable light on the economic dimensions of these imbalances. In 1806, for example, 65 percent of the 1,294 *gens de couleur* in Port Louis who reported their livelihood were women, while one occupation, that of seamstress or dressmaker, accounted for no less than 55 percent of the 1,294 occupations in question.[18] Facts such as these suggest that the marginal status of *gens de couleur* was, at least in part, a product of the ways in which free colored social and economic structures interacted with one another. Nowhere are the nature and dynamics of this interaction more apparent than in the realm of land acquisition and ownership.

In Mauritius, as in the New World, the acquisition of real property was crucial to free colored attempts to carve out a significant place for themselves in colonial society. Mauritian *gens de couleur* acquired land through the grant or purchase of public lands, as gifts and bequests from family, friends, and former masters, and by private purchase. The total number of these transactions is impossible to determine because many of them were handled privately and remain hidden from view. Between 1748 and 1810, however, the colonial land office recorded approximately 410 grants and sales of public land to free persons of color, and these documents and their accompanying petitions provide us with an initial opening from which we may begin to view the workings of free colored society.

Only a handful of free persons of color received grants of public land before Compagnie rule came to an end in 1767. Most of these grantees were individuals of some consequence to the colony's social, economic, or political life. Elizabeth Sobobie Béty (or Bétia), who received the first land grant made to a free person of color (1758), was the daughter of the king, and later herself briefly the queen, of Foulepointe, an important center for French slavers operating along the east coast of Madagascar.[19] Other early free colored recipients of these grants, such as Louis LaViollette, an interpreter for the Compagnie in Madagascar, and Manuel Manique, *cydevant maître d'hôtel du gouvernement*, were also persons who occupied or had served in positions of importance to the colony's economic and administrative well-being.[20]

The number of grants made to *gens de couleur* began to increase significantly after the establishment of royal government in 1767. Like the Compagnie, the royal regime used land grants to create or cement ties with certain segments of the free colored population. One-half of the grants to *hommes de couleur* during the 1770s, for example, were made to *noirs de détachement*, that is, to those men charged with the capture of fugitive slaves. Other recipients included interpreters, government functionaries, and important seamen. While many more such grants were made during the 1780s to persons with no apparent ties to the colonial government, at least one-quarter of the *hommes de couleur* who received grants during this decade were or had been in government service.

While grants such as these helped to lay the foundation upon which free colored social and economic mobility would ultimately rest, we must remember that this foundation remained a modest one into the early nineteenth century. *Gens de couleur* received only 15 percent of grants made during the 1770s and 1780s, and their involvement in this particular sphere of colonial life continued to be limited when public lands began to be sold off early in the 1790s. No more than 17 percent of all such sales between 1807 and 1810, for example, were made to free persons of color. The arpentage in free colored hands was even less than these figures might suggest. In 1788, *gens de couleur* owned a mere 3.5 percent of all inventoried land; in 1806, after almost forty years of active involvement in the public and private real estate markets, free colored holdings amounted to only 7.1 percent of all inventoried land.

The size and location of these public land grants and sales underscore the fact that the colony's free population of color possessed only limited resources at the dawn of the nineteenth century. More than four-fifths of the properties in question encompassed less than 1 arpent, or 1.043 acres. Approximately two-thirds of these properties were also located in Port Louis or Mahébourg where, as in the Caribbean, most of these plots covered no more than several hundred square meters, an area large enough only for the erection of a small house, workshop, or boutique, and perhaps the establishment of a modest garden.[21]

Mauritian *gens de couleur* also began to acquire real property during the mid-eighteenth century through bequests and donations and by private purchase. As was noted earlier, the full extent of this activity is impossible to ascertain for the simple reason that many of these transactions were handled privately. On numerous occasions, however, free persons of color called upon local notaries to document these transactions, which they often did in considerable detail. The survival of thousands of notarial acts from this era provides an exceptional vantage point from which we may begin not only to chart the economic fortunes of the colony's free population of color in some detail, but also to inquire how *gens de couleur* mobilized the resources they needed to acquire ever-greater quantities of land and other kinds of property.

Free persons of color first purchased houses and the occasional plot of land on their own account no later than the late 1740s. A sample of 543 transactions drawn from the acts of six notaries active between 1737 and 1820 indicates, however, that their involvement in the local real estate market remained somewhat limited until the 1790s. A great majority of the property transfers recorded before 1780 involved the sale of houses (*cazes*) and outbuildings such as kitchens and sheds, which were frequently situated on public land in Port Louis. *Cazes* tended to be small one- or two-room structures, often only several hundred square feet in area, and frequently constructed of boards and covered by wooden shingles or straw thatching. While some of the buildings changing hands had been in their owner's possession for years, others were clearly regarded as investments to be bought and then quickly sold if a reasonable profit could be made on the sale. Both whites and *gens de couleur* dealt in these structures. Between 1748 and 1779, for example, five notaries documented seven sales in which free persons of color bought buildings from white colonists, twelve sales in which they bought buildings from other free persons of color, and seventeen transactions in which they sold buildings to local whites.

While *gens de couleur* occasionally purchased land on their own account during the mid-eighteenth century, the real beginnings of free colored involvement in the local real-estate market date to the 1770s. Notarial acts from this era indicate that the pattern of these private purchases was much the same as it had been for their acquisition of public lands; transactions involving small plots in the colony's urban areas, and especially in Port Louis, outnumbered those involving larger rural tracts by a substantial margin. This activity continued on a rather modest scale until the 1790s when the number of private transactions involving *gens de couleur* began to increase dramatically. This increase is not unexpected; between 1788 and 1806, the free colored population would triple in size. However, population growth was not the only, or even the most important, factor which contributed to this increased activity. The notarial record suggests that growing numbers of these individuals were venturing into the local real-estate market because of their increasing ability to mobilize the capital resources needed to do so. More specifically, the increasing regularity with which they paid the full purchase price for land at the time of a sale's formal completion suggests that, especially after the 1780s, more and more *gens de couleur* enjoyed a certain degree of fiscal solvency, if not financial independence.

*Gens de couleur* obtained the capital they needed to purchase land, houses, and other property such as slaves from various sources. In some instances, freedmen and women were the beneficiaries of generous gifts or bequests from former masters such as François Desveau who, in addition to confirming the freedom of Hélène, the natural daughter of Roze, *négresse de caste indienne*, on December 28, 1763, bequeathed her the sum of 20,000 livres.[22] The following year, Nicolas Auclair's last will and testament not only freed Susanne, *négresse de caste malgache*, and her six children on the day of his death, but also stipulated that she was to receive his plantation as well as all of his slaves, livestock, furniture, and other personal possessions.[23] In other instances, individuals such as Louis LaViollette enjoyed lifetime annuities from former employers or masters.[24] Colonists such as Antoine Codère also occasionally loaned money to *gens de couleur* such as Jacques Lambert, *noir libre créol de l'Amérique*, to underwrite the purchase of houses, land, or slaves.[25]

It is difficult to determine the extent to which the economic fortunes of the local free population of color rested upon white largesse. The notarial record indicates clearly that the long-term economic well-being of some free persons of color and their families or heirs may be traced to the actions of former masters or other white benefactors. The case of Marie Rozette, an Indian freedwoman who owned 156 arpents of land and had at least 113,000 livres in cash assets at her disposal in 1790, is a stunning case in point.[26] Other evidence suggests, however, that many more free persons of color could count only upon modest amounts of support from local whites, and often upon none at all. A survey of the manumissions recorded by the notary Antoine Gombaud between November 5, 1790, and December 4, 1795, suggests, for example, that most of the slaves freed by whites during these years received no more than 3,000 livres at the time of their manumission. The loans recorded by five notaries between 1748 and 1819 provide additional evidence of this general state of affairs: white colonists were the lenders of record in only nineteen of fifty-seven acts involving free persons of color.

*Gens de couleur* accordingly looked elsewhere for the capital they needed. Those who already owned land, houses, or slaves drew upon the profits that could be made from the sale of their property. Certain kinds of employment could be highly remunerative for those fortunate enough to obtain it; for managing his plantation, Vivien de Carmasson agreed that Baptiste, *noir malabar libre*, would receive one-half of the estate's produce.[27] Individuals such as Pauline, *indienne*, invested occasionally in maritime ventures, especially when they were guaranteed a 30 percent return on their investment.[28] Rents were another important source of income for individuals like Marie Louise Eléonore Volatsara, who acknowledged receipt on January 28, 1786, of 8,830 livres from Delaux Verogue for the use of her slaves.[29] Still others, such as Françoise, *négresse libre*, loaned compatriots the money they needed to buy a plot of land and a slave to work it.[30] As the numerous land grants and sales to members of the Pitcha or Pitchen family between 1774 and 1807 attest, in still other instances *gens de couleur* drew upon familial resources or capitalized upon quasi-familial ties to secure the funds they needed.

While these examples demonstrate that some *gens de couleur* were able to acquire the means that allowed them to buy land, including extensive tracts in the rural districts, the modest amount of land in free colored hands *circa* 1806 confirm that the capital resources available to the free colored population as a whole remained rather limited well into the early nineteenth century. Even when free persons of color managed to purchase large tracts of land, they were often unable to mobilize the funds they needed to clear their land and bring it fully into production. Their inability to do so stemmed in part from the fact that the population as a whole seems to have had to rely rather heavily upon its own financial resources for developmental capital. The necessity of doing so is suggested by the fact that thirty-three of the fifty-seven loans referred to earlier entailed free colored borrowers going to other *gens de couleur* for the money they needed. However, even when free colored moneylenders could be found, it is apparent that most of these persons had limited discretionary funds at their disposal. As we shall see, a great majority of the colony's *gens de couleur* relied upon the service sector of the local economy for their livelihood during the late eighteenth and early nineteenth centuries, and many of these individuals possessed little or no property of consequence.

Land was not the only resource of importance to Mauritian *gens de couleur*. Like their American counterparts, the island's free men and women of color also bought and sold slaves, gave and received them as gifts, and bequeathed them to family and friends. Just when and how *gens de couleur* first acquired slaves remains to be determined, but free colored ownership of slaves was a fact of colonial life no later than 1755

Table 8. *Slave-ownership by free colored households, 1776–1826*

| Locale | Year | Households | Number of slaves per household (percent) | | | |
|---|---|---|---|---|---|---|
| | | | None | 1–2 | 3–4 | 5+ |
| Colony-wide | 1776 | 475 | 64.8 | 20.6 | 7.8 | 6.8 |
| | 1780 | 563 | 64.7 | 17.1 | 8.3 | 9.9 |
| Port Louis | 1776 | 343 | 63.0 | 26.5 | 7.0 | 3.5 |
| | 1780 | 360 | 60.5 | 22.8 | 10.3 | 6.4 |
| | 1805 | 1,532 | 31.5 | 39.8 | 15.5 | 13.2 |
| | 1806 | 1,666 | 39.5 | 35.9 | 13.6 | 11.0 |
| All rural districts | 1776 | 132 | 69.7 | 5.3 | 9.8 | 15.2 |
| | 1780 | 203 | 71.9 | 6.9 | 4.9 | 16.3 |
| Plaines Wilhems | 1788 | 28 | 14.3 | 46.4 | 17.9 | 21.4 |
| | 1810 | 161 | 24.8 | 24.8 | 16.2 | 34.2 |
| | 1819 | 248 | 29.0 | 24.6 | 14.9 | 31.5 |
| | 1825 | 261 | 29.5 | 29.9 | 14.9 | 25.7 |
| | 1826 | 245 | 23.7 | 34.7 | 12.6 | 29.0 |

*Sources:* CAOM: G¹ 473 – Recensement général de l'Ile de France, 1776; G¹ 474 – Recensement général de l'Ile de France, 1780.

MA: KK 3 – Recensement des populations blanche et libre, Port Louis (1805); KK 5 – Recensement des impositions de l'an XII, populations blanche et libre (25 mars 1806); KK 7 – Recensement des populations blanche et libre, Plaines Wilhems (1810–12); KK 8 – Recensement des populations blanche et libre, Plaines Wilhems, 1819; KK 13 – Recensement des populations blanche et libre, Plaines Wilhems, 1825; KK 15 – Cadastre des Plaines Wilhems. Populations blanche et libre (1826); KK 46 – Recensement de l'Ile de France, 1788.

when Louis Moutou, *noir malabard libre*, freed Catherine, *noire créolle*, and her mother on the eve of his marriage to Catherine.[31] The extent of free colored slave-ownership was first revealed in the census of 1776 when *gens de couleur* were reported to own 623 slaves.[32] Twelve years later, free persons of color held 2,162 bondsmen.[33] This number continued to increase over the years, to 7,908 in 1806 and to at least 8,163 three years later.[34]

A closer examination of these censuses provides additional insight into the dynamics of free colored slave-ownership. In the first instance, these censuses reveal not only that the number of slaves held by free persons of color increased between the mid-1770s and 1806, but also that slave-ownership became much more widespread within the free colored population as a whole (see table 8). By 1810, two-thirds or more of free colored households owned at least one slave compared to only one-third

Table 9. *Age and sex of slaves owned by free persons of color, 1776–1809*

| Locale | Year | (Percent) | | | | No. |
| | | Men | Women | Boys | Girls | |
|---|---|---|---|---|---|---|
| Port Louis | 1776 | 47.8 | 47.5 | 2.8 | 1.9 | 316 |
| | 1780 | 40.8 | 35.9 | 13.2 | 10.1 | 395 |
| | 1788 | 37.1 | 39.8 | 11.9 | 11.2 | 1,128 |
| | 1809 | 41.5 | 31.5 | 14.1 | 12.9 | 2,731 |
| Rural districts | 1776 | 49.5 | 32.3 | 11.4 | 6.8 | 307 |
| | 1780 | 52.6 | 31.5 | 9.5 | 6.4 | 454 |
| | 1788 | 51.9 | 29.3 | 11.0 | 7.8 | 1,034 |
| | 1809 | 51.2 | 24.2 | 13.4 | 11.2 | 5,432 |

*Sources:* CAOM: G¹ 473; G¹ 474; G¹ 505, No. 9 – Relevé du cadastre général de l'Isle de France fait pour l'année 1809 d'après les Recensemens fournis par les habitans.
    MA:     KK 46.

of all such households some thirty years earlier. The number of households controlling large numbers of slaves also increased significantly. In 1776, only seven free colored households in the entire colony were reported to own ten or more slaves; by 1805, Port Louis alone sheltered at least thirty-six such households.[35] Changes in the master–slave ratio also confirm the increasing pervasiveness of slave-ownership within the free population of color. *Gens de couleur* had outnumbered their slaves by a two-to-one margin in 1776, but by 1806 a rough parity would exist between these two populations.

In addition to becoming an integral part of free colored life by the early nineteenth century, the pattern of slave-ownership became more complex with the passage of time. While *gens de couleur* in Port Louis and the rural districts mirrored one another in certain respects (e.g., comparable percentages of households owning no bondsmen in 1776 and 1780), the Plaines Wilhems censuses indicate that the rural households owning slaves tended to hold larger numbers of bondsmen than did their urban counterparts. Other data point to changes in these patterns of ownership over time. During the 1770s and 1780s, for example, the slaves held by free persons of color were distributed more or less evenly between Port Louis and the rural districts. By 1806, however, rural *gens de couleur* owned a disproportionately large percentage of all slaves. Changes in the demographic structure of these urban and rural slave populations can also be discerned. As table 9 reveals, the relative parity between the sexes that characterized the servile population owned by free colored residents of Port Louis during the 1770s and 1780s was not

Table 10. *Economic condition of rural free persons of color, 1776–1825*

| | | | Percentage of households owning | | | |
|---|---|---|---|---|---|---|
| Locale | Year | Households | No land<br>No slaves | Slaves<br>only | Land<br>only | Land &<br>slaves |
| All rural districts | 1776 | 132 | 54.5 | 4.5 | 15.2 | 25.8 |
| Plaines Wilhems | 1776 | 9 | 88.9 | — | — | 11.1 |
| | 1788 | 28 | 14.3 | 60.7 | — | 25.0 |
| | 1819 | 248 | 23.8 | 37.9 | 5.2 | 33.1 |
| | 1825 | 261 | 24.5 | 28.0 | 5.7 | 41.8 |
| Plaines Wilhems<br>households:[a] | | | | | | |
| Male-headed | 1825 | 40 | 10.0 | 20.0 | 2.5 | 67.5 |
| Female-headed | 1825 | 111 | 19.8 | 30.6 | 5.4 | 44.2 |

*Note:* [a] Comprised of two or more persons residing together.
*Sources:* CAOM: G$^1$ 473.
      MA:     KK 8; KK 13; KK 46.

replicated in the rural districts, where males consistently outnumbered females by a substantial margin. Several decades later, male slaves continued to outnumber female slaves in the rural districts, while in Port Louis there are indications that the earlier sexual parity was giving way to a pattern which echoed that prevailing in the countryside.

These differences come as no surprise given what we know about free colored economic life at this time. Free colored properties in the rural districts were usually substantially larger than those in Port Louis, and their owners obviously required more manpower to bring them into production. Many rural *gens de couleur* actively worked their land, and their income from farming, coupled with their ability to use their land as collateral for loans, made it likely that they had, or at least had easier access to, the financial resources which allowed them to acquire the labor they needed.

Although free persons of color in the countryside accordingly enjoyed some advantages over their urban cousins in this regard, access to economic resources could still vary widely from one household to another (see table 10). The distribution of public land grants and sales among free colored men and women between 1770 and 1810, together with data from Plaines Wilhems, suggests that a free colored household's access to assets could depend to at least some extent upon whether it was headed by a man or a woman. *Femmes de couleur*, for example, not only acquired a disproportionately small number of the public lands granted or sold before 1810, but also often received substantially smaller tracts than did *hommes de couleur*.[36] The subdivision of the Grand Reserve during the first decade of the nineteenth century graphically illustrates this fact of economic life; only seven of the twenty-four tracts sold to *gens de couleur* were purchased by women. Plaines Wilhems census data confirm that male-headed households probably controlled a disproportionately large percentage of free colored economic resources in the rural districts by the mid-1820s, if not before. These data also suggest that slaves were a more important asset than land in many rural female-headed households.

The fortunes of Port Louis's free colored residents, like those of their country cousins, varied widely. Almost 30 percent of the city's free colored households owned no taxable property in 1806, while another 41 percent of these households possessed either bondsmen or real property, but not both. Even those *gens de couleur* fortunate enough to possess both real property and slaves were often persons of rather modest means, as the appraised value of their possessions and the rates at which they were taxed demonstrate (see table 11). Almost two-thirds of the slaves owned by the city's free colored population in 1806 were subject to a capitation tax of only 10 livres, while a comparable percentage of white-owned slaves were taxed at the rate of 20 livres per head.[37] The appraised value of urban properties provides additional evidence of this general state of affairs; three-fifths of the free colored households owning some kind of real property in 1806 had holdings valued at less than $250. The value of free colored real property in the city that same year totaled only $247,879 compared to $2,582,765 for the city's white inhabitants.

In Port Louis, as in the rural districts, the nature of free colored social structure helps to explain these low levels of capitalization and proprietorship. The extent to which women of color outnumbered *hommes de couleur* in Port Louis has already been noted, as has the numbers of slaves held by urban households and the limitations which the small size of urban properties imposed upon their owners. These data indicate that *femmes de couleur* throughout the island depended more heavily upon slaves in their daily struggle for survival than did *hommes de couleur*. The demographic structure of the slave population owned by the free colored residents of Port Louis suggests, furthermore, that slave-ownership may have been as much a liability as it was an asset for many free women of color. In many instances, *gens de couleur* in Port Louis made their living or supplemented their income by renting out their slaves, 60 percent of whom were women and children who commanded significantly lower rents than did adult males. Just how marginal a resource these slaves may have been is suggested by two additional facts: the great majority of free colored households owning slaves held only one or two bondsmen,

Table 11. *Economic condition of free persons of color in Port Louis, 1806*

| Households owning | No. | No. of slaves taxed at | | Appraised value of property[a] | | | | | |
|---|---|---|---|---|---|---|---|---|---|
| | | 10 livres | 20 livres | None given[b] | $1–249 | $250–499 | $500–999 | $1,000 + |
| No property/slaves | 491 | — | — | — | — | — | — | — |
| Slaves only | 511 | 790 | 298 | — | — | — | — | — |
| 1–2 slaves | 379 | 457 | 50 | — | — | — | — | — |
| 3–5 slaves | 108 | 251 | 143 | — | — | — | — | — |
| 6–10 slaves | 21 | 70 | 79 | — | — | — | — | — |
| 11+ slaves | 3 | 12 | 26 | — | — | — | — | — |
| Property only | 167 | — | — | 36 | 105 | 11 | 8 | 7 |
| Property & slaves | 497 | 1,114 | 783 | 28 | 230 | 107 | 62 | 70 |
| 1–2 slaves | 220 | 283 | 39 | 19 | 146 | 32 | 14 | 9 |
| 3–5 slaves | 179 | 446 | 227 | 6 | 68 | 48 | 29 | 28 |
| 6–10 slaves | 70 | 270 | 313 | 2 | 13 | 22 | 12 | 21 |
| 11+ slaves | 28 | 115 | 204 | 1 | 3 | 5 | 7 | 12 |
| Total | 1,666 | 1,904 | 1,081 | 64 | 335 | 118 | 70 | 77 |

*Notes:*
[a] Real estate and/or buildings.
[a] Indicates ownership of a house, often described as a straw hut (*paillote*), of no discernible value.
*Source:* MA: KK 5.

Table 12. *Occupations of Port Louis's free colored residents, 1776–1828*

| Occupational category | Distribution within free colored population (percent) | | | Percentage of all persons so employed | | |
|---|---|---|---|---|---|---|
| | 1776 | 1805[a] | 1828[a] | 1776 | 1805[a] | 1828[a] |
| Agriculture | 0.3 | 2.6 | 2.0 | 33.3 | 28.8 | 37.9 |
| Business & commerce | 1.6 | 3.0 | 14.7 | 4.8 | 10.2 | 45.2 |
| Clerical & managerial | 6.3 | 4.9 | 6.8 | 35.9 | 39.0 | 66.5 |
| Crafts & trades | 66.8 | 77.7 | 67.3 | 35.3 | 71.3 | 84.8 |
| Gov't/public service | 10.6 | 0.2 | 1.0 | 18.5 | 1.9 | 15.2 |
| Maritime | 9.0 | 4.5 | 3.6 | 45.2 | 25.0 | 53.3 |
| Professional | 0.3 | 0.2 | 1.0 | 1.9 | 3.1 | 13.7 |
| Miscellaneous[b] | 5.1 | 6.9 | 3.6 | 12.8 | 65.6 | 61.2 |
| Sample/Total | 368 | 1,293 | 1,771 | 26.8 | 49.0 | 65.2 |

*Notes:*
[a] For the eastern and western suburbs combined. Residents of these suburbs are not always described specifically as persons of color. However, since these suburbs are the sites of the former *Camp des noirs libres* and *Camp des malabars*, it is assumed that their residents were largely *gens de couleur*.
[b] Including persons described as laborers, infirm or invalid, or retired.
*Sources:* CAOM: G¹ 473.
      MA:    KK 3; KK 20 – Recensement des populations blanche et libre, Port Louis (1828–29).

and often these slaves were not chattel who could be exploited unconditionally, but family members whose freedom had not yet been purchased or otherwise secured.

The ways in which *gens de couleur* earned their living sheds additional light on free colored economic marginality during the last decades of French rule. Free persons of color practiced a wide variety of professions, but a small range of occupations accounted for most free colored employment. In 1776, two-thirds of Port Louis's free colored population worked in a craft or trade such as blacksmithing, carpentry, cooperage, masonry, or tailoring. Thirty years later, an urban work force that had more than tripled in size continued to depend heavily upon the service and artisanal sector of the local economy for its daily bread (see table 12). Even in the rural districts, service and related occupations apparently accounted for an important part of free colored employment. Such was the case in Plaines Wilhems *circa* 1810 where 39 of the 138 heads of household who reported their profession claimed one that was not agricultural in nature.[38]

By the end of the first decade of the nineteenth century, *gens de couleur*

Table 13. *Projected value of free colored economic resources and activities, 1806–1830*

| Category | 1806 | | 1829–30 | |
| --- | --- | --- | --- | --- |
| | Projected total value | % Total from GDC[a] | Projected total value | % Total from GDC[a] |
| Agriculture | $1,456,023 | 4.9 | $3,476,357 | 11.8 |
| Cloves | 16,964 | 0.3 | 10,523 | 19.1 |
| Coffee | 12,318 | 5.3 | 7,119 | 11.3 |
| Cotton | 121,321 | 3.6 | 72 | 100.0 |
| Grains | 184,340 | 13.9 | 131,935 | 31.0 |
| Root crops[b] | 472,558 | 8.0 | 415,453 | 19.7 |
| Sugar | 648,522 | 0.4 | 2,911,255 | 9.7 |
| Land | $6,745,020 | 7.1 | $6,800,550 | 13.4 |
| Livestock | $465,309 | 5.2 | $1,097,494 | 16.0 |
| Cattle | 238,980 | 3.4 | 681,870 | 15.2 |
| Goats/sheep | 12,459 | 10.2 | 5,136 | 25.3 |
| Horses | 151,050 | 6.0 | 169,650 | 14.2 |
| Mules/donkeys | 62,820 | 9.3 | 225,000 | 19.2 |
| Pigs | — | — | 15,838 | 21.7 |
| Slaves | $8,490,440 | 13.0 | $9,726,640 | 20.7–28.8 |
| Total | $17,156,792 | 9.8 | $21,101,041 | 16.6–20.4 |

*Notes:*
[a] *Gens de couleur.*
[b] Manioc and potatoes.
*Sources:*  CO 172/42 – Tableaux Nos. 24, 25, 27, 30, 31, 33, 34.
         d'Unienville 1885–86, Vol. I, pp. 52–228, as corrected.
         Milbert 1812, Vol. II, p. 233 bis.

had become an integral part of the island's economic landscape, owning more than 7 percent of all inventoried land and nearly 15 percent of the colony's slaves. Their ability to carve out this small, but distinct, place for themselves in the colony's economic life may be traced to several developments. One of these was their ever-increasing involvement in agriculture; by 1809, free persons of color were farming more than 9 percent of all cultivated land. Rapid population growth was another factor; by 1810, one in every ten of the island's inhabitants was a free person of color and *gens de couleur* accounted for more than 50 percent of all free persons in the colony. This growing demographic presence manifested itself in other ways; by 1805, free persons of color comprised one-half of an urban work force that had almost doubled in size during the preceding three decades. While most of these urban workers still relied upon the service sector, which they now dominated, for their livelihood, this was also a sector that had flourished during the heady days of the late eighteenth century. Lastly, as the numerous testaments and donations in the notarial record from this era attest, these individuals took great care to ensure that the assets they had accumulated were protected and preserved for the future use of their kith and kin.

It is impossible to determine precisely the value of free colored possessions or economic activity. An estimate of the value of the land, slaves, and livestock owned by *gens de couleur* and of the produce for which they may have been responsible suggests, however, that the free population of color accounted for approximately 10 percent of the island's agricultural and related wealth by 1806 (see table 13).[39] This modest place in the local economy comes as no surprise given what we know about the structure of free colored social and economic life and about the restrictions which limited the scope of free colored economic activity during the late eighteenth and early nineteenth centuries. Evidence of these limitations is not hard to find. In 1770, to cite one prominent example, the eighteen *noirs de détachement* who received land grants at Réduit were specifically prohibited from cultivating spices or other export commodities.[40] The impact of such prohibitions was evident thirty-five years later when less than 10 percent of the land being cultivated by free persons of color was devoted to cash crops such as cloves, coffee, and indigo. In other instances, the limitations upon free colored economic life were more subtle but no less pronounced. The preoccupation with commerce and trade between 1770 and 1810 restricted the range of activities in which an undercapitalized and predominately female population could hope to participate. The dramatic growth of the island's slave population during the same period also served to limit the opportunities many *gens de couleur* might have otherwise had to secure gainful employment in either the agricultural or maritime sectors of the local economy.[41]

While the advent of British rule in 1810 had an immediate impact upon the political and economic life of the Ile de France as a whole, its initial effect upon the colony's free population of color was much less pronounced. *Gens de couleur* were not released from the legal disabilities under which they had to live and work; restrictions on their gathering in public, for instance, remained in place, and they continued to be subject to heavier fines than whites for breaking the same law. The general pattern of free colored social and economic life also stayed much as it had been during the last years of French rule. The community's demographic structure remained seriously unbalanced; in 1817, adult men comprised less than one-fifth of all *gens de couleur* while children accounted for more than one-half of the population. The

Table 14. *Economic condition of the free population of color, 1776–1830*

| | (Percent) | | | | | | |
|---|---|---|---|---|---|---|---|
| | 1776 | 1780 | 1788 | 1806 | 1809 | 1825 | 1830 |
| Total inventoried land | 1.3 | 1.3 | 3.5 | 7.1 | 7.4 | 11.3 | 13.4 |
| Total land under cultivation | 1.0 | 1.9 | 2.8 | 7.7 | 9.1 | 14.3 | 13.0 |
| Cloves | — | — | — | 0.3 | 1.1 | 8.1 | 15.4 |
| Coffee | — | — | — | 5.3 | 6.5 | 11.2 | 11.3 |
| Cotton | — | — | — | 3.5 | 3.6 | 15.1 | — |
| Grains | — | — | — | 28.5 | 13.3 | 23.9 | 46.7 |
| Indigo | — | — | — | 1.9 | 1.5 | 18.9 | — |
| Manioc | — | — | — | 8.0 | 8.7 | 17.6 | 22.0 |
| Miscellaneous crops | — | — | — | 8.6 | 13.1 | 18.8 | 24.8 |
| Sugar cane | — | — | — | 0.4 | 0.1 | 4.1 | 7.5 |
| Total livestock | 2.2 | 2.3 | 5.3 | 6.2 | 6.5 | 18.2 | 17.8 |
| Total slaves | 2.5 | 3.0 | 5.4 | 13.0 | 14.7 | — | — |
| Total vehicles | — | — | — | — | 2.5 | 5.7 | 10.4 |
| Total industries[a] | — | — | — | — | — | 4.6 | 17.6[b] |

*Notes:*
[a] Lime kilns, stills, and sugar mills.
[a] For Pamplemousses and Grand Port only.
*Sources:* BB 1825, p. 291.
　　　　　CAOM: G[1] 473, G[1] 474, G[1] 505.
　　　　　d'Unienville 1885–86, Vol. I pp. 52–228, as corrected.
　　　　　Kuczynski 1949, pp. 760–73.
　　　　　MA: KK 46.
　　　　　Milbert 1812, Vol. II, p. 233 bis.

service sector likewise continued to be the locus of free colored economic life.

By the mid-1820s, however, there are clear indications that things were changing for the colony's free population of color. The 1828 Port Louis census revealed that only one-half of the city's *gens de couleur* now earned their living by providing personal services – as bootmakers, hatmakers, seamstresses, servants, wigmakers, etc. – compared to the 66 percent who had done so in 1805. One in seven of these urban residents now claimed employment in business or commerce compared to the mere 3 percent who had done so a quarter of a century earlier. The number of *gens de couleur* in managerial and clerical positions had also increased, albeit at a much more modest rate.

Distinct signs of change can also be detected in the countryside where *gens de couleur* not only controlled substantially more land by 1825 than they had two decades earlier, but also figured much more prominently in agricultural life (see table 14). The arpentage in free colored hands increased again noticeably between 1825 and 1830; a 22 percent increase in livestock and a tripling of the number of carts, carrioles, and carriages owned by free persons of color during the same period likewise point to this population's growing presence and prosperity. Figures on the number of slaves owned by *gens de couleur* colony-wide are unavailable after 1809, but the growing numbers of slaves held by the free colored residents of Plaines Wilhems during the 1810s and 1820s suggest that *gens de couleur* may have owned 20 percent or more of all slaves by 1830. The Plaines Wilhems data likewise confirm the growing pervasiveness of slave-ownership among free colored households. More than one-third of the district's households owned at least a slave or two in 1826, compared to 25 percent of such households some fifteen years earlier. The number of households in the district owning five or more slaves had also increased, from fifty-five in 1810 to seventy-one in 1826.

These changes were closely linked to the development of the local sugar industry. The transformation of white-owned estates into sugar plantations, especially after 1825, and the attendant withdrawal of whites from food production offered *gens de couleur* an opportunity to become increasingly important as producers of the basic foodstuffs needed in the colony. The only production figures we have from this era convey some sense of how important this free colored activity had become by the late 1820s. More specifically, in 1829, free colored agricuturalists produced 36 percent of the island's corn, 23 percent of its potatoes, 19 percent of its manioc, 10 percent of its wheat, and 19.5 percent of its garden produce and miscellaneous grocery items.[42]

However, *gens de couleur* did not limit themselves solely to producing foodstuffs. The first decade of the nineteenth century witnessed not only the initial expansion of the island's sugar industry, but also the first hints of free colored involvement in this particular sector of the colonial economy. As table 14 indicates, only a few arpents of free colored land were planted in cane during the first quarter of the century. Following the repeal in 1825 of the preferential tariff on West Indian sugar entering Britain, *gens de couleur* moved to take advantage of the opportunities created by this act, albeit on a much smaller scale than their white neighbors. There are even indications that some free colored planters may have been as productive as their white counterparts, if not more so; although *gens de couleur* controlled no more than 7.5 percent of all land planted in cane in 1830, these planters may have accounted for as much as one-tenth of the value of the 1829–30 crop. Even if the value of free colored sugar production was less than has been projected in table 13, the fact that almost two-fifths of all free colored land under cultivation in 1830 was planted in such a highly remunerative crop demonstrates that sugar was becoming an important source of income for some *gens de couleur* as the 1820s drew to a close.

The free colored population's ability to exploit these opportunities depended upon access to and control of land, labor, and capital and, as the career of Baptiste Sebelin illustrates, some rural *gens de couleur* clearly commanded adequate supplies of all three during the early nineteenth century. Between August 18, 1811, and December 11, 1816, Sebelin not only bought a herd of cattle for $1,900 and 27.25 arpents for $900, but also sold eight slaves for $1,300 and four parcels of land totaling 44.25 arpents for $1,134.[43] The Plaines Wilhems censuses provide additional confirmation that members of this rural population possessed the means they needed to become and remain active players on the local agricultural scene. Victorine Demay, for one, owned forty-two slaves and 156 arpents of land in 1819; six years later, her property included a total of fifty-four slaves.[44] Other of the district's *gens de couleur* not only acquired more land and slaves during these years, but also committed substantial resources to developing their properties. Henriette Jouan, for example, owned twenty slaves between 1810 and 1812; by 1819, she held thirty-one slaves and had 60 of her 65 arpents under cultivation. Six years later, she owned 70 arpents and had increased the number of slaves in her possession to thirty-six. Françoise Fanon's story is much the same. In 1819, she owned twenty-nine slaves, fourteen more than she had in 1810–12, and was farming 39 of her 50 arpents; six years later, she owned one less slave but now farmed 52 of the 60 arpents in her possession.[45]

The success of Baptiste Sebelin, Henriette Jouan, Françoise Fanon, and others like them clearly sprang in part from their willingness to reinvest their earnings to expand their operations. Additional details about their lives have yet to be uncovered, so the exact means by which they originally established themselves must remain somewhat conjectural. The career of Jacques Momimes suggests, however, that long-term residence in a locale was one key to free colored success in the countryside. The records of Guillaume Balteau reveal not only that Momimes bought and sold land in Rivière du Rempart over a twenty-year period beginning in 1794, but also that his continued residence in the district allowed him to take quick advantage of any opportunities that presented themselves, as when Joseph Jean LeJuge began to sell off portions of an 849-arpent estate in 1800; Momimes was able to acquire a 24-arpent tract almost immediately for only $280.[46] Various members of the Rioux family did likewise, purchasing a total of 64 arpents from LeJuge between 1800 and 1811.[47]

If long-term residence in the countryside was one factor that could contribute to free colored success, another was the careful husbanding of the assets that had been acquired. Formal gifts (*donations*) and the terms of last wills and testaments attest to the importance many *gens de couleur* placed upon protecting their patrimonies and ensuring that their property remained in the "family" even when an individual apparently had no blood relatives living in the colony. The actions of Marie Gassin are an illustrative case in point. On May 5, 1808, Marie gave her godson, Jean François, 15 arpents she had purchased some six weeks earlier for $500; five years later, she gave him another tract of 9 arpents.[48] Early in 1817, Marie bequeathed to Jean François the ten slaves she had purchased just seven days earlier and stipulated that the balance of her estate, which consisted of additional land and slaves as well as her personal possessions, was to go to her 8-year-old god-daughter, Elise Gigette.[49] Marie's decision to name Elise's uncle as executor of her estate underscored her determination to secure the future of her "children."

Port Louis likewise housed substantial numbers of *gens de couleur* of some economic consequence by the mid- and late 1820s. Evidence of the improving economic fortunes of the city's free population of color is not hard to find. Slave-ownership had become increasingly common among urban households by the early nineteenth century, and the number of slaves held by the city's free colored inhabitants continued to increase, from 3,944 in 1806 to 5,918 in 1827.[50] Data from the city's western suburb, the site of the old *Camp des noirs libres*, also suggest that more free colored households owned larger numbers of slaves than ever before.[51] Tax and census records similarly point to an improving standard of living for many urban free persons of color. The total value of free colored immovable property in the city, for example, increased from $247,879 to $638,300 between 1805 and 1828. The number of free colored urban households which owned property valued from $500 to $999 increased markedly, from 10.5 to 18 percent of all such households, during this same period, while the percentage of these households owning property valued at $1,000 or more doubled, from 11.6 to 23.8 percent.[52]

The ability of Port Louis's *gens de couleur* to command such resources raises the question of the extent to which they participated in the agricultural sector of the local economy. The notarial record demonstrates that some of the city's free colored residents were involved in various aspects of rural life no later than the early nineteenth century. Some *gens de couleur* followed in the footsteps of Benjamin Broudon, who paid $300 in 1810 to lease a 20-arpent estate in Pamplemousses, together with two houses and ten slaves, for a period of five years.[53] Others bought and sold land in the rural districts on a regular basis. These transactions could involve considerable arpentage and substantial sums of money; when Baptiste Louis purchased more than 40 arpents, together with the houses, buildings, and crops thereon, from Louis Hercule, another *homme de couleur*, in 1809, he paid $2,000 for the privilege of becoming a landowner.[54] While we do not know what Baptiste subsequently did with his property, other new free colored estate-owners clearly set about the business of farming their holdings. Such was clearly the case with Babet, *négresse libre*, who not only bought 15 arpents from Jean Dioré in early 1810, but also eight of his slaves to work the land in question.[55]

Our only opportunity to gauge the extent of this activity comes at the very end of the period under consideration. More specifically, the Port Louis census of 1828–29 reveals that 127 of the city's free colored residents, or slightly more than 6 percent of those enumerated, owned more than 10,150 arpents in the countryside, or 28 percent of all free colored land in the colony. These properties tended to be relatively large; an overwhelming majority of them encompassed at least 5 arpents, while 44 percent of the total number covered an area of 20 arpents or more. The census also indicates that 70 percent of these properties were situated in Pamplemousses, Plaines Wilhems, and Rivière du Rempart, districts that had been home to significant numbers of free colored agriculturalists since the latter part of the eighteenth century.

In addition to reporting on the size and location of these holdings, the 1828–29 census sheds light on the nature and extent of the ties that existed between *gens de couleur* living in Port Louis and those residing in the rural districts. The census reveals, in the first instance, that those of Port Louis's free colored residents who owned property both in the city and in the countryside controlled significant resources. The value of the property in Port Louis held by the 127 individuals who fall into this category was $102,350, a sum equal to 16 percent of the value of all free colored property in the city. Nearly one-third of these persons owned property in Port Louis worth $1,000 or more, while at least thirteen people held property valued at $2,000 or more. The value of the rural properties held by these 127 persons is unknown, but projections based upon the average selling price of undeveloped land at this time point to a minimum value of $158,000 to $211,000.

Members of this free colored economic elite earned their livelihood in various ways. Of the city's 117 residents who owned property valued at $1,000 or more and reported their occupation in 1828–29, 29 percent described themselves as a merchant, shopkeeper, or businessman, 47 percent practiced a craft or trade, and the remaining 24 percent earned their living from an assortment of occupations. A striking feature of this economic elite is the apparent failure of free colored merchants and businessmen, regardless of the value of the property they owned in the city, to purchase land in the rural districts. Only eight such individuals were reported as having done so, most of whom had acquired tracts of less than 20 arpents. Fully one-half of the investment in rural property by urban *gens de couleur* came instead from craftsmen and artisans.

The presence of large numbers of craftsmen and artisans among the city's wealthiest *gens de couleur* demonstrates that dependence upon the local service sector was not necessarily an impediment to free persons of color making or improving upon their fortunes. The large number of artisans among free colored rural landowners living in Port Louis, the apparent reluctance of free colored business and commercial interests to become involved in agriculture, and the small percentage of free colored urban residents who owned land in the countryside also suggest, however, that whatever ties may have existed between the free colored population's urban and rural components remained highly personalized. As time would tell, the apparent failure to develop institutionalized links between town and country would place many *gens de couleur* at a distinct disadvantage when the colony's social and economic landscape began to be transformed again during the 1840s.

Other developments contributed to the growing ability of Mauritian *gens de couleur* to capitalize upon the opportunities created by the sugar revolution and improve the quality of their lives. More specifically, there are clear indications by the late 1820s that many of the demographic anomalies that had characterized free colored social structure earlier in the century were becoming less pronounced. Adult men comprised almost one-fourth of the free colored population in 1830, compared to less than 14 percent in 1819. The proportion of children declined as well, from a high of 62 percent of the population in 1819 to less than 44 percent in 1830. The ethnic and cultural fragmentation that had marked early free colored society also became less pronounced as the population became increasingly creolized.[56]

These trends suggest that, by the late 1820s, the local free population of color was acquiring a degree of social structural stability which it had lacked since at least the 1780s, if indeed it had existed before then. This development had profound implications for the free colored community, especially one for which there is evidence of growing internal socio-economic stratification. Mr. Marcenay's "exposé" of 1827, for example, makes it quite clear that the colony's *gens de couleur* were not sharing equally in the relative prosperity of the times. Other sources confirm the existence of a relatively well-to-do free colored elite by the mid-1820s.[57] As their agitation during the 1820s against the color bar demonstrates, this elite was eager to enhance its standing in colonial society and, moreover, possessed the means to give substance to its claims to respectability. Conforming to white social values, especially in the realm of family life, was a strategy that free populations of color in the New World commonly used to achieve this end, and Mauritian *gens de couleur* were no different than their American counterparts in this regard. Reliable information on the conjugal status of Mauritian free men and women of color does not exist, but the limited data at our disposal make it reasonable to assume that the demographic trends noted above facilitated the creation of growing numbers of legally recognized families.[58] This formal sanctioning of familial relationships not only meant enhanced social status, but also ensured that many of the colony's *gens de couleur* enjoyed greater legal protection of their hard-won property.

By 1830, the Mauritian free population of color had clearly become an important component of colonial social and economic life. *Gens de couleur* comprised more than two-thirds of the island's free inhabitants and one-fifth of its total population and controlled perhaps one-fifth, if not more, of the island's agricultural wealth.[59] As the Commission of Eastern Enquiry's report attests, this social and economic clout was matched by a growing political presence. There can be little doubt that an appreciation of the community's economic achievements contributed to the Commission's decision in 1828 to recommend the immediate abolition of the local color bar.

The implementation of this recommendation the following year brought an end to the practice of identifying free persons of color as such in public and private documents. As a result, the free population of color became a much less readily identifiable entity within the larger Mauritian matrix. Its presence and power can still be discerned, however, especially during the late 1830s and early 1840s as colonists sought to come to terms with the consequences of slave emancipation in 1835 and the collapse of the apprenticeship system four years later. During the post-emancipation period, free persons of color were to wield the social and economic power they had developed with great effect, helping to frustrate planters' attempts to drive their former apprentices back on to the sugar estates. The ability of *gens de couleur* to do so stemmed in part from the fact that many of them could offer these new freedmen viable alternatives to working on white-owned sugar estates. In so doing, they would help not only to sweep away the last formal vestiges of slavery, but also to set the stage for further transformations in Mauritian social and economic life.

# 5 The general desire to possess land: ex-apprentices and the post-emancipation era, 1839–1851

The almost total absence of the Emancipated Race from Plantation labour is a striking feature in our social economy. They are now to be sought for in the principal Towns and their neighbourhood, or in retired spots, where they have located themselves in straggling hamlets deriving an easy subsistence from the produce of the ground which they cultivate, and from the rearing of Poultry and other Stock which they carry to the market of Port Louis; sometimes from very distant quarters of the Island. They also traffic in Fire wood and Charcoal – and huckstering and peddling are favorite pursuits. I visited some of these settlements – they wear an appearance of comfort and independence – their inmates are generally orderly and well conducted but they prefer ease to work – and unstimulated to labour beyond what their necessities demand, they abandon all field work for hire, which unfortunately they consider to be a degraded occupation, and which in their own minds they cannot disconnect from the old system of compulsory labour. This feeling is imbibed by their children whom they bring up to follow callings similar to their own or some trade or handicraft; so that until the Immigrants become denizens of the soil, to which every possible encouragement is given, Planters may be said to be entirely dependent upon foreign labour for the cultivation of their Estates ...

Governor Higginson to Earl Grey, October 14, 1851[1]

On March 25, 1839, Governor Sir William Nicolay wrote to Lord Glenelg, the Secretary of State for the Colonies, about his plans to increase the size of the island's police force and almost double the police department's budget. His reason for doing so was straightforward: "on account of the approaching final termination of the praedial apprenticeship."[2] To underscore the need for these measures, the governor forwarded a report by John Finniss, the Chief of Police, on the recent and rather dramatic increase in the number of thefts and robberies in the colony. According to Finniss, the reason for this crime wave was equally straightforward: many apprentices were trying to acquire the means that would allow them to avoid the "dishonor" of not purchasing their freedom before the apprenticeship system came to an end.[3]

Governor Nicolay and police chief Finniss were not the only persons concerned about the possible threat to public order posed by the impending emancipation of more than 53,000 apprentices. James Backhouse reported that during his visit to the colony in 1838 he had "often heard strong fears expressed, that after the emancipation, there would be no safety living in the island ..."[4] Such consternation was not unexpected, given the colony's experience with slavery, and especially its tradition of maroonage. Large numbers of apprentices had continued to run away from their masters after the formal abolition of slavery in 1835, a fact of life that only reinforced local apprehensions about what these "servants" might do upon their final emancipation.[5] However, as events subsequently proved, these fears proved to be unfounded. Less than two weeks after the formal termination of the apprenticeship system on March 31, 1839, Edward Baker informed the Rev. William Ellis that emancipation had "passed off without the slightest disturbance."[6] Governor Nicolay seconded this observation several weeks later when he informed Lord Glenelg that "The conduct of the late apprentices, speaking of them as a mass, has been in a most extraordinary degree quiet and orderly."[7]

Although a much-feared collapse of public order did not materialize, emancipation was nevertheless a traumatic experience for many colonists because, as Edward Baker reported, "many thousands of Blacks" refused to work for their former masters on the same terms as indentured Indians.[8] Proprietors such as Th. Cordouan and Mme. Senneville complained bitterly to their district magistrate that most of their former apprentices had abandoned their estates; Cordouan also observed that frequently it was only the illness of a family member that had delayed the departure of those few apprentices who remained.[9] Governor Nicolay verified in early May that a "great number of large sugar estates have been almost wholly abandoned by the former apprentices."[10] While the governor hoped that many of these individuals would return to the estates once the novelty and excitement of freedom had waned, he admitted that the colony would still have to deal with "an enormous decrease" in the number of its agricultural workers. To many local planters and merchants, the withdrawal of more than one-half of the colony's agricultural work force from active labor augured nothing but disaster, all the more so since emancipation followed hard on the heels of the suspension of Indian immigration to the colony. The "actual and immediate want of hands to gather the crops," they were quick to note, placed them "in imminent peril of losing a great portion of the produce of their properties ..."[11]

Despite the government's interest in maintaining the integrity of the local agricultural work force, its attempts to force the colony's new freedmen to remain on the sugar estates would meet with little success.

Only 4,000–5,000 ex-apprentices agreed to work as agricultural laborers in 1839, most of whom did so only because they had no where else to go or had been coerced or tricked into signing contracts by local magistrates.[12] The following year, hardly any former apprentices could be found on the sugar estates. While some freedmen eventually returned to the plantations, the number who did so would remain small. Of the 48,330 ex-apprentices and their descendants enumerated in 1851, just 4,461 lived or worked on a sugar estate.[13]

As many observers of Mauritian life appreciated, the successful ex-apprentice withdrawal from plantation labor had profound social and economic consequences, some of which were readily apparent by the mid-1840s. In 1846, Governor Sir William Gomm noted not only that these new freedmen were now employed in a wide range of occupations, but also that "a gap would be left, ill to be supplied in the Community, if they relinquished these various pursuits of their choice."[14] Historians of Mauritius, however, have either ignored the emancipated population or, at best, viewed ex-apprentices as unimportant players on the colonial scene who were soon overshadowed by Indian immigration.[15] The reasons why the island's ex-apprentices managed to leave the sugar estates remain unexplored, while attempts to reconstruct their lives during the post-emancipation era have been limited to describing the legal or quasi-legal dimensions of their activities.[16] This failure to do little more than sketch the general outlines of ex-apprentice life may be traced to the reliance upon a small number of official sources for information about this population, to a reluctance to probe beyond the conceptual parameters imposed by this limited body of archival materials, and to an unwillingness to compare the experience of Mauritian freedmen with that of ex-apprentices elsewhere in the post-emancipation world. In at least one instance, the end result has been the mischaracterization of the colony's new freedmen as serfs.[17]

Ex-apprentices in the Caribbean, by comparison, are the subject of increasing scholarly interest. Historians have examined the post-emancipation era in Belize, British Guiana, Jamaica, the Leeward Islands, Surinam, and Trinidad in varying degrees of detail.[18] These studies reveal a similar pattern to post-emancipation developments in many colonies: planters and colonial authorities tried to force ex-apprentices to continue working as estate laborers; their failure to do so often spurred the importation of large numbers of Asian indentured laborers to work in the cane fields; and the attendant rise of free black peasantries fostered the complex class relations that influence Caribbean life to the present day.

If there is a consensus about the general course of events in the wake of emancipation, the same cannot be said about the dynamics of change during this period. Kevin Smith has observed that the diverse experience of these colonies has resulted in a fragmented understanding of how and why the post-emancipation world took the shape that it did. The debate about the degree of continuity or discontinuity between the pre- and post-emancipation eras perhaps best illustrates how limited our understanding of this period continues to be. Until the late 1970s, historians tended to see the uninterrupted social, economic, and political dominance of local planters, the continuing dependence of colonial sugar industries upon the international market, and the persistent conflict between planters and their ex-slave or immigrant workers as proof that the substance of colonial life remained essentially unchanged after emancipation. Recent scholarship has challenged this view and argued that there were marked differences between these two eras, differences which stemmed from the ability of subordinate groups in these societies to influence the course of local events after 1838.[19]

Land and labor are at the heart of this debate, and there is a considerable diversity of opinion about the relative importance of each of these factors. While some have argued that labor supply and control was crucial to determining the fate of Caribbean peasantries, surprisingly little research has been conducted on many aspects of post-emancipation labor relations. Historians concede, for instance, that the withdrawal of ex-apprentice women and children from local labor markets had a major impact upon the plantation sector of colonial economies. The consequences of their withdrawal on local economic life nevertheless remain poorly understood, as do the impact of changes in gender relations upon other areas of ex-apprentice and colonial life.[20]

If the mists of time continue to obscure a fuller understanding of post-emancipation labor relations, some light has been shed on the extent to which access to and control of land shaped the contours of ex-apprentice social and economic life. Early work on this topic argued the importance of land-to-labor ratios in determining how colonies adjusted to the new realities of the post-emancipation era.[21] Recent scholarship challenges this argument, holding instead that control of land was the crucial variable that determined not only whether planter attempts to dominate their former apprentices succeeded or failed, but also the speed at which free black peasantries came into existence.[22] The extent to which slaves had access to provision grounds, developed marketing systems, and institutionalized pre-capitalist attitudes and economic structures number among the variables that governed the rise of these peasantries.[23]

This debate over the ways in which access to and control of land shaped the post-emancipation world has contributed to a more sophisticated understanding of developments during this era. However, one consequence of this preoccupation with land and labor has been a failure to explore other aspects of the ex-apprentice experience. All too often, the picture we have of these populations is one in which ex-apprentices seemingly existed in relative isolation from the larger socio-economic milieu of which they were an integral part. References to free populations of color and their role in facilitating the rise of free black peasantries, for example, are rare.[24] The relationship between ex-apprentices and Asian indentured laborers likewise remains largely unexplored. Lastly, the economic context within which these peasantries came into being remains only partially researched. The often dramatic transformation of colonial economies during the first half of the nineteenth century, for example, are usually analyzed only in terms of changes in the world sugar market or in levels of metropolitan investment.[25] Despite evidence that slaves and *gens de couleur* often controlled significant financial resources by the 1830s, little attention has been paid either to the impact that their mobilization of domestic capital resources may have had upon these developments or to the ways in which micro- and macro-economic forces interacted with one another.[26]

The course of events in Mauritius after March 31, 1839, illustrates the need to consider these issues more fully. As was noted earlier, attempts to compel the colony's new freedmen to return to the cane fields failed, in part because the Colonial Office, sensitive to pressure from abolitionist groups, repeatedly struck down vagrancy ordinances designed to force these individuals to sign labor contracts.[27] After Indian immigration resumed late in 1842, the incentives to mobilize ex-apprentice labor waned rapidly. While these developments clearly facilitated the ex-apprentice withdrawal from plantation agriculture, colonial sources still opined that ultimately "the cause of their unwillingness to return is beyond the control or influence of any class of the community, and even of the Government itself."[28] Comments such as this suggest that reconstructing the history of post-emancipation Mauritius cannot ignore the socio-economic realities of the day, realities that included a financially troubled sugar industry and the existence of a large and well-established free population of color.

The fortunes of the colony's new freedmen, like those of the local free population of color, depended upon their ability to mobilize capital, to acquire land, and to exploit the economic opportunities that presented themselves during the late 1830s and early 1840s. The full extent of their participation in colonial life would not be revealed until 1846, but there were indications before 1839 that many apprentices sought to follow in the footsteps of their free colored cousins. The decline in the size of this population between 1835 and 1839 is one such indicator. On the eve of abolition, the colony had housed 66,613 slaves. Four years later, however, the number of apprentices had declined to 53,230, in part because many had purchased or otherwise secured their freedom before the apprenticeship system came formally to an end. According to Special Magistrate C. Anderson, a total of 9,000 apprentices obtained their freedom between 1835 and 1839, the vast majority of whom did so after 1837.[29]

Unfortunately, it is impossible to verify the accuracy of Anderson's report. The notarial record confirms that many apprentices secured their freedom before April, 1839, but it is silent about the extent of this activity. What is clear is that the years after 1835 witnessed a precipitous decline in the size of the apprentice and ex-apprentice population, the magnitude of which is suggested by the fact that only 38,049 of the 49,365 persons described as "ex-apprentices" in the census of 1846 declared themselves to have been among those emancipated in 1839.[30]

A high mortality rate, which reportedly averaged 3.2 percent a year from 1835 through 1846, clearly contributed to this trend.[31] Governor Sir William Gomm attributed this high rate to a combination of factors, including the large number of aged freedmen, the disparity between the sexes, a "headlong rush into intemperance and universal indulgence" after emancipation, and the effects of epidemic disease, especially smallpox.[32] Age and disease were undoubtedly the most important of these factors. Information about the age structure of the ex-apprentice population is unavailable before 1846, but data on manumitted slaves during the 1820s suggest that one-fifth, if not more, of the colony's new freedmen were probably forty years of age and above by the late 1830s. A report in the 1846 census that 18.5 percent of all ex-apprentices were reputedly fifty years of age or older suggests that this estimate is within reasonable limits.[33] In a day and age when the life expectancy of most persons in many parts of the world was forty years or less, the death of significant numbers of ex-apprentices because of "old age" is accordingly not an unexpected development, especially among a population in which many had been subjected to a rigorous servitude.

In his annual report for 1856, Governor J.M. Higginson observed that ex-apprentices suffered more from epidemic disease than any other segment of the local population,[34] and there can be little doubt that the harshness of the slave regime magnified the impact disease had on these new freedmen. Dysentery, typhoid, and enteric fevers plagued the island's inhabitants, and periodic epidemics of smallpox, cholera, and influenza remained a part of life well into the nineteenth century. Smallpox was brought largely under control after vaccination was introduced early in the nineteenth century, but outbreaks still occurred in 1820, 1844–45, and 1855–56. One-half of the 1,013 victims of the 1855–56 epidemic were freedmen and their descendants.[35] Cholera was another major threat, and a severe epidemic in 1854 killed 8,496 people, the largest proportion of whom came from among the ranks of the colony's "ex-apprentices."[36]

The demographic crisis that afflicted the ex-apprentice population in the immediate wake of emancipation appears to have come to an end by the mid-1840s. Governor Gomm informed London early in 1846 that he had no reason not to presume that ex-apprentices were generally "thriving at this day,"[37] and census data confirm that this population's size had stabilized at approximately 49,000. A mortality rate that averaged only 1.3 percent a year between 1846 and 1851 contributed to this increasing demographic stability.[38] Other indications that ex-apprentices were now more or less holding their own include increasing numbers of children and a diminution of the earlier imbalance between the sexes. Children accounted for 34 percent of all "ex-apprentices" in 1851 compared to 26 percent just five years earlier, a trend that also explains the steady movement toward greater sexual parity within the population as a whole.[39]

The large-scale relocation of the island's new freedmen after 1839 magnified the impact of this early demographic crisis. Most contemporary observers of colonial life believed that this population movement began only after emancipation, but Blue Books from the late 1830s suggest that significant numbers of apprentices and/or ex-apprentices were well on the move by 1837–38, many of whom found their way to Port Louis.[40] Correspondence from Plaines Wilhem attests that this process rapidly gained momentum after emancipation. Th. Cordouan, for one, informed Armand Hugnin in late April that only 30 of the 130 apprentices formerly in his charge remained on his estate.[41] About the same time, Mr. Fortenay reported the departure of 92 of the 181 apprentices who had resided on "Plaisance" estate.[42] Shortly thereafter, William Saunders advised Hugnin that a "large number" of persons had been seen traveling at night on the main road to Vacoas, then one of the district's more remote areas, and that he had every reason to believe that ex-apprentices were establishing themselves there illegally.[43] We will never know how many of the district's ex-apprentices were on the move at this time, but the reports Hugnin solicited from eighteen estate-owners about the immediate consequences of emancipation reveal that at least 1,015 freedmen, or nearly one-fifth of the district's apprentice population, had abandoned their homes and former masters within several weeks of acquiring there freedom.[44]

This exodus became one of increasing complexity. Captain J.A. Lloyd, the Surveyor-General, distinguished four "classes" of ex-apprentices in 1840: those wandering from one part of the island to another with no settled place of residence, those residing in Port Louis or Mahébourg and along the island's roads, those squatting on public lands near the seashore, and those who had migrated to the colony's dependencies.[45] Census data reveal that the propensity before 1839 for apprentices or freedmen to gravitate toward Port Louis soon gave way to a movement away from Port Louis and heavily cultivated districts such as Pample-mousses and Rivière du Rempart to less developed parts of the island. Their reason for doing so was simple and straightforward: the areas in question were ones "in which they can purchase plots of ground at a cheaper rate, or find it easier to occupy them without purchase."[46]

To many colonists, the desire of ex-apprentices to own or occupy a plot of land seemed to be inconsistent with their refusal to continue working on the sugar estates. Frequent note was made of the fact that freedmen equated field labor with their former servitude, and that their desire to act as free men supposedly precluded returning to the land. Some, such as Captain Lloyd, laid the blame for this state of affairs at the feet of the colony's freedwomen:

Their feelings & opinions of the word "slavery" is so intimately blended with the culture of the soil and the use of the degrading "pioche" that *liberty* to them *must* be wholly independent of any field labour whatever – They live therefore in hundreds dependent on their husbands, brothers, cousins &c. and the main repugnance of the black may be attributed to the unceasing efforts on the part of the women in dissuading them from other work than fishing, &c. or/what is the acme of their pride/keeping a shop.[47]

Others charged that governmental incompetence, the lack of an adequate police force, and the reputed ease with which ex-apprentices could satisfy their "scanty and simple wants" allowed them to lead such independent lives.[48] The reasons why Mauritian freedmen were able to translate their concept of liberty into freedom from estate labor were, however, far more complex than observers of colonial life – and later historians – believed them to be. At the heart of these developments would be what one magistrate characterized as "the general desire of these people ... to possess land."[49]

While some ex-apprentices moved to Port Louis to look for work after emancipation, many others remained in the rural districts, where their activities were a subject of considerable interest to planters and local authorities. William Saunders, for one, advised Armand Hugnin not only that large numbers of ex-apprentices were settling near Vacoas, but also that several apprentices formerly in his service now resided on a nearby property without the owner's consent.[50] Besides recounting how his former apprentices could be found all over the colony, Th. Cordouan noted that some of these individuals were living on small properties, some of which were near his own estate.[51] Mme. Senneville, in turn, complained bitterly to Hugnin about her new neighbors who, she reported, lived in miserable shacks and supported themselves by stealing her sugar cane, wood, vacoas, fruits, and vegetables which they sold in town.[52]

As these reports suggest, the movement by ex-apprentices onto the land was a complex process, one aspect of which was that some new freedmen simply squatted on unoccupied public and private land. It is impossible to determine how many former apprentices did so, but substantial numbers seem to have been involved. Early in May, 1839, for example, Armand Hugnin was asked to investigate reports that two or three thousand ex-apprentices were illegally occupying land in Plaines Wilhems. Hugnin found that these reports were exaggerated, but did not elaborate further.[53] Squatting remained a serious problem a year later when Captain Lloyd observed that the largest of the four "classes" he had identified was composed of the "numberless" trespassers to be found on the *pas géométriques*.[54]

The details of this activity remain largely hidden from view. Some freedmen apparently moved quickly to formalize their occupation of a particular piece of land, but the number who did so remains unknown. With respect to the leasing of Crown lands by ex-apprentices, Captain Lloyd noted only that title deeds had been made out and the lands in question had been occupied despite the fact that the lessees had "neither paid the expences to Gov$^t$ of such deeds nor ... paid one shilling of annual rent."[55] The extent to which squatting on privately owned land was formalized in a like manner is even more difficult to ascertain. The records of four notaries active at this time contain only a few private leases, in none of which were ex-apprentices identified specifically as the lessee of record.

This lack of documentation does not mean, of course, that planters did not lease or otherwise attempt to exercise some measure of control over the land being squatted upon. There is good reason to believe that informal understandings or oral contracts became a regular part of rural life immediately after emancipation. If leases made during the mid-1840s are any kind of guide to the terms of these agreements, both squatters and landowners may have sought to protect their respective interests by entering into *de facto* sharecropping arrangements. An 1845 report on conditions in Grand Port confirms that such agreements were not unknown during the early 1840s.[56]

While significant numbers of freedmen squatted on vacant properties or leased plots of land after emancipation, those described as being of a "better class" soon began to purchase tracts on which to raise maize, vegetables, and poultry.[57] Once again, it is impossible to determine how many ex-apprentices fell into this category, but accounts of colonial life from the mid-1840s make regular mention of these small landowners. The Rev. A. Denny, for one, observed in July, 1845, that while many ex-apprentices lived in and about Port Louis, "the majority occupy small allotments of land in remote parts of the island."[58] Local officials echoed Denny's comments, and Governor Gomm would subsequently inform London that these individuals were "benefitting the Community while they work for their own advantage."[59]

The plots in question tended to be small, usually encompassing only one or two arpents, although occasionally former apprentices purchased tracts of twenty or more arpents. The price of these properties varied widely, from as little as $10 an arpent in more remote parts of the island to $100 for an arpent of uncleared land and $200 for an arpent of cultivated land in rich agricultural districts such as Pamplemousses and Rivière du Rempart. A striking feature of these sales is the fact that the plots being sold were frequently described as being part of a larger property. The size of these *terrains plus considérables* or *plus étendus* varied widely. The two arpents Colas, *ci-devant apprenti de Mr. Collard*, purchased from Mr. Jean Leclair were part of a 40-arpent tract, while the one arpent Perrine Arlequin, *ci-devant apprenti de Mr. Bruniquel*, bought from Mr. Pierre Severin came from a 7-arpent tract.[60] In some cases, the *terrain plus considérable* covered an arpent or less. In still other instances, these plots came from established estates such as "Mon Repos" in Plaines Wilhems, "Minissy" in Moka, and "St. Félix" in Savanne, each of which encompassed at least several hundred arpents.

This subdivision of established estates and other properties in the wake of emancipation heralded the beginnings of an event of considerable consequence in nineteenth-century Mauritian life – the *petit morcelle-ment*. Unlike the *grand morcellement* that began later in the century, the *petit morcellement* is a largely unknown development in Mauritian history. Contemporary accounts of colonial life, for example, are surprisingly reticent about this activity despite both its scale and its novelty. The failure of colonial authorities to take a sustained interest in the island's emancipated population is one reason why the extent and dynamics of this process have remained undescribed and unanalyzed. Other reasons include the widely held view among historians of Mauritius that ex-apprentices played little or no role in shaping the course of events during the mid-nineteenth century, and the attendant failure to explore developments during this era.

The turmoil of the immediate post-emancipation era contributed to an official reluctance to investigate the details of ex-apprentice life. Only in late 1845, on the eve of a colony-wide census, were civil commissioners and stipendiary magistrates asked to report upon the freedmen residing in their districts. On the subject of ex-apprentice landownership, most of these reports echoed that of South Pamplemousses' Peter Heyliger, who declared simply that "Settlements of half an acre, to two and three, have in almost every part of this District been made, and that at high prices."[61] Only Moka's Denis Beaugendre noted that some of these plots had been acquired as a result of estate *morcellement* or that this activity had led to the formation of small villages,[62] while just two of these officials reported on the extent of ex-apprentice landownership. According to F. Giblot Ducray, 577 of the 2,526 ex-apprentices living in Savanne were proprietors who tilled their own land.[63] Jonathon Davidson observed in turn that ex-apprentices had purchased 161 acres in Grand Port over the preceding three years at a cost of almost £1,392, "all of which has been paid, together with the expenses of the deed of sale and title, with very few exceptions . . ."[64]

Local notaries, on the other hand, were keenly aware of these developments. The late 1830s and early 1840s witnessed an explosion in the number of land sales being handled by their offices, many of which involved the subdivision of estates and other large properties. A sample of more than 900 transactions drawn from the acts of four notaries active at this time indicates that while the large-scale subdivision of properties that characterized the *petit morcellement* did not begin before late 1838, some proprietors were contemplating such activity several years prior to emancipation. Mme. Jeanne Françoise Sollied, for one, started to sell off portions of a 72-arpent estate in Pamplemousses late in 1836, with the first two plots going to Hypolite Le Bon dit St. Aulaire and Charles Agathe, both of whom were probably *gens de couleur*.[65] As the end of the apprenticeship system drew close, the subdivision of properties began in earnest as individuals such as Mme. Eugène Giblot Ducray started to sell off one and two arpent plots from a 104-arpent estate she owned in Plaines Wilhems.[66] Mr. Louis Fortuné Desbieux soon followed in Mme. Ducray's footsteps and disposed of portions of the ten arpents in Pamplemousses he had acquired just several months earlier.[67] Several weeks later, Dlle. Françoise Provençal did likewise as she sold the first of many plots from the 25-arpent estate she had owned in Plaines Wilhems

Table 15. *Land sales during and after the petit morcellement, 1839–1859*

| Period | Size of plots[a] (percent) | | | | | | % PDIF[b] | No. | Annual average |
|---|---|---|---|---|---|---|---|---|---|
| | <1.0 | 1–1.9 | 2–2.9 | 3–4.9 | 5–9.9 | 10+ | | | |
| 1839–40 | 13.6 | 36.4 | 27.3 | 10.2 | 8.0 | 4.5 | 75.0 | 88 | 44 |
| 1841–42 | 12.8 | 37.9 | 27.4 | 13.7 | 5.5 | 2.7 | 83.1 | 219 | 110 |
| 1843–46 | 6.3 | 40.7 | 27.7 | 13.0 | 10.2 | 2.1 | 93.4 | 332 | 83 |
| 1847–48 | 12.2 | 40.0 | 25.2 | 8.7 | 12.2 | 1.7 | 96.5 | 115 | 58 |
| 1849–50 | 8.5 | 31.0 | 42.2 | 12.7 | 2.8 | 2.8 | 97.2 | 71 | 36 |
| 1851–59 | 24.7 | 36.6 | 26.9 | 5.4 | 4.3 | 2.1 | 94.6 | 93 | 10 |
| Total/average | 11.3 | 38.3 | 28.3 | 11.6 | 8.0 | 2.5 | 90.0 | 918 | — |

*Notes:*
[a] Arpents.
[b] Purchase price paid in full at the time of a sale's formal completion.
*Sources:* MA: NA 80, 83, 84, 85.

Table 16. *Size of properties subdivided during and after the* petit morcellement, *1839–1859*

| Period | Arpents | | | | | Not specified[a] | Terrains[b] |
|--------|--------|--------|--------|--------|--------|--------|--------|
| | < 10 | 10–24.9 | 25–49.9 | 50–99.9 | 100 + | | |
| 1839–40 | 1 | 3 | — | 6 | 5 | 6 | 21 |
| 1841–42 | 4 | 5 | 3 | 3 | 2 | 14 | 31 |
| 1843–46 | 2 | 9 | 5 | 6 | 12 | 19 | 53 |
| 1847–48 | — | 2 | 1 | 1 | 2 | 6 | 12 |
| 1849–50 | — | — | — | 1 | 1 | 1 | 3 |
| 1851–59 | 1 | 2 | 3 | 1 | — | — | 7 |
| Total | 8 | 21 | 12 | 18 | 22 | 46 | 127 |

*Notes:*
[a] Described simply as a *terrain plus étendu* or *plus considérable*.
[b] Number of properties being subdivided for the first time.
*Sources:* MA: NA 80, 83, 84, 85.

since 1821.[68] The scale of this activity increased dramatically after April, 1839, so much so that a major restructuring of rural social and economic relations was clearly under way by the end of 1840.

The notarial acts at our disposal indicate that the process which began in earnest in 1839–40 accelerated rapidly between 1841 and 1842 when the number of sales each year seems to have reached its peak (see table 15). Although the pace of this activity apparently slackened somewhat after 1842, the growing number of properties undergoing subdivision reveals that the *petit morcellement* remained very much a part of colonial life through 1846 (see table 16). In 1847, however, the intense activity of these earlier years began to wane noticeably and, by 1850, the *petit morcellement* had run its course. Properties continued to be subdivided during the 1850s and 1860s, but this activity remained modest in scale and often intermittent in nature.

The decision to subdivide these properties was a deliberate one, but the notarial record is silent about owners' reasons for doing so. Contemporary observers are equally reticent; even Denis Beaugendre, who seems to have paid particularly close attention to what was going on in Moka, offered no explanation why estates were being broken up and sold piecemeal. The reasons for the *petit morcellement* must therefore be inferred from the available documentation. Fortunately, the acts which recorded the size, location, price, and relevant particulars of the lands being sold also noted the residence, occupation, and other personal data about the participants in these transactions, information that makes it possible to discern not only the reasons why ex-apprentices purchased these plots, but also the considerations that shaped landowners' decisions to sell off their property.

As in the Caribbean, some of the purchases by ex-apprentices during the *petit morcellement* were undoubtedly intended to formalize their occupation of land which they claimed as their own. Douglas Hall, Michel-Rolph Trouillot, and Richard Sheridan have pointed out that the struggle for control of slaves' provision grounds was an important factor in shaping post-emancipation developments in some West Indian colonies.[69] The extent to which Mauritian slaves had access to such grounds is unknown, but scattered references indicate that the colony's bondsmen owned large numbers of pigs, goats, and chickens, and that trusted slaves were allowed to market fruits, vegetables, and other produce.[70] These reports suggest not only that substantial arpentage may have been allocated to slaves as provision grounds, but also that continued control of these grounds was a matter of concern to some ex-apprentices.

If some freedmen sought to acquire legal title to land in which they already had a vested interest, others opted to acquire uncleared or vacant land, often in more remote parts of the island.[71] Their decision to do so stemmed, at least in part, from their desire to remove themselves as far as possible from the places associated with their former servitude.[72] However, while many Mauritian freedmen changed their place of residence after 1839, the notarial record indicates that any attempt to correlate the relocation of the ex-apprentice population with their subsequent territorial acquisitions must be carefully qualified. More specifically, the record indicates that at least 75 percent of those persons who purchased land during the *petit morcellement* resided in the same district in which the land they were buying was located.

This propensity of Mauritian freedmen to reside in the general vicinity of the plots they were purchasing is not unexpected. Post-emancipation Caribbean history is replete with examples of ex-apprentices who, despite an intense desire to disassociate themselves from all vestiges of their former condition, nevertheless continued to live in relatively close proximity to the estates on which they had once labored as slaves. Their reasons for doing so are not difficult to fathom. Complex webs of social, economic, and psychological ties that had been created over the years were not easily or readily dismantled, their place of origin notwithstanding. There is no reason to suppose that many Mauritian freedmen were any less hesitant about cutting themselves adrift, especially in uncertain times. Moreover, many estates included large areas of uncleared or unused arpentage, precisely the kind of land that estate-owners would be

Table 17. *Occupations of persons purchasing land during and after the* petit morcellement, *1839–1859*

| Occupational category | (% Distribution within period) | | |
| --- | --- | --- | --- |
| | 1839–42 | 1843–48 | 1849–59 |
| Agriculture/landowner | 19.4 | 25.4 | 23.1 |
| Business & commerce | 2.1 | 2.0 | 2.9 |
| Clerical & managerial | 0.8 | 2.0 | 1.0 |
| Crafts & trades | 39.4 | 39.7 | 42.3 |
| Ex-apprentice | 16.0 | — | — |
| Laborer | 2.4 | 4.0 | 8.6 |
| Personal service | 13.1 | 13.5 | 8.6 |
| Miscellaneous[a] | 6.8 | 13.4 | 13.5 |
| Total | 381 | 657 | 208 |

*Note:* [a] Includes persons with no stated profession.
*Sources:* MA: NA 80, 83, 84, 85.

inclined to sell if the need to do so arose and which former apprentices would be inclined to acquire, particularly if they had lived on or near the estate and knew the land in question. We do not know how much undeveloped arpentage was available *circa* 1839–40, but the fact that only 74,839 of 272,022 inventoried arpents were under cultivation in 1830 suggests that considerable amounts of land fell into this category.[73]

There were other practical reasons for many freedmen to remain on the periphery of plantation life, not the least of which were the opportunities for temporary employment. Planters complained repeatedly about the high wages their former apprentices could command during the post-emancipation labor crisis, and although most ex-apprentices continued to refuse to sign long-term contracts, many agreed to work on a part-time basis to earn enough money to meet their immediate needs.[74] The services of skilled workmen were especially in demand, and the notarial record suggests that many of these individuals capitalized upon the opportunities afforded them to improve their socio-economic status by purchasing land (see table 17).

The willingness of many freedmen to live in relative proximity to the estates on which they had once been enslaved cannot be explained, however, solely in terms of their connections to or dependency upon these estates. The rural districts also housed a sizable and well-established free population of color. While many whites asserted that *gens de couleur* and slaves regarded one another with suspicion, if not antagonism,[75] others noted that the relationship between elements of these two populations was often one of close cooperation and mutual support. Eugène Bernard observed, for example, that the only reason many of the bondsmen who had been manumitted during the 1820s did not die of hunger was because they had been fed by slaves living on the great estates.[76]

Post-emancipation sources attest to this continuing cooperation between *gens de couleur* and the colony's new freedmen, noting that many of the ex-apprentices who left the sugar estates readily found refuge and employment with free colored smallholders.[77] Mme. Senneville revealed some of the details of this activity when she complained that one near-by small landowner had no fewer than nine ex-apprentices working on his 4 arpents while she had been able to retain the services of only six of the sixty apprentices formerly attached to her estate.[78] A year later, Captain Lloyd confirmed that "in preference to hiring themselves to a respectable planter, they will probably obtain a small piece of ground, from a coloured or black petty proprietor, on the conclusion of working for him ..."[79] On the eve of the 1846 census, district authorities reported that many ex-apprentices continued to find employment with these small farmers.[80]

The conduct of Mauritian planters during this period, like that of their former apprentices, was shaped by several considerations, the most pressing of which was the need to deal with the loss of a substantial portion of the labor force upon which their economic survival depended. The 30,000 apprentices involved in sugar production on the eve of emancipation had accounted for 55 percent of the colony's agricultural work force. Only 4,000 to 5,000 freedmen had been induced or compelled to remain on the estates after March, 1839, and by mid-1840 they too had withdrawn from regular plantation labor. The impact of their withdrawal was compounded by the fact that it followed hard on the heels of the suspension of Indian immigration late in 1838, and it was against this backdrop of a severe and possibly long-term labor shortage that Mauritian estate-owners began to contemplate the subdivision and sale of their property.

While these developments triggered the *petit morcellement*, the reasons why large numbers of estate-owners decided to subdivide and sell off portions of their property are less clear. Several contemporary accounts imply that the decision by some landowners to do so stemmed from their willingness to satisfy the desire of many ex-apprentices to own their own land. Such intimations of altruism say a great deal about how planters wished to be perceived by humanitarian and abolitionist groups and the Colonial Office, but they provide little insight into what estate-owners hoped to accomplish by subdividing their properties. They shed even less light on the reasons why *morcellement* continued long after the post-emancipation labor crisis apparently came to an end in 1843.

These proprietors' motives must therefore be inferred from what we know about the different phases of the *petit morcellement*. The relevant chronology was outlined earlier: the large-scale subdivision of properties that began in 1839–40 expanded rapidly during 1841–42, and then continued at a strong pace until 1847 when this activity began to wane, before ending by 1849–50. Closer scrutiny of the notarial record reveals often subtle changes in the nature of this activity. The years from 1843 through 1846, for example, witnessed a marked increase not only in the number of properties undergoing *morcellement* for the first time, but also in the number of large estates being subdivided (see table 16, p. 117). The post-1842 era also found many more properties being subdivided that had been in their owners' possession for relatively long periods of time. One-half of the properties subdivided between 1839 and 1842 had been in their owners' hands for less than three years when the first sales from them were made; almost 57 percent of those subdivided between 1843 and 1848, on the other hand, had been in their owner's hands for at least five, and often for more than ten, years before the advent of *morcellement*.

An important feature of the immediate post-emancipation era was the need by planters to bring some measure of order to a seemingly chaotic countryside, a need that coincided with the desire of many freedmen to acquire land of their own. Large numbers of ex-apprentices had occupied vacant land after emancipation, often near estates where their presence was perceived to be a threat not only to public order, but also to the estate's economic viability. As was noted earlier, some landowners responded by leasing the land in question or entering into informal share-cropping agreements. The notarial record indicates that their willingness to do so was part of a conscious strategy to restructure local socio-economic relationships so as to facilitate the reconstitution of an agricultural work force at a time when their ability to coerce laborers was circumscribed. While there is no evidence to date that planters expected these sharecroppers or lease-holders to plant or cultivate cane, there can be little doubt that such arrangements encouraged the creation of a work force which, although semi-permanent at best, was nevertheless immediately at hand. The decision by some proprietors to sell off parts of their estates was a logical extension of this need to establish as stable a work force as local conditions would allow.

The extent of *morcellement* activity at specific points in time provides additional confirmation of planters' intentions in this respect. Despite losing the services of most of their former apprentices early in 1839, many planters had reason to believe that the labor crisis confronting them, although severe, would nevertheless be one of relatively short duration. A significant number of freedmen had been induced or compelled to remain on the estates after emancipation and, like Governor Nicolay, many estate-owners no doubt anticipated that other ex-apprentices would return to agricultural labor once the euphoria of liberation had dissipated. There was also reason to expect that Indian immigration might resume without undue delay, given the governor's strong support for doing so. Under these circumstances, the modest level of *morcellement* activity during 1839 and 1840 may be regarded as a qualified response to the exigencies of the day. By late 1840, however, hopes for a speedy resolution to this labor crisis faded as the finality of the ex-apprentice withdrawal from regular estate labor became increasingly apparent and the resumption of Indian immigration remained very much in doubt. The result was a dramatic increase in *morcellement* during 1841 and 1842, as estate-owners moved to protect their interests by vigorously encouraging the development of a peasantry which, although legally free, would still be bound, if only indirectly, to plantation life.

The Government of India's decision late in 1842 to lift the ban on Indian emigration to Mauritius has been regarded as a watershed event in the island's history. By most accounts, the importation of tens of thousands of Indian laborers that began in 1843 brought an end to the post-emancipation labor crisis and set the island's sugar industry back on the road to prosperity. Immigration figures appear to substantiate such claims; more than 34,500 indentured laborers reached the island during 1843 alone, a multitude which far exceeded the number of apprentices who had worked in the cane fields on the eve of emancipation. However, as both the notarial record and official reports from 1845–46 attest, the *petit morcellement* nevertheless continued apace.

Any assertion that the resumption of Indian immigration brought an end to the colony's post-emancipation economic crisis must accordingly be viewed with skepticism. A careful review of immigration data likewise suggests that the immediate impact of renewed immigration on this crisis can be easily overstated. Despite the massive influx of indentured laborers during 1843, substantially lower and often widely fluctuating levels of Indian immigration during subsequent years, coupled with the movement by thousands of Indians off the sugar estates once they had completed their "industrial residence," meant that the colony's agricultural work force did not return to its pre-emancipation size until the late 1840s. Given these impediments to the rebuilding of an adequate work force, the decision by some proprietors to continue facilitating the establishment of a resident peasantry near their estates comes as no great surprise.

These developments underscore the need to examine the workings of the post-emancipation world in terms other than just those of labor supply and/or relations. Unlike many historians of nineteenth-century colonial plantation systems, Mauritian authorities understood only too well that access to or control of adequate amounts of capital was of equal, if not greater, importance to the survival of a plantation regime. In 1843, for example, Governor Gomm expressed his concern about the fiscal distress being experienced by some planters and noted that "relief could not be effectually afforded in such extreme cases by the mere temporary assistance of Government in whatever shape tendered."[81] Three years later, the governor would report that despite good sugar crops, the presence of a stable and expanding agricultural work force, reduced labor costs, and a general sense that the island was in a state of "advancing prosperity," the colony continued to be plagued by a serious capital liquidity problem.[82]

Gomm's remarks highlight the need to examine the *petit morcellement* in light of the financial problems that many planters had to face during the mid-nineteenth century. These problems, as chapter 1 detailed, stemmed from the local sugar industry's heavy dependence upon domestic capital. Although the industry attracted metropolitan investment during the second quarter of the nineteenth century, this investment remained fitful, as British investors withdrew at the slightest hint of uncertainty, especially over the supply of labor. The suspension of Indian immigration late in 1838 and the termination of the apprenticeship system several months later accordingly spelled an end to the boomlet of the early 1830s. Investors returned to the colony after the resumption of Indian immigration, but several years later Governor Gomm was once again referring to the "extensive individual embarrassment among the agricultural and commercial bodies [that] has formed the topic of numerous addresses forwarded to your Lordship through my hands." This problem, he observed, arose from the fact that local "proprietors of the soil [are] incompetent with their own means to work out all the profits of which their estates were susceptible."[83]

The notarial record reveals some of the ways in which financial considerations helped to shape the *morcellement* process. In the first instance, the circumstances which surround the subdivision of "Bagatelle," "Cancaval," and "Minissy" estates during the early 1840s indicate that their owners sought to establish the kind of "tenant plantations" being created in other parts of the post-emancipation colonial world. In addition to providing planters with a means to mobilize and exercise some measure of control over a resident work force, such plantations were, as Nancy Virts has pointed out, capable of the economies of scale needed to survive in a world without slavery.[84] Secondly, there can also be little doubt that many proprietors regarded *morcellement* as a means of extracting the substantial amounts of cash in ex-apprentice hands for their own use. More than 90 percent of those who purchased *morcellement* lands after 1843 paid the purchase price in full at the time of the sale's formal completion (see table 15, p. 116). *Gens de couleur*, by comparison, had done so in only 65 percent of such transactions during the late eighteenth and early nineteenth centuries.

We will never know exactly how much cash Mauritian apprentices controlled, but considerable sums seem to have been involved. The cost of acquiring an adult apprentice's services ranged from $200 to $250 between 1835 and 1839, a fact which suggests that the 9,000 apprentices who reportedly purchased their freedom before emancipation spent at least $1,800,000 to do so. Notarial acts confirm that individual apprentices possessed or had access to significant financial resources. Dame Vve. François Pilot's apprentice Pauline, for one, paid the full purchase price of $100 for the 4 arpents she purchased in 1836, while Tristan Fogarthy prevailed upon Robert Edie, a merchant, to loan him $102 toward the cost of securing his early release from Mme. Corpet's service.[85]

That Mauritian apprentices could command such resources is not completely unexpected. Many slaves either had skills that could be used to generate income on their own account or had access to provision grounds and were able to market their produce. The value of this market activity cannot be determined, but some sense of its possible magnitude is suggested by what we know about slave productivity in the Caribbean at this time. Jamaican bondsmen, for instance, not only dominated local food production by 1832, generating 94 percent of the £900,000 realized by this sector of the colony's economy, but also accounted for more than one-quarter of the island's gross domestic product of £5,500,000 sterling.[86] Slaves in the Windward Islands likewise exercised a virtual monopoly over the local food, fuel, and fodder markets, and may have held as much as one-half of all money in circulation.[87]

That the colony's new freedmen had significant fiscal resources at their disposal may also be inferred from the speculative nature of some early *morcellement* activity. One of the more striking features of the *morcellement* process before 1843 is the relatively large number of properties that had been in their owners' hands for only a short period of time before undergoing subdivision. Of the thirty-six properties under consideration during this period, twelve had been purchased less than a year before the onset of *morcellement*, while eighteen belonged to their owners for less than three years before subdivision began.

The financial incentives to subdivide an estate could be considerable. Returns of 100–200 percent on original investments were common for both large and small landowners who engaged in *morcellement*. Dlle. Françoise Provençal, for example, made $413 between late 1838 and early 1841 from the sale of 19.5 of the 25 arpents she had purchased in 1821 for $200. M. and Mme. Pierre Leclos, in turn, realized $2,506 between mid-1840 and early 1847 from the sale of 42.5 of the 62 arpents they had purchased in October, 1838, for $1,000. In some instances, the measured rate at which landowners such as M. and Mme. Remi Pierre Léonard Morel sold off small plots was undoubtedly intended to alleviate the kind of liquidity problems to which Governor Gomm referred. The Morels began to sell off sections of a 110-arpent estate in November, 1842, and continued to do so until at least February, 1854.

The demand for land, coupled with the financial rewards for satisfying that demand, often encouraged the further subdivision of the small plots created by *morcellement*. Emile Zéphir's activities are a representative case in point. On May 18, 1841, Zéphir paid $125 to M. and Mme. Eugène Dombreu for a 5-arpent tract from the *terrain plus considérable* they had started to subdivide earlier in the year. The following year, Zéphir turned around and sold 4 of the 5 arpents in question for a total of $250. At least five other persons who purchased comparable tracts from the Dombreus did likewise. This process of sub-*morcellement* often continued still further. On May 25, 1841, Fidale Robin purchased 3.5 arpents from the Dombreus for $140 cash.[88] The following January, he sold 1.5 arpents from this tract to Mlle. Phrasie Ariotte, who paid $50 down toward the purchase price of $75.[89] Two and a half months later Mlle. Ariotte, in turn, sold off portions of this property to Benjamin Moujava and Mlle. Geneviève Félix, each of whom purchased 0.5 of an arpent for $32.50 cash.[90]

The colony's new freedmen were not the only participants in this process. The countryside housed a large free colored population by the 1830s, and the notarial record indicates that *gens de couleur* also participated actively in the *petit morcellement*, both as purchasers of the plots being sold and as owners of the properties being subdivided. The full extent of this free colored activity is difficult to gauge because notarial acts no longer specified the background or social status of the persons involved as they had done before 1830. As such, *gens de couleur* can often be distinguished from ex-apprentices only on the basis of problematic criteria such as surname, occupation, place of residence, and details about the land in question.

With this thought in mind, we may note that sixteen of the ninety-six properties subdivided between 1839 and 1848, or approximately one-

Table 18. *Social characteristics of persons purchasing land during and after the* petit morcellement, *1839–1859*

| Purchaser | Distribution within period (percent) | | |
|---|---|---|---|
| | 1839–42 | 1843–48 | 1849–59 |
| Individual male | 45.2 | 31.0 | 42.2 |
| Individual female | 18.9 | 20.6 | 18.0 |
| Male and female[a] | 24.9 | 27.6 | 19.9 |
| Family[b] | 8.0 | 18.9 | 16.9 |
| Other[c] | 3.0 | 1.9 | 3.0 |
| No. = | 301 | 428 | 166 |

*Notes:*
[a] Joint purchase by a man (or men) and a woman (or women) whose legal relationship to one another is unknown.
[b] Any combination of persons related by blood or marriage, e.g., husband and wife, parent and child, siblings, and other persons reported explicitly as being related to one another.
[c] Joint purchase by two or more men or by two or more women whose legal relationship to one another, if any, is unknown.
*Sources:* MA: NA 80, 83, 84, 85.

sixth of the sample under consideration, apparently belonged to free persons of color. While these properties were scattered throughout the countryside, nearly one-third of them were located in Grand Port, a district where *gens de couleur* were particularly well established. The properties in question varied greatly in size, from as few as 4 to almost 92 arpents, with more than two-thirds of the total encompassing 25 arpents or less. Their owners included a carpenter, a dressmaker, a mason, an officer in the merchant marine, a tailor, two "farmers," and eight "land-owners." Several of these individuals, including Dlle. Javotte Tranquille and Alexis Bertrand dit Alexis Cato, numbered among the first land-owners to participate in the *petit morcellement*, while others such as Dlle. Pélagie Attenon, Dlle. Marie Louis Jacques, and Mlle. Lisette Panglos were among the last.

Other data culled from the notarial record provide additional insights into the nature of free colored involvement in this process. Chapter 4 revealed that the free population of color controlled a significant percentage of the colony's agricultural wealth by 1830, and the high rates of payment-in-full in *morcellement* transactions undoubtedly reflect, at least in part, the ease with which *gens de couleur* mobilized the capital needed to exploit the opportunities that presented themselves in the wake of emancipation. The substantial number of landowners and agricultur-alists among those acquiring land during this era (see table 17, p. 119) is consistent with significant free colored participation in this process. The social characteristics of the persons purchasing land at this time likewise point to significant free colored involvement in the *petit morcellement* (see table 18). The greater involvement of married couples and family units in this process after 1842 is consistent with the greater degree of social structural stability that prevailed within the free colored population as a whole by the 1830s. When viewed in their totality, these various data suggest that free colored involvement in the *petit morcellement* became especially pronounced after 1842, precisely that point in time when the sugar industry's liquidity problems would have made tapping into the substantial financial resources held by the local free population of color a particularly alluring option to many planters.

Although local authorities observed that "many" former apprentices held land by the mid-1840s, any sense of the number who did so remained unreported until 1846 when a census was taken of the island's inhabitants. This census, as well as that taken in 1851, distinguished three groups among the colony's residents – ex-apprentices, indentured Indian immigrants, and the "general population" composed of all other persons regardless of their ancestry, birthplace, or nationality – and organized its data accordingly. While these censuses shed a fair amount of light on various aspects of post-emanicpation life, the problematic nature of some of these data also means that the resulting picture is a somewhat limited one. The 1846 census commissioners noted, for example, that "ex-apprentices" were identified only on the basis of individual declarations to that effect, and that this "class" did not include those persons who acquired their freedom between 1835 and 1839.[91] While former *gens de couleur* accounted for a great majority of the "general population," probably at least one-fourth of this group were persons of European and Asian ancestry, a fact which necessarily limits its use in determining the extent of free colored involvement in the *petit morcellement*. Lastly, neither census elaborated upon the criteria used to distinguish between similar occupations, one consequence of which is a degree of uncertainty about some of the changes that took place between 1846 and 1851.

The ex-apprentice withdrawal from plantation labor after emancipation was the subject of considerable comment, and the 1846 census reveals that the passage of time had not altered this state of affairs; freedmen and their children accounted for a miniscule 1.3 percent of contractual estate workers that year. This continuing refusal to work regularly on the island's sugar plantations did not, however, preclude involvement in other areas of agricultural life. More than 4,300 ex-apprentices earned their living from non-estate agriculture of some kind,

90 percent of whom apparently did so as "gardeners." The number of gardeners who owned their land cannot be ascertained, but it is reasonable to assume that some of these individuals had purchased *morcellement* plots.

The census of 1846 also reported the presence of 4,116 "independent proprietors" in the colony, 58 percent of whom were former apprentices. The criteria for distinguishing independent proprietors from other landowners were not reported, but the income or property qualifications for such a designation were probably relatively high. The use to which these properties were put remains unreported, although there is reason to believe that many of these independent proprietors engaged in truck-farming for the local market. If nothing else, the existence of this rather large group of freeholders by 1846 underscores the fact that a sizable number of the colony's freedmen had been able to exploit the opportunities created during the post-emancipation era.

The movement of many of these ex-apprentice landowners into truck-farming comes as no surprise. Food shortages were a regular source of concern throughout the eighteenth century, and famine had frequently been kept at bay only by the importation of rice from India and cattle from Madagascar. The problems of feeding the island's inhabitants increased during the early nineteenth century as white plantation owners allocated ever-increasing amounts of land to sugar production. Although *gens de couleur* had stepped into this breach, they had been unable to satisfy the demand for foodstuffs, all the more so as they too devoted more and more of their arpentage to sugar; by 1830, almost 40 percent of free colored land under cultivation was planted in cane. The advent of Indian immigration, with its attendant requirements that planters furnish their indentured workers with regular rations, strained local food supplies still further, while the high cost of imported food placed a significant burden upon often shaky planter finances.

The labor and liquidity crises of the late 1830s and early 1840s exacerbated this problem and encouraged not only the continued *morcellement* of properties, but also the rapid rise of a class of ex-apprentice gardeners and truck-farmers. Contemporary accounts of colonial life indicate that large numbers of freedmen used their new holdings to grow bananas, maize, manioc, sweet potatoes, and other fruits and vegetables, and to raise poultry or swine. While many obviously did so for their own sustenance, local officials reported that substantial amounts of this produce also found its way to market, and especially to the market in Port Louis. The scale of this activity was such that Governor Gomm wrote to the Colonial Secretary early in 1846 that "the Bazaar of Port Louis, so meagrely supplied in former years, now daily affords an

Table 19. *Ex-apprentice occupations, 1846–1851*

| Occupation | % Distribution within year | | % All persons so employed | |
|---|---|---|---|---|
| | 1846 | 1851 | 1846 | 1851 |
| Agriculture | 18.4 | 26.6 | 10.7 | 11.8 |
| Commerce | 1.5 | 1.5 | 18.5 | 12.1 |
| Crafts & trades | 30.6 | 39.3 | 51.4 | 43.8 |
| Domestic service | 18.2 | 15.0 | 50.3 | 33.5 |
| Gov't civil service | 0.6 | 0.5 | 20.3 | 12.0 |
| Independent proprietor | 9.1 | 3.3 | 57.9 | 25.0 |
| Laborer[a] | 18.4 | 10.8 | 59.5 | 35.7 |
| Maritime | 3.0 | 2.9 | 42.5 | 46.3 |
| Professions[b] | 0.2 | 0.1 | 3.2 | 1.0 |
| Total | 26,243 | 23,610 | 29.0 | 22.6 |

*Notes:*
[a] Non-sugar estate.
[b] Includes educated persons.
*Sources:* 1846 Census, para. 24 and Appendix No. 9; 1851 Census, p. 8 and Appendix No. 8.

abundant display of wholesome fruits and vegetables."[92] The governor would repeat his observation later that same year, adding that this activity was a decided benefit to the colony.[93]

While many freedmen earned their living from gardening, a great many more pursued other livelihoods. Ed. Kelly, the Stipendary Magistrate for Port Louis, spoke for many of his official colleagues when he noted that large numbers of ex-apprentices kept body and soul together by peddling firewood, fish, fruits, grass, and vegetables, by working as longshoremen on the Port Louis docks, and by allegedly stealing poultry, fruit, and vegetables almost every night.[94] Ex-apprentices also figured prominently among the island's craftsmen, artisans, and domestic servants (see table 19). Skilled workmen tended to work on sugar estates where they commanded high wages and were described as being the "most regular and orderly at work" of the various "classes" of freedmen.[95] Ex-apprentice fishermen, hawkers, and peddlers, on the other hand, were generally deemed to be "irregular" workers who seldom stayed in the same employer's service for long.

The impact of this activity upon both the colonial economy and the quality of ex-apprentice life is difficult to assess. Except for sugar and its by-products, agricultural production figures are non-existent for this era, and reports on governmental revenues are silent about the taxes, license fees, and other charges paid by the different segments of the island's population. Contemporary accounts likewise shed little real light on these questions. When they were asked in late 1845 to comment upon the "increase in knowledge and wealth" among the colony's ex-apprentices, district commissioners and stipendiary magistrates did little more than intone the standard litany that these individuals remained ignorant, lazy, and given to hedonism. Others, however, opined that ex-apprentices had carved out an important place for themselves in colonial life. Governor Gomm stated firmly in his report for 1846 that they had become "a thriving and improving class of the colonial population ... filling a middle station between the common field labourer and easy employer ... with fair profit to themselves and advantage to the community."[96] Independent observers were equally impressed. The Reverend A. Denny, for one, held that ex-apprentice smallholders could be counted among the "30,000 persons of color forming a middle class and fast rising in wealth & consequence."[97]

Such favorable assessments, although overstated, were not without some basis in fact. The 1846 census revealed that former apprentices figured prominently in certain areas of local economic life, accounting as they did for a substantial proportion of the colony's gardeners, independent proprietors, and skilled workmen. Within the space of just a few years, however, the seemingly halcyon days of the mid-1840s had vanished. Dr. Frederic Mouat reported in 1852 that many of the freedmen who had squatted on small plots of land lived "in a state bordering on misery and starvation."[98] A decade later, observers despaired openly about the ex-apprentice population's future. In 1864, Bishop Vincent Ryan dismissed the colony's freedmen and their children with the curt observation that they were "generally very degraded, very ignorant, and sometimes very destitute."[99] Two years later, Governor Sir Henry Barkly would write that "a large proportion of the ex-apprentices have never been tempted by high wages or the ambition of raising their children in the social scale to abandon the life of indolent ease to which they betook themselves and their families after emancipation."[100] While the governor acknowledged that former apprentices were still "useful to a certain extent" as market gardeners, he nevertheless concluded that they added little, "in proportion to their numbers, to the exportable produce and wealth of the Colony."

Comments such as these could easily be dismissed as another example of the prejudice directed toward freedmen and their descendants throughout the nineteenth-century colonial world. At a minimum, the tone of these remarks betrays a certain lack of understanding about the role small proprietors played in local economic life. However, their agreement about the impoverished condition of many former apprentices suggests that the patterns of economic activity that characterized the immediate post-emancipation era began to change during the late 1840s and early 1850s. The precipitous decline in ex-apprentice independent proprietors, from 2,388 to 778 between 1846 and 1851, is the most visible manifestation of these changes. An increase in the number of such proprietors within the general population during this same period suggests that some freedmen, like some depressed castes in India, successfully manipulated the census in order to enhance their standing in colonial society.[101] While their ability to do so may help to explain why the number of these proprietors within the general population rose from 1,728 to 2,213 between 1846 and 1851, the magnitude of the ex-apprentice decline and the absence of a corresponding increase within the general population point to deeper structural changes in the fabric of colonial life.

Other data also point to a restructuring of ex-apprentice economic life during the late 1840s. These years witnessed, among other things, the return of a sizable number of former apprentices or their children to plantation life. The island's sugar estates had housed only 486 ex-apprentices in 1846; by 1851, that number soared to 5,161, 35 percent of whom reportedly worked as agricultural laborers.[102] While the number of ex-apprentice craftsmen and artisans remained relatively constant between these two censuses, by 1851 these individuals comprised a noticeably smaller percentage of the colony's skilled workmen than they had six years earlier. The failure of ex-apprentices engaging in commerce to hold their own likewise indicates that many of the colony's freedmen either had lost or were losing ground as the second half of the nineteenth century began.

Contemporary observers readily attributed such developments to the purported ex-apprentice propensity toward "idleness." Government officials, planters, and merchants complained repeatedly about the indolence of the colony's freedmen. Captain Lloyd, for example, described one of his four "classes" of new freedmen as being composed of "an alarming proportion of idlers," while another such class was filled with persons living "in a state of comparative idleness."[103] Similar sentiments colored colonists' perceptions about ex-apprentice employment, or lack thereof. The refusal of ex-apprentices to work for what many estate-owners considered to be exorbitant wages was a topic of bitter commentary during the mid-1840s, as was the continued unwillingness of freedwomen to leave their husbands, homes, and families and return to work.[104]

These stereotypical views were so pervasive that reports which castigated freedmen for their indolence openly ignored the fact that children accounted for a significant percentage of those ex-apprentices without work, or that the unemployment rate within the general population was higher than it was among the colony's freedmen. Occasionally, however, officials such as Emile Magon demonstrated some awareness, if not understanding, of the complexities of post-emancipation economic life. Magon, while acknowledging that the wives of well-paid, skilled workmen generally stayed at home and tended to their families, also noted that some worked as seamstresses and washerwomen.[105] Implicit in his remarks is the suggestion that even relatively well-off ex-apprentice families had to engage in more than one kind of economic activity to support themselves.

The apparent need of such families to earn their living from several different sources underscores the failure of many freedmen to consolidate their position in the post-emancipation order. Their failure to do so may be traced to several factors. In the first instance, as the concern about ex-apprentice "idleness" and their movement to more remote parts of the island after emancipation attest, many freedmen sought to minimize their involvement in various areas of colonial life. Their reason for so doing, like that of their counterparts in the Americas, was simple and unequivocal: to have as little as possible to do with anything reminiscent of their previous status. This ethos, while neither unexpected nor irrational, nevertheless perpetuated cultural values that not only discouraged ex-apprentice participation in the mainstream of colonial economic life, but also contributed to an unwillingness or inability to exploit the opportunities that presented themselves in the wake of emancipation.

The options open to many freedmen were further circumscribed by the nature of ex-apprentice social organization, and especially by the marked age and sex disparities that prevailed during the late 1830s and early 1840s. The social structural instability inherent in such a system was, in turn, compounded by the demographic collapse and geographical relocation that occurred in the wake of emancipation. While the notarial record demonstrates that some freedmen acted quickly to stabilize and formalize familial relationships after they became free, local authorities intimated that social relationships within the ex-apprentice population as a whole nevertheless remained unsettled well into the 1840s, if not beyond. Félix Ducray, for one, reported that the former apprentices living in Savanne rarely married the women with whom they cohabited.[106] Denis Beaugendre discerned a growing desire by ex-apprentices in Moka to marry and legitimize their children, but admitted that such progress was slow and confined largely to freedmen who had been born in Madagascar or Africa.[107] "The Creole youth of both sexes," he observed, "have an aversion to be bound by any ties that would bring them into Subjection." *Morcellement* data indirectly corroborate these reports. More specifically, we may note that the number of purchases made by couples who do not seem to have been legally married remained relatively high and constant over time, and that the increase in the number of families who purchased *morcellement* plots after 1842 notwithstanding, more than one-half of all such sales continued to be made to individual men or women (see table 18, p. 126).

The failure of ex-apprentices to consolidate their position during the 1840s may also be linked to the withdrawal of many freedwomen from direct involvement in local economic life. Women comprised 40 percent of the adult ex-apprentice population in 1846, but accounted for only a quarter of those persons who declared an occupation. Even those with a profession remained outside the mainstream of economic life; only one in seven was reported to be an independent proprietor, while domestic service, dressmaking, and laundering accounted for four-fifths of all female employment. Once again, *morcellement* data provide indirect confirmation of this general state of affairs; individual women acquired only one-fifth of the plots sold during the *petit morcellement*.

The failure of these women to participate actively in the colonial economy had profound implications for the ex-apprentice population as a whole. Their decision to stay at home and care for their husbands and children served, at a minimum, to inhibit the process of capital accumulation within the larger emancipated community. This was a serious problem for a population in which many had only modest resources, especially since the archival record indicates that *femmes de couleur* may have played a prominent role in shaping free colored economic fortunes earlier in the century. The consequences of this failure to acquire greater capital resources became readily apparent during the late 1840s, when the number of ex-apprentice independent proprietors plummeted by two-thirds as these landowners were forced to sell their property for ready cash. In some instances, this failure to accumulate adequate financial reserves left ex-apprentices, and freedwomen in particular, with no other option but to return to plantation agriculture. A disproportionately large percentage of the unemployed ex-apprentices who returned to the sugar estates during the late 1840s and early 1850s would, in fact, be women.

A final factor which governed ex-apprentice fortunes during the late 1840s was the resumption of Indian immigration in 1842 and the subsequent massive influx of indentured laborers into the colony. From its very beginning, colonial authorities hoped that Indian immigration would have a "salutory effect on the mind of the ex-apprentices" by giving them a "more concrete notion of things."[108] As several magistrates ultimately acknowledged, this expectation remained unfulfilled. Ed.

Kelly, for example, noted late in 1845 that despite the arrival of 57,000 indentured laborers since 1843, "I have never observed the Slightest disposition to jealousy on the part of the ex-apprentices towards the Indians, neither do I think the introduction of the latter, has been prejudicial to them in any way."[109]

Within the space of only a few years, however, this situation began to change dramatically as ever-increasing numbers of Old Immigrants completed their industrial residence and left the sugar estates to earn their living from non-agricultural pursuits. The census of 1851 revealed, for instance, that one of every seven persons employed in commerce, trade, and manufacturing was now of Indian origin. Substantial numbers of Indian immigrants were also to be found among the colony's domestic servants, peddlers, and gardeners, occupations which hitherto had been dominated by ex-apprentices or characterized by a sizable ex-apprentice presence. Ten years later, another census demonstrated that Old Immigrants had made significant inroads into many areas of local economic life, one consequence of which was that "the children of former slaves" soon numbered among those trying to hold their own by taking advantage of the educational opportunities they had previously ignored.[110]

In the years after 1851, ex-apprentices disappeared as a distinct entity within both the Mauritian body politic and the archival record. Colonial officials, preoccupied with the tens of thousands of Indian immigrants in their midst, paid less and less attention to a community whose numbers declined still further with the passage of time. Annual reports during the early 1850s did little more than note the number of ex-apprentice births and deaths, and after 1857 even this information ceased being reported. By 1861, the difficulties of distinguishing former apprentices and their children from the rest of the colony's non-Indian colored inhabitants were such that the census commissioners decided to count all remaining ex-slaves and their descendants as members of the general population.[111]

The last expression of official interest in Mauritian freedmen came five years later when Governor Sir Henry Barkly was asked to report on conditions in the colony. The governor's report says much about local perceptions of both ex-apprentices and the changes that had taken place since emancipation. Like other colonial administrators of his day, Barkly expressed his concern about the moral, as well as the social and economic, condition of the island's non-white inhabitants. Like later historians, he also viewed developments since the mid-1830s largely through the prism of Indian immigration. In the governor's eyes, immigration had not only quadrupled the colony's revenue and population, but had also "raised to comparative affluence hundreds of thousands of labourers, who in their native land could never have earned above a precarious subsistence, and has further saved the emancipated negroes from retrograding into barbarism, and afforded to their descendents a fair prospect of raising themselves in the scale of civilized life."[112] Blinded by prejudice and the concerns of the day, the governor spoke for many who did not understand the nature of the transformations to which he referred, much less comprehend that the forces which had driven the *petit morcellement* were already setting the stage for an even more dramatic restructuring of Mauritian social and economic relationships.

# 6 The regenerators of agricultural prosperity: Indian immigrants and their descendants, 1834–1936

With respect to the fear of a superabundance of Immigrants, Your Excellency may be assured, that there will never be a superabundance of Agricultural laborers, so long as they can leave the Estates at pleasure, by paying the light monthly tax of Four shillings, which ought, in our opinion, to be at least Ten Shillings.

That there is, no doubt, a large Population of do-nothings, who have quitted the estates to avoid work, and we believe, that they will continue to do so under present facilities, where the climate is so genial, and the means of subsistence so easy. The Planters ask for Agricultural, or as Lord Grey properly designates them "Industrial Laborers." They do not ask to overstock the Colony with Shopkeepers, Cake-sellers and "bazardiers." If these people were really to do the work they came here purposely to do, the cost of Immigration would have nearly ceased. The Planter is not to blame for this.

Address to Sir William Gomm by W.W. West, M. Baudot, and Ed. Rouillard, April 20, 1847[1]

On June 10, 1855, Indian immigrant no. 152,217 arrived at Port Louis aboard the *Bushire Merchant* from Calcutta. Twenty-eight years old when he stepped ashore, the young man subsequently known as Seewoodharry Bhaguth was of the Kurmi caste and came originally from the village of Soondurpore Korreeanea in Patna district.[2] While the reason why he left India remains unknown, three years after his arrival Seewoodharry was free of his obligation to complete five years of industrial residence. On August 27, 1858, he entered into partnership with two other Old Immigrants to establish a store in Grand Port.[3] By 1866, Seewoodharry, now described regularly as a landowner in notarial acts, was actively purchasing, leasing, and clearing large tracts of land in Plaines Wilhems. For the next fifteen years, until his death in 1881, he would continue to figure in the district's economic life as a merchant, landowner, and businessman of some consequence. In this capacity, he not only helped to inaugurate the large-scale subdivision of sugar estates and other properties known as the *grand morcellement*, but also heralded the active role Indian immigrants were to play in this process of social and economic transformation.

The assertion that Indian immigrants played an important role in shaping the colony's fortunes during the nineteenth century is not new. Contemporary observers of Mauritian life readily acknowledged that the colony's economic survival depended upon immigrant labor, a conclusion echoed in later histories of the island. Governor J.M. Higginson, for example, asserted in 1852 that immigration was "the corner-stone of Mauritian prosperity, the mercury that raises and depresses the spirits of the planters, the lever regulating all the operations of agriculture, which are checked or advanced according to the extent and certainty of the supply of labour."[4] The governor repeated these sentiments in subsequent annual reports, as did later occupants of Government House such as William Stevenson and Sir Henry Barkly. In 1858, Stevenson would describe immigration as "the regenerator of agricultural prosperity," an opinion seconded eight years later by Barkly, who observed that the island's commercial, as well as its agricultural, prosperity had been maintained and enhanced by the introduction of Indian immigrants.[5]

This positive assessment of immigration's impact upon colonial life was matched by the belief in some circles that indentured laborers themselves numbered among the beneficiaries of what emigration had wrought. From its very beginning, proponents of the so-called "coolie trade" held that agricultural labor in other parts of the British Empire would allow tens of thousands of disadvantaged Indian men, women, and children to improve the quality of their lives. Not only would the opportunities created by emigration permit them to escape the grinding poverty of their overpopulated homeland, these apologists argued, but labor on colonial plantations would also improve their physical and moral condition.

Not everyone, however, subscribed to this view. Humanitarian and anti-slavery groups quickly condemned indentured labor as little more than a "new system of slavery." The abuses to which the earliest immigrants to the island were subjected and the subsequent suspension of emigration to Mauritius late in 1838 heightened fears that slavery was simply being resurrected in another guise. Government supervision of the indentured labor trade when immigration resumed four years later did not calm these suspicions. Claims and counterclaims about the treatment of the Indians working in Mauritius continued to circulate until 1872 when a Royal Commission was appointed to look into the matter. Their investigations soon led the Commissioners to state that they had been unable to discern "the great physical, moral, and intellectual advance accruing to Indians which is asserted to be the consequence of their immigration to Mauritius."[6]

These themes dominate much of the literature on indentured labor systems during the nineteenth and early twentieth centuries.[7] The extent to which indentured laborers were or were not "free" has remained a subject of particular interest and debate. The attendant preoccupation with cataloguing the disabilities under which these workers lived or with enumerating the opportunities for self-improvement they would not otherwise have had is one reason why so many important questions about the immigrant experience remain unasked and unanswered. Despite occasional attempts to do more than simply engage in such recitatives, there continues to be a marked unwillingness to explore the social and economic context within which these lives were lived. A reluctance to view these men and women as playing any other role in colonial life than that of "laborer" only compounds this problem.

These problems are readily apparent in Mauritian studies where histories of the island have focused basically upon how and why indentured laborers reached the colony and the most obvious or sensational details of the immigrant experience.[8] The social and economic transformations of the late nineteenth century remain largely undescribed, while the dynamics of these changes have been analyzed only in the most general of terms. Auguste Toussaint, for one, viewed these changes as little more than the logical outcome of the various external and internal forces to which the colony had been subjected since the 1860s.[9] Raj Virahsawmy, in turn, has argued that these changes stemmed from the transition after 1870s from a semi-capitalist plantation economy to an agrarian capitalist economy.[10] More recently, M.D. North-Coombes characterized nineteenth- and early twentieth-century Mauritian political economy as having both capitalist and pre-capitalist features which fostered the rise of a semi-proletarianized peasantry.[11] In each instance, the dynamics of this era's most important development – the *grand morcellement* and the concomitant rise of an Indian small planter class – have remained unexplored. The relationship between these developments and the local sugar industry's financial condition likewise remains shrouded by the mists of time.

Access to and control of land was as crucial to Indian immigrant attempts to enhance their standing in the Mauritian colonial order as it had been for the island's *gens de couleur* and ex-apprentices. The archival record reveals that immigrants numbered among the colony's landowners by the early 1840s, but the nature and extent of their activity has remained hidden from view. Colonial officials paid little attention during the first decades of immigration to those aspects of Indian life that did not bear directly upon their service as indentured laborers or their potential threat to public order. The commissions that investigated immigrant living and working conditions did likewise. The 1872 Royal Commission of Inquiry, for example, did little more than acknowledge that some Old Immigrants had acquired property during the 1860s. Only when the *grand morcellement* became an increasingly visible part of the colony's social and economic landscape during the late nineteenth century did local authorities begin to take serious note of Indian land ownership. However, despite their growing awareness of this phenomenon, officials frequently failed to report the kinds of information which are crucial to understanding when and how *morcellement* began and why it took the shape that it did. So we must turn once again to the notarial record to reveal the dynamics of this process.

The importance of this record to our understanding of this era in Mauritian history cannot be overemphasized. No other contemporary source allows us to examine the relationship between those who bought and sold land in such detail. The colonial government's desire to exercise tight control over its Indian population further enhances the value of these acts. Every indentured laborer reaching the island was issued a "ticket" upon his or her arrival, the number of which was recorded in an immigration register, together with a substantial amount of personal information about the ticket-holder in question. In addition to noting an immigrant's name, age, sex, and caste, these registers often recorded an individual's exact place of origin in India, his or her marital status, and the name and ticket number of their spouse and any children who accompanied them. Subsequent entries might include the dates of an individual's marriage, registration as an Old Immigrant, return to India, or death. These data, coupled with the fact that notaries regularly recorded ticket numbers after 1854–55, allow us not only to chart the *grand morcellement*'s course, but also to explore the ways and means by which immigrants ordered their social and economic relations with one another and with other segments of the colony's population.

Because notarial acts did not regularly identify Old Immigrants as such until the mid-1850s, the date when Indians who had completed their industrial residence first purchased land is difficult to ascertain. A survey of approximately 10,000 acts recorded by three notaries active from 1838 through 1849 suggests that one of the earliest such transactions dates to mid-1841 when Moutou Daca bought two of the 6.95 arpents owned by Jean Louis L'Herminette.[12] Purchases of land by persons who we may reasonably assume were Old Immigrants began to be recorded in mid-1843, when Seckzorip, a laborer and native of Nassirabad, and

Table 20. *Indian immigrant land purchases, 1840–1889*

| Period | Individual plots[a] (percent) | | | | | | No. | % PDIF[b] |
| | < 1.0 | 1–1.9 | 2–2.9 | 3–4.9 | 5–9.9 | 10 + | | |
|---|---|---|---|---|---|---|---|---|
| 1840–49 | 15.4 | 26.9 | 26.9 | 15.4 | 11.5 | 3.9 | 26 | 69.2 |
| 1850–59 | 52.8 | 18.6 | 12.9 | 10.0 | 4.3 | 1.4 | 70 | 87.1 |
| 1860–69 | 43.5 | 30.6 | 9.7 | 3.2 | 6.5 | 6.5 | 62 | 83.9 |
| 1870–79 | 55.7 | 17.2 | 9.0 | 3.3 | 2.5 | 12.3 | 122 | 66.4 |
| 1880–89 | 38.2 | 25.7 | 11.8 | 9.6 | 5.9 | 8.8 | 136 | 76.5 |
| Average | 45.2 | 22.8 | 11.8 | 7.2 | 5.1 | 7.9 | 416 | 76.0 |

| Period | Morcellement plots[c] (percent) | | | | | | No. | % PDIF |
| | < 1.0 | 1–1.9 | 2–2.9 | 3–4.9 | 5–9.9 | 10 + | | |
|---|---|---|---|---|---|---|---|---|
| 1860–69 | 40.7 | 27.7 | 18.1 | 7.7 | 2.6 | 3.2 | 155 | 79.4 |
| 1870–79 | 60.5 | 29.1 | 6.3 | 2.2 | 1.5 | 0.4 | 271 | 93.0 |
| 1880–89 | 50.2 | 30.5 | 10.6 | 6.3 | 1.3 | 1.1 | 616 | 97.7 |
| Average | 51.4 | 29.8 | 10.6 | 5.5 | 1.5 | 1.2 | 1,042 | 87.8 |

*Notes:*
[a] Arpents. Excludes plots acquired as a result of the subdivision of larger properties.
[b] Purchase price paid in full at the time of the sale's formal completion.
[c] Arpents. Only plots acquired as a result of the subdivision of larger properties.
*Sources:* MA: NA 80, 83, 84, 85, 102, 112, 119.

Seckmarali, a laborer from Dakka, purchased portions of a 22-arpent tract in Grand Port.[13] Other Indian laborers soon followed in their footsteps. Like Seckzorip and Seckmarali, a few of these individuals purchased sections of properties that were being subdivided but, in general, Old Immigrants do not appear to have participated actively in the *petit morcellement*.

Indian involvement in the local real estate market increased noticeably in late 1847 and 1848, as many of the first wave of post-1842 immigrants completed their industrial residence, acquired Old Immigrant status, and left the sugar estates to earn their living in business, commerce, domestic service, and other walks of life. The notarial record reveals that Old Immigrants continued to purchase small plots of land, usually encompassing less than 2 arpents, at a sustained but modest rate during the 1850s and early 1860s (see table 20). The natural disasters that befell the island between 1864 and 1868 slowed this process of land acquisition, but by the early 1870s Old Immigrants were not only purchasing land again, but also doing so in numbers which heralded the advent of the *grand morcellement*.

The beginning of the *grand morcellement* has previously been dated to late 1880 when a property in Flacq belonging to Mme. Joseph Dioré was divided into twenty-two lots.[14] While the early 1880s clearly witnessed the subdivision of a growing number of sugar estates and other properties, the notarial record demonstrates that what transpired at this time was, in many respects, simply a continuation of the process that had begun some forty years earlier during the *petit morcellement*. Although the *petit morcellement* came to an end *circa* 1848, properties nevertheless continued to be subdivided, albeit on a much smaller scale than before. The notaries Adolphe Macquet and Elisé Liénard, for instance, recorded the subdivision during the 1850s of at least nine properties which ranged from 6 to 140 arpents in size.

The late 1850s and early 1860s witnessed a limited resurgence in *morcellement* activity. Macquet and his colleague, Laurent Raoul, for example, facilitated the subdivision of fourteen properties in various parts of the island between 1860 and 1865. These properties, like those sub-subdivided during the 1850s, tended to be of rather modest size; half of the tracts in question contained fewer than 10 arpents, while the largest encompassed no more than 78 arpents. As the circumstances which surround the subdivision of properties such as "Le Hochet," the "Terrain Ganet," and "La Ménagerie" attest, some of this activity was closely associated with the rapid growth of a resident Old Immigrant population in and around Port Louis. Most of the sales from these three tracts were of small house plots which contained no more than several hundred square meters.

The natural disasters of the mid-1860s, and especially the malaria epidemic of 1867–68, curtailed this surge of immigrant involvement in the local real estate market, but only temporarily so. Old Immigrants resumed purchasing small plots of land again by the early 1870s, while the subdivision of a limited number of properties also continued. The pace of this activity quickened, however, around 1875, as increasing numbers of properties began to undergo *morcellement*. Equally important, the notarial record reveals that Indians were now intimately involved in this process, both as *de facto* agents for Franco-Mauritian estate-owners and as large landowners in their own right. These developments confirm that the beginnings of the *grand morcellement* date to *circa* 1875, and not to late 1880 as previously supposed.

Careful thought and planning went into the subdivision of these properties. When Seewoodharry Bhaguth purchased a 312-arpent tract from Augustin Perrier in 1875, he declared his intention of subdividing the land in question.[15] Perrier agreed on the condition that the land had to be sold for at least $50 an arpent. The sale of other large properties to

Table 21. *Value of real property acquired by Indian immigrants and Indo-Mauritians, 1864–1931*

| | Average annual value of property acquired | | | Average annual net value of specie imports/ exports (Rs.) |
|---|---|---|---|---|
| Period | Total value (rupees) | % TVPCH[a] | Net value (rupees) | |
| 1864–1887 | 222,615 | — | — | +1,118,680 |
| 1888–1894 | 1,217,097 | — | — | +853,837 |
| 1895–1900 | 1,716,251 | — | — | +1,204,348 |
| 1901–1904 | 1,529,489 | 33.6 | +465,102[b] | −768,170 |
| 1905–1909 | 1,242,931 | 24.5 | +466,264 | +334,401 |
| 1910–1914 | 2,415,678 | 29.4 | +495,305 | +579,339 |
| 1915–1919 | 5,370,588 | 33.3 | +1,387,896 | +242,594 |
| 1920–1924 | 9,311,477 | 37.0 | +2,794,595 | +1,704,466 |
| 1925–1929 | 4,027,622 | 35.2 | −376,589 | −1,089,376 |
| 1930–1931 | 1,783,980 | 35.7 | −601,542 | −964,250 |

*Notes:*
[a] Total value of property changing hands.
[b] For 1904 only.
*Sources:* AR 1900, p. 6. PP 1902 LXV [Cd. 788–5].
    PP 1901 CVI [Cd. 4984], pp. 78–81; 1914–16 LXXIX [Cd. 7786], pp. 90–93; 1924 XXIV [Cmd. 2247], pp. 99–102; 1929–30 XXX [Cmd. 3434], pp. 141–42; 1937–38 XXVII [Cmd. 5582], p. 148.
    RMD 1904–31.

Indian entrepreneurs frequently included similar declarations and terms. Such was the case when Auguste Blaize sold Matapoorsad and his partners two sections of "Belle Mare" estate in Flacq in 1881 and another three tracts in Rivière du Rempart the following year; Matapoorsad's reservation of the right to subdivide most of the 478 arpents in question was agreed to by Blaize on the condition that this arpentage could not be sold for less than Rs. 100 ($50) an arpent.[16]

The *morcellement* process steadily gained momentum during the 1880s and early 1890s. By 1895, the scale of this activity was such that Acting Governor C.A. King Harman not only characterized its increasing pace as "inevitable," but also noted that the colony's sugar factories were being improved to handle the canes produced by the growing number of Indian small planters.[17] The following year, Governor Charles Bruce estimated that at least one-fourth of the year's sugar crop had been produced by these small planters.[18] In 1897, the president of the Chamber of Agriculture also acknowledged that the parceling out of land was proceeding on a large scale, an observation given substance by a Protector of Immigrants' report that Indians had added 23,243 arpents worth more than Rs. 4,600,000 to their holdings between 1894 and 1896.[19]

The rapidly increasing value of the real property acquired by Indians during the latter part of the nineteenth century underscores the extent of this activity. Indian investment in real estate skyrocketed during and after the late 1880s; in the space of only six years (1888–94), immigrants paid out Rs. 8,519,676 for land, or almost 60 percent more than the Rs. 5,342,760 they had spent for similar purchases between 1864 and 1887. Indian involvement in the local real estate market continued to increase as the century drew to a close; between 1895 and 1900, immigrants invested another Rs. 10,297,509 in land. The advent of a new century brought no let-up in this activity as immigrants and their Indo-Mauritian descendants continued to invest significant sums in land well into the 1920s (see table 21).

Indian money found its way into Mauritian agriculture by other means as well. The notarial record reveals, among other things, that Old Immigrants began to lease land no later than 1850. While most of these early leases covered the use of plots encompassing only 1 or 2 arpents for just a year or two, in some instances substantial tracts were rented for extended periods of time. In one of the earliest such transactions on record, Nareyna, a laborer who had arrived during the immigration of 1834–38, rented 25 arpents already planted in cane for four years at an annual cost of $150.[20] Other Old Immigrants such as Mungroo, no. 5324/ 54,248, were soon renting even larger properties for longer periods of time. When Marie and Clémence Morel came to terms with him in April, 1859, Mungroo acquired the use of 49 arpents for nine years for $4,171.50.[21] The total value of these leases cannot be ascertained, but some sense of the scale of this activity is suggested by the 1872 Royal Commission's report that 5,256 Indians were known to have leased land to or from another party between 1864 and 1871, and that the value of these transactions was estimated to be £122,000.[22]

The absence of detailed information about sugar industry finances and the difficulties of ascertaining how much money was in circulation in any given year makes it difficult to assess the impact which Indian investment in land had on late nineteenth- and early twentieth-century Mauritian economic life. Some sense of its possible importance can be gauged if the combined net value of specie imports and Indian land purchases is regarded as a rough index of domestic capital liquidity. As table 21 indicates, the modest level of immigrant involvement in the local real estate market before the mid-1880s probably had a correspondingly limited impact upon sugar industry finances. There is reason to believe, however, that immigrant investment in real property became increasingly important to the industry's financial well-being as the colony's economic crisis deepened after the mid-1880s. By 1900, if not before, Indians may have accounted for as much as one-third of the value of all property changing hands. Equally important, the net value of Indian holdings continued to increase, often at a substantially higher rate than the net value of specie imports.

The ability of Indian immigrants and their children to play an ever-more active and important role in colonial economic life as the nineteenth century drew to a close was an impressive accomplishment. Their investment of more than Rs. 24,000,000 in real property between 1864 and 1900 is all the more striking given the low wages paid to agricultural workers and the high cost of land relative to laborers' incomes. The average estate worker, for example, earned only Rs. 7.40 a month between 1877 and 1881 and, as chapter 3 details, the penalties for sickness, absence from work, etc., frequently reduced a laborer's take-home pay by 20 to 30 percent. While wages increased after the turn of the century, penalties and deductions of 15 to 20 percent or more remained a regular part of economic life for many agricultural workers. At the same time, acquiring even a small plot of land could be an expensive undertaking depending upon the location and quality of the property in question and the circumstances of its sale. The price of land during the late 1870s ranged from several hundred to more than Rs. 1,000 for an arpent that had been cleared and brought into production. The closing of the agricultural frontier during the late 1870s and early 1880s, together with the growing demand for land, ensured that real estate prices in general, and the cost of prime agricultural land in particular, remained high.

These economic facts of life indicate that the *grand morcellement* and associated developments cannot be understood without examining the various ways and means by which Indian immigrants capitalized upon the opportunities that presented themselves during the latter part of the nineteenth century. As the history of the colony's free colored and ex-apprentice populations demonstrates, doing so must include a careful consideration of immigrant social and economic organization. We must also remember that the economic crisis that began to take shape during the 1860s was not without precedent in Mauritian history. The ability of some Old Immigrants to carve out a place of consequence for themselves in the colonial order must accordingly be viewed in light of the attempts by *gens de couleur* and ex-apprentices to exploit similar opportunities to their own advantage. At the same time, we must not forget that, despite these opportunities, large numbers of *gens de couleur* and freedmen did not become economically independent, or even improve their standard of

Table 22. *Indian representation in occupations, 1846–1931*

| Occupation | (Percent) | | | | | | | | | |
|---|---|---|---|---|---|---|---|---|---|---|
| | 1846 | 1851 | 1861 | 1871 | 1881 | 1891 | 1901 | 1911 | 1921 | 1931 |
| Agriculture | 84.8 | 84.6 | 91.6 | 96.3 | 96.9 | 91.9 | 95.2 | 93.0 | 92.0 | 94.2 |
| Commerce | 3.0 | 31.2 | 47.9 | 65.3 | 60.8 | 58.8 | 57.8 | 60.5 | 65.0 | 54.9 |
| Crafts & trades | 6.1 | 11.7 | 18.0 | 14.7 | 13.7 | 12.3 | 11.7 | 28.9 | 34.1 | 23.6 |
| Domestic service | 36.7 | 44.7 | 68.4 | 67.5 | 60.8 | 56.2 | 57.5 | 47.3 | 46.4 | 50.5 |
| Independent proprietor | 0.1 | 4.9 | 6.2 | 19.1 | 26.9 | 46.5 | — | — | — | — |
| Professions[a] | 3.0 | 10.8 | 23.9 | 19.9 | 25.5 | 23.1 | 22.7 | 31.2 | 42.4 | 37.6 |

*Note:* [a] Includes, in 1846, 1851 and 1861, those described as "other educated persons" and in government service.
*Sources:* 1846 Census, para. 24; 1851 Census, p. 8; 1861 Census, pp. 14–17; 1871 Census, Appendix No. 18; 1881 Census, Appendix No. 12; 1891 Census, pp. 23–27; 1901 Census, pp. 30–35; 1911 Census, pp. xv–xvii; 1921 Census, pp. 21–22; 1931 Census, pp. 15–16.

living over the long term. Numerous Indian immigrants would likewise fail to escape from the poverty that came with confinement on the margins of Mauritian economic life.

The archival record is silent about many aspects of early immigrant life in Mauritius. Visitors to the island during the 1840s and early 1850s paid little attention to the colony's Indian population, and local authorities tended to ignore those aspects of immigrant life that did not bear directly upon their status as agricultural laborers or their ability to pose a threat to public order. Occasionally, however, brief notes were made about Indian life away from the plantations. One of the earliest such reports dates to 1844 when the local Immigration Committee observed that the failure of Indian estate laborers to renew their contracts stemmed from the ease with which they could carry on a trade or work either on their own account or for small landowners.[23] Three years later, Messrs. West, Baudot, and Rouillard complained bitterly to Governor Gomm about the number of Indians earning their living from non-agricultural pursuits.[24] Several months later, the Immigration Committee likewise reported that immigrants who had withdrawn from estate labor preferred "to devote themselves to labour of a lighter and more attractive or profitable kind" such as petty trade, huckstering, and raising goats, pigs, and poultry.[25]

The extent of this activity first became apparent during the census of 1846. While the census confirmed that the overwhelming majority of Indians in the colony earned their living as agricultural laborers, it also indicates that immigrants were already to be found in all non-agricultural sectors of local economic life, albeit often only in small numbers. Subsequent censuses would document the exodus of ever-greater numbers of immigrants from the sugar estates upon completion of their industrial residence (see table 22). Their pursuit of new livelihoods would, however, be subject to constraints. Relatively few Old Immigrants, for example, found work in the skilled trades (see table 23). In other occupational categories, such as the civil service and the professions, the Indian presence grew steadily, but at a slower rate than in areas such as commerce and trade.

These trends illustrate the differential impact of Old Immigrant economic activity. On the one hand, the massive influx of indentured laborers from the mid-1840s through the 1850s minimized whatever short-term consequences the loss of Old Immigrant labor might have had on the sugar industry. On the other hand, the decision by Old Immigrants to forsake plantation labor began to disrupt existing patterns of economic life, especially for the colony's Creole inhabitants, that is, those of African descent.

Table 23. *Distribution of occupations within the Indian population, 1846–1931*

| Occupation | (Percent) | | | | | | | | | |
|---|---|---|---|---|---|---|---|---|---|---|
| | 1846 | 1851 | 1861 | 1871 | 1881 | 1891 | 1901 | 1911 | 1921 | 1931 |
| Agriculture | 83.6 | 77.7 | 72.7 | 65.2 | 67.6 | 72.9 | 78.8 | 73.9 | 64.0 | 73.5 |
| Commerce | 0.1 | 1.6 | 2.8 | 7.8 | 7.7 | 9.0 | 8.4 | 10.7 | 17.8 | 9.7 |
| Crafts & trades | 2.1 | 4.3 | 4.5 | 3.2 | 2.9 | 3.1 | 3.0 | 8.1 | 10.4 | 5.2 |
| Domestic service | 7.7 | 8.2 | 8.4 | 11.2 | 9.6 | 7.6 | 8.6 | 5.6 | 5.0 | 8.2 |
| Independent proprietor | [a] | 0.1 | 0.3 | 0.6 | 1.1 | — | — | — | — | — |
| Professions[b] | 0.2 | 0.5 | 1.1 | 0.8 | 1.2 | 1.2 | 1.2 | 1.7 | 2.8 | 3.4 |
| Other[c] | 6.3 | 7.4 | 10.4 | 11.5 | 10.4 | 5.1 | — | — | — | — |

*Notes:* [a] Less than 0.1 per cent. [b] Includes, in 1846, 1851, and 1861, those described as "other educated persons" and in government service. [c] Mostly laborers.

*Sources:* See table 22.

While many *gens de couleur* and ex-apprentices had become small proprietors during the *petit morcellement*, many more had continued to earn their living from the local service sector, and it was this segment of the general population which bore much of the brunt of the Old Immigrant abandonment of agricultural labor. As the censuses of 1851 and 1861 attest, Creoles began to be displaced from many of the occupations they had hitherto dominated. By 1851, to cite several prominent examples, Indians already comprised one-half of the colony's 1,215 carters, 40 percent of its 495 hawkers and peddlers, almost one-third of its 2,250 shopkeepers, and nearly 29 percent of its 2,142 laundrymen and laundrywomen. A decade later, Old Immigrants would account for almost 92 percent of all carters, more than 88 percent of hawkers and carriers, nearly one-half of the colony's shopkeepers, and more than one-half of its laundrymen and women.

The rapidly growing Indian presence in these occupations reflected the fact that not only were increasing numbers of Old Immigrants plying these trades, but also that the number of Creoles pursuing these livelihoods was declining. The number of carters within the "general" population, for example, dropped from 607 in 1851 to only 166 in 1861; the number of Indian carters, on the other hand, soared from 608 to 1,885 during the same period. Changes of comparable magnitude can also be discerned in other representative occupations. The number of hawkers and peddlers within the general population dropped from 300 in 1851 to 190 in 1861, while the number of Indians engaging in these activities rose from 195 to 1,451 during the same period. The number of Indian and Creole washermen and washerwomen rose and fell in a like manner, from 613 to 1,290 and from 1,529 to 1,179 respectively.

These developments point to a significant restructuring of domestic economic relationships that came to full fruition during the 1850s and undercut the attempt by many former *gens de couleur* and ex-apprentices to establish a significant independent presence in the colonial economy. The impact of these changes was perhaps most pronounced among small agriculturalists. Almost 40 percent of the colony's 7,012 "gardeners" were of Indian origin as early as 1851. A decade later, only 1,368 of 5,737 gardeners belonged to the general population. This process accelerated with the passage of time; by 1871, only 683 of 8,196 gardeners were non-Indian, and in 1881 members of the general population accounted for a mere 2 percent of the island's 10,222 gardeners.

This displacement of Creoles from many areas of local economic life may be traced to several factors. In the first instance, the sheer weight of numbers quickly gave Indian immigrants an advantage in an economy which depended so heavily upon inexpensive labor. Planters had complained at length about the high wages ex-apprentices commanded during the immediate post-emancipation period, and the dramatic increase in the size of the local labor pool, especially during the 1850s, allowed planters to begin lowering wages. This trend, coupled with the continuing reluctance of many ex-apprentices to return to full-time estate labor, limited their ability to tap into a wage-labor market worth hundreds of thousands of pounds each year. By the 1860s, the massive influx of indentured labor was having a pronounced impact even in those professions where relatively few Old Immigrants were to be found. In 1871, the Protector of Immigrants reported that the average monthly wage of many Old Immigrant artisans and tradesmen had declined since 1860, sometimes dramatically so.[26] The wages paid to Creoles in these same professions can only have come under similar pressure.

A second, related, factor that limited the ability of many Creoles to compete successfully was a lack of adequate financial resources. Although many of the reports prepared by colonial authorities in 1845–46 implied that ex-apprentices were either prospering or capable of doing so in the near future, some local officials painted a much darker picture of contemporary realities. Emile Ravel, for one, described most of Rivière du Rempart's freedmen as being impoverished, if not destitute.[27] His comments would be echoed by others, such as Dr. Frederic Mouat who noted *circa* 1852 that most of the freedmen who had squatted on small patches of land after emancipation lived "in a state bordering on misery and starvation."[28]

The annual reports of the Government Savings Bank likewise suggest that many Creoles possessed limited fiscal resources. The Bank, which began operations in 1837, had been established to encourage "provident habits among the lower classes of society," and especially among apprentices who accounted for 211 of 369 depositors during its first year of operation.[29] The Bank's reports reveal, for example, that the average amount in the account of a "Mauritian," that is, a non-Indian, agricultural laborer, between 1851 and 1855 varied from as little as £3 to slightly more than £8 a year, while that of Indian laborers during the same period ranged from £18 to £21 each year. The disparity between the financial resources at the disposal of these two populations is even more striking when the amounts standing to the credit of all agricultural laborers at the end of the year during this five-year period are compared; Mauritians averaged £303 each year compared to £11,399 for their Indian counterparts. The value of the deposits held by Indian laborers is equally impressive when compared to those standing to the credit of artisans and mechanics (approximately £4,542) and domestic servants (approximately £7,327), many of whom, according to the Bank's president, were of African ancestry.[30]

The rapidly changing composition of the colony's gardening population during the late 1840s and 1850s underscores the consequences that could flow from the inability of many Creoles to control significant capital resources and the ability of some Old Immigrants to amass such resources. While the extent to which Creole gardeners owned their own land remains unknown, the notarial record leaves little doubt that many of the early sales of land to Old Immigrants were made by such Creole smallholders. That these peasant proprietors often possessed limited economic resources even in the best of times is also suggested by the fact that many of the plots sold to Old Immigrants had remained uncleared years after their purchase during the *petit morcellement*. The economic realities of the day make it reasonable to conclude that increasing numbers of Creole proprietors had no option but to sell some or all of their land as they struggled to hold their own during the 1850s. The only persons who would have been interested in these small plots and, moreover, who would have had the ready cash to purchase them, were the colony's Old Immigrants.

If necessity compelled some Creole landowners to sell their property, in other instances these proprietors clearly sought to capitalize upon the Old Immigrant desire to own land. In April, 1847, to cite but one example, Adonis Adrien and the Dlles. Sophie and Irma Anna sold the one arpent they had acquired in 1841 for $40 to Ramsamy, a merchant and native of Madras, for $170.[31] The speculative nature of some of this activity is even more apparent in transactions such as that of February 19, 1848, when Dlle. Gertrude Emma Allard sold 6 arpents to Corindavel Nareyena for $85; Dlle. Allard had purchased the tract in question only eighteen days before for $48.[32] Creole smallholders were also to be found subdividing their properties. Some of these tracts, such as that divided among several former residents of Calcutta by Elie Labonté and his wife late in 1852, had been purchased ten years earlier during the *petit morcellement*.[33] The 8.5 arpents subdivided by Hippolyte Pierre dit Hippolyte Godin in 1855, on the other hand, had been purchased just two years earlier.[34]

Members of the Creole community also entered into leases with Old Immigrants as a way of generating income while retaining control of their assets. The full extent of this activity will never be known, but the notarial record at least reveals something of the nature of these transactions. The provisions of such leases could be rather generous, as when Caivenaigon and Songol rented 3.5 arpents for five years from Dlle. Melon Adèle in March, 1851, for $37.50 a year. In addition to the land in question, the lessees acquired the use of a house on the property, an arpent already planted in maize and manioc, 3,000 feet of vacoas, and various fruit trees.[35] Proprietors such as Porphire Paul Emile Sénèque also engaged occasionally in the *de facto* subdivision of their property by signing long-term leases with multiple tenants.[36]

In certain respects, the movement by Old Immigrants onto the land during the 1840s and 1850s paralleled that by *gens de couleur* during the late eighteenth and early nineteenth centuries and by ex-apprentices during the *petit morcellement*. In all three instances, the properties being acquired tended to be small, usually encompassing no more than 2 arpents, and often much less than that. Like their Creole counterparts, the Old Immigrants who purchased land generally resided in the same district in which their new property was located. In other respects, however, Old Immigrant activity differed significantly from that of the colony's Creole inhabitants. Women, for instance, comprised a much smaller percentage of the immigrants who acquired individual plots of land during and after the 1840s than had been the case among *gens de couleur* and ex-apprentices. The number of sales made to families at this time was also noticeably lower among Indians that it had been among the Creole population. Similar patterns would also characterize immigrant activity during the *grand morcellement* (see table 24).

Such differences are not unexpected given the demographic structure of these populations. As has already been noted, the Creole community had achieved a certain degree of social structural stability by the mid-nineteenth century. The sexual disparity within the Indian immigrant population, on the other hand, continued to be a source of considerable concern to colonial and imperial officials. The need to correct the serious imbalance that existed between the sexes during the first years of Indian immigration soon led to official mandates that a certain percentage of all immigrants had to be women. However, despite these dicta, the difficulties of engaging or otherwise inducing the requisite numbers of women to migrate to the colony meant that the Indian population remained disproportionately male for an extended period of time. These differences are also not unexpected, given the different cultural traditions which prevailed in each of these populations. While women had participated actively in free colored social and economic life, the great majority of immigrant women remained confined to the subservient roles in family and community life that had been their customary lot in India.[37]

If demographic and cultural considerations explain some of the differences in Creole and Indian patterns of land acquisition during the mid-nineteenth century, others may be traced to variations in the

Table 24. *Social characteristics of Indians purchasing land, 1840–1889*

| Purchaser | (% Distribution within decade) | | | | |
|---|---|---|---|---|---|
| | 1840–49 | 1850–59 | 1860–69 | 1870–79 | 1880–89 |
| Individual Plots[a]: | | | | | |
| Individual male | 73.1 | 51.4 | 61.3 | 46.1 | 63.7 |
| Individual female | 7.7 | 2.9 | 12.9 | 7.8 | 3.0 |
| Male and female[b] | 7.7 | 25.7 | 11.3 | 11.8 | 5.9 |
| Family unit[c] | 3.8 | 5.7 | 1.6 | 13.7 | 12.6 |
| Other[d] | 7.7 | 14.3 | 12.9 | 20.6 | 14.8 |
| No. = | 26 | 70 | 62 | 102 | 135 |
| *Morcellement* plots: | | | | | |
| Individual male | — | — | 46.2 | 34.9 | 51.0 |
| Individual female | — | — | 5.9 | 4.2 | 7.8 |
| Male and female | — | — | 26.1 | 24.9 | 8.3 |
| Family unit | — | — | 13.4 | 15.9 | 19.1 |
| Other | — | — | 8.4 | 20.1 | 13.8 |
| No. = | — | — | 119 | 189 | 528 |

*Notes:*

[a] Excludes land acquired as a result of the subdivision of properties during the *petit* or *grand morcellement*.

[b] Joint purchase by a man (or men) and a woman (or women) whose legal or quasi-legal relationship to one another, if any, is unknown.

[c] Any combination of persons related by blood or marriage, e.g., husband and wife, parent and child, siblings, and other persons reported explicitly as being related to one another.

[d] Joint purchase by two or more men or by two or more women whose legal relationship to one another, if any, is unknown.

*Sources:* MA: NA 80, 83, 84, 85, 102, 112, 119.

structure and organization of economic life of these two communities. Census data highlight one such difference of long-term consequence: the existence of a sizable business and commercial community within the immigrant population from a relatively early date. Furthermore, the notarial record indicates that many more Indian merchants and businessmen participated in the buying and selling of land than did their Creole counterparts. While the roster of Creole men and women who purchased land during and after the *petit morcellement* includes those who earned their living from commerce and trade, the number of these entrepreneurs remained small compared to the number of like-minded persons in the immigrant community. Equally important, Indian merchants and businessmen would remain actively involved in the local real estate market as the *grand morcellement* got under way (see table 25).

The local free population of color had included persons of Indian

Table 25. *Occupation of Indians purchasing land, 1840–1889*

| Occupation | (% Distribution within decade) | | | | |
| --- | --- | --- | --- | --- | --- |
| | 1840–49 | 1850–59 | 1860–69 | 1870–79 | 1880–89 |
| Individual Plots:[a] | | | | | |
| Agriculture | 12.5 | 22.9 | 62.5 | 65.6 | 53.9 |
| Business/commerce | 33.3 | 31.4 | 25.0 | 17.7 | 20.4 |
| Crafts & trades | 20.9 | 15.7 | 7.5 | 10.4 | 11.8 |
| Domestic service | — | 1.2 | 2.5 | 5.2 | 0.7 |
| Laborer | 25.0 | 27.7 | — | 1.1 | 6.6 |
| Miscellaneous | 8.3 | 1.2 | 2.5 | — | 6.6 |
| No. = | 24 | 83 | 40 | 96 | 152 |
| *Morcellement* plots: | | | | | |
| Agriculture | — | — | 41.1 | 51.3 | 44.5 |
| Business/commerce | — | — | 29.0 | 16.2 | 7.7 |
| Crafts & trades | — | — | 12.2 | 10.8 | 11.6 |
| Domestic service | — | — | 2.8 | 1.4 | 1.4 |
| Laborer | — | — | 9.3 | 18.0 | 32.1 |
| Miscellaneous | — | — | 5.6 | 2.3 | 2.7 |
| No. = | — | — | 107 | 222 | 560 |

*Note:* [a] Excludes land acquired as a result of the subdivision of properties during the *petit* or *grand morcellement*.

*Sources:* MA: NA 80, 83, 84, 85, 102, 112, 119.

ancestry who earned their living from commerce and trade but, as the Port Louis census of 1805 reveals, only a handful of Indian *gens de couleur* did so. Shortly after the advent of British rule, however, the origins of a distinctly Indian business and commercial presence can be discerned as merchants from the sub-continent reached the island's shores and quickly became involved in colonial economic life, including the developing sugar industry. One of the first to do so may have been Runtongee (or Ratangee) Bickagee, a Parsi merchant who apparently arrived in 1811 to serve as the Imam of Muscat's agent on the island.[38] These individuals could be persons of considerable means and credit-worthiness. When Annassamy, *négoçiant indien*, formalized his 1822 purchase of two plantations encompassing 765 arpents, together with 285 slaves, a steam-driven sugar mill and its appurtenances, fifty-five head of cattle, twelve mules, seven carts, and other items, he paid $20,000 down toward the purchase price of $178,850, and agreed to pay off the balance at the rate of $22,770 a year for five years with a final payment of $45,000 on September 30, 1829.[39] Annassamy subsequently acknowledged a loan of $20,000 from Rama Tiroumoudy, with whom he shared ownership of the "Bon Espoir" estate in Rivière du Rempart.[40] Other merchants, such as Pestonjee Manackjee, soon followed in Bickagee and Annassamy's footsteps and established themselves as businessmen and land owners of consequence.[41]

While the activities of men such as Bickagee, Annassamy, Tirou-moudy, and Manackjee heralded the establishment of an influential Indian business community with ties to important commercial centers in Bengal, Gujerat, and Tamilnad, and foreshadowed that community's growing involvement in the local sugar industry, it is important to remember that their careers were not representative of the great majority of Indian immigrants who engaged in trade and commerce during the mid-nineteenth century. The 1851 census reported the presence of only seven Indian merchants and commercial agents in the colony, and while that number increased to thirty-three by 1861, Indians still accounted for only 12 percent of all such persons. Despite further growth in their numbers during the 1860s and 1870s, Indians still comprised less than one-third of the colony's merchants and commercial agents by 1881. For every Bickagee and Annassamy, there were hundreds of Indian shop-keepers, hawkers, and peddlers in the colony who, like Rugbhur, no. 287,668, possessed only limited resources. Rugbhur, who undertook on June 14, 1875 to peddle notions and other items for a period of two years and five months, had to rely upon Ramsoroop, no. 356,881, to provide the $30 he needed to capitalize his venture.[42]

Although many of the Old Immigrants who engaged in commerce and trade controlled limited assets even in the best of times, the rapid expansion of this commercial population during the mid-nineteenth century nevertheless had profound implications for the local economy. The activities of Gungaram Beekoosing, no. 51,158, illustrate the impact that even shopkeepers of modest means could have upon a locality. During 1859, Gungaram leased 7 plots of land encompassing more than 14.5 arpents, all of which were apparently planted in canes, for a period of five years at annual rents which varied from $8 to $28. He soon transferred five of these leases to a local planter at a considerable profit to himself. In July of that same year, he also assumed responsibility for a 30-arpent section of the "Crombleholme" estate. According to the terms of this lease, Gungaram undertook not only to pay the owners an annual rent of $210 for six years, but also to clear and plant cane on the land in question by the end of the year and to take care of a neighboring stand of canes already belonging to them.[43]

The establishment of an extensive network of Indian shopkeepers and petty traders throughout the island provided many rural inhabitants, both Indian and non-Indian, with greater access to banking and credit services that had hitherto been unavailable in the countryside. What we know about the activities of Durmalingum, no. 95,335, who ran a store at L'Escalier in Grand Port, demonstrates that many of these individuals were at the center of a web of financial services that helped to lubricate the gears of daily economic life. At the time of his death in 1867, Durmalingum held merchandise, livestock, and other items worth $642.20, several tracts of land valued at $750, and $3.16 in cash. However, this property accounted for only 22 percent of his assets. A substantially larger percentage of his estate consisted of a credit from Alexandrine Capricieuse in the amount of $68.50 and the $3,532.27 owed to him by various persons. These outstanding accounts included 189 promissory notes worth $2,350.42 from thirty-three individuals, only seven of whom were Indian immigrants. While the value of these notes varied from as little as a few cents to as much as $72.20, most of them were for amounts of $7 to $10. Many of his clients had only one outstanding note, but in a several instances Durmalingum held from 10 to 15, and even as many as 25, notes from one person.[44]

Another important component of Durmalingum's estate was his share in several plantings of sugar cane on the 38 arpents which he and Seevajoundachetty Lingachettee had leased piecemeal from Ernest Azor in December, 1866. The value of this share – $1,390.44, or some 22 percent of his total assets – highlights the increasingly visible role Indian merchants, shopkeepers, and traders were beginning to play in the sugar industry by the late 1860s and early 1870s. In addition to buying sugar estates or smaller tracts already planted in cane on their own accord, Indian commercial men could also be found helping planters to under-write the costs of production. The partnership formed by Myanne Rayapa, a landowner and *cultivateur* in Grant Port, and Samoumouta-poullé, a shopkeeper living in Savanne, on December 15, 1848, for a period of seven years was an early harbinger of this involvement. According to the terms of this pact, Samoumoutapoullé agreed to advance the wages needed to hire a laborer to work the 4.75 arpents owned by Rayapa, 3.75 of which were already planted in cane, together with another $68 to cover miscellaneous production costs.[45] In return, Samoumoutapoullé was to receive one-half of all proceeds from the sale of the crop, which he was also responsible for selling.

Other partnerships preserved in the notarial record attest to the increasing ability and willingness of Indian commercial interests to become involved in financing local sugar estates. Only a few years after Rayapa and Samoumoutapoullé became partners, Pery Tamby Vel-laydon, a Mahébourg shopkeeper, extended a $1,300 line of short-term credit to Léonard Jean Pierre and Amédée Fricain as part of an agreement covering the operation of the property known as "Bellevue" until October 31, 1856.[46] As in the Rayapa–Samoumoutapoullé accord, Vellaydon assumed responsibility for selling the sugar crop in Port Louis and, furthermore, was delegated to use the proceeds from the crop's sale to settle an outstanding debt of $1,250 against the 150-arpent estate. By the early 1860s, some Indian businessmen were involved in financing sugar estate operations. Early in 1860, for example, Mylapoor Moonisamy, a merchant and landowner who resided in Port Louis, loaned $12,000 to Jean François Chavrimoutou and Tatouvon Maniacara for the express purpose of covering their production costs. Later that same year, Moonisamy advanced another $6,000 to Chavrimoutou for the same purpose.[47]

The size and composition of the immigrant business community during the 1850s and 1860s precluded large-scale Indian commercial involvement in the sugar industry before the latter part of the century. Businessmen such as Vellaydon and Moonisamy nevertheless established the precedents other Indian entrepreneurs would follow. The notarial record demonstrates that one of the reasons individuals such as Seewoodharry Bhaguth and Matapoorsad would play such an active role in the *grand morcellement* stemmed from the fact that, like Annassamy, Manackjee, Vellaydon, and Moonisamy, they too could mobilize large sums of ready cash. Matapoorsad, for example, paid $7,000 down toward the $10,000 purchase price of the 103-arpent section of "Belle Mare" he bought from Auguste Blaize in June, 1881.[48] On other occasions, these entrepreneurs paid the full purchase price at the time of a sale's formal completion. Seewoodharry and Monogilal did so in 1878 when they purchased 156 arpents from James Currie for $6,000 (Rs. 12,000), and again the following year when they paid Messrs. Constantin, Naz, and Edwards $15,000 for three tracts of land totaling 158 arpents.[49]

Financing for these purchases came from various sources, one of which was loans from planters, local financial institutions, and other Indian businessmen in the colony. The extent to which planters underwrote such ventures is difficult to ascertain, but individual estate-owners such as André Bourgault du Coudray were not averse to doing so; on January 9, 1877, du Coudray loaned $4,000 to Indur, no. 203,091, a peddler, and his wife, Dowtuteea, no. 188,248, so they could pay off the balance due on 15 arpents they had purchased the day before.[50] Seven years later, Soobanah, no. 290,024, persuaded The Mauritius Fire Insurance Company to loan him Rs. 40,000 for various and sundry purposes.[51] The following year, Soobanah and his partner, Adee Reddy, secured the loan of an additional Rs. 26,000 from Henry Smith, a Plaines

Wilhems landowner.[52] In other instances, Indian businessmen were the ultimate source of capital, as was the case early in 1875 when Essack Mamode, a Port Louis merchant, advanced $18,400 to Goorachand Lalla, Seewoodharry Bhaguth, Soomessur, and Monogilal.[53]

In addition to borrowing money, these entrepreneurs also drew upon the profits generated by their other enterprises. Both Goorachand Lalla and Seewoodharry contracted to clear extensive tracts of forest during the mid-1860s, and they continued to do so through the 1870s. The scale of this activity is best illustrated by their joint purchase in 1873 of the rights to clear 1,771 arpents in Plaines Wilhems for $10,000.[54] Like countless other local proprietors, these entrepreneurs also speculated in land. Such undertakings could be quite lucrative, as Pestonjee Manackjee's sale of the sugar estate he created in 1849–50 demonstrates; the properties which originally cost him $7,250 were sold in 1851 for $17,000.[55]

High rates of return were not the only reason for such speculation. As another transaction involving Seewoodharry Bhaguth demonstrates, the possibility of dramatically improving short-term capital liquidity could overshadow the profit motive *per se*. More specifically, Seewoodharry purchased 131 arpents from Eugène Mancel in April, 1878, for Rs. 7,884, but paid only Rs. 1,000 down and agreed to pay the outstanding balance in four equal payments of Rs. 1,721, due every six months, plus 9 percent interest. Nine months later, Seewoodharry sold the same tract to Célicourt Antelme for Rs. 8,876.75, which gave him a nominal profit of Rs. 922.75, or 11.7 percent, on his original investment.[56] Probably of greater consequence to Seewoodharry, however, was the additional operating capital which this sale placed in his hands. Antelme agreed to pay Rs. 3,713.75 down upon completion of the requisite formalities, the net result of which, assuming that Mancel had been paid the sum due to him on October 3, 1878, was to leave Seewoodharry with Rs. 917 more in cash assets (or an increase of almost 33 percent) than he had originally spent on this property.

As Seewoodharry's career demonstrates, still another factor which helped to ensure these entrepreneurs' success was their ability to cultivate and maintain an extensive web of business relationships within both the Indian and non-Indian communities. By the time of his death in mid-1881, Seewoodharry had dealt with the entire spectrum of colonial society, from the most humble of day-laborers to members of the colony's social, economic, and political elite. Between 1864–81, he purchased or leased land worth more than $37,000 from prominent Franco-Mauritian landowners such as Emile Déroullède and Augustin Perrier, Indian shopkeepers such as Essackjee Ismaël, and sirdars such as

Oodit, no. 171,201. During the same period, he also sold property worth more than $12,300 to the likes of James Currie, a merchant and landowner, and Célicourt Antelme, a member of the Council of Government, leased a large tract of land to Ally Mamode, a Port Louis merchant, and made loans totaling more than $4,000 to landowners such as Pierre Bacy and his wife, carpenters such as Rodolphe Lareservée, and small shopkeepers and businessmen such as Moorghen, no. 295,437, and Gooljar, no. 221,180.

A willingness to share risks and cooperate in the protection of their mutual interests was a third factor which contributed to the success of these entrepreneurs. In addition to buying property and borrowing money together, Goorachand Lalla, Seewoodharry Bhaguth, Monogilal, and Soomessur entrusted one another with their power of attorney to manage their affairs when they were temporarily absent from the colony. During 1878, to cite but one example, Monogilal and Seewoodharry both sold land on Goorachand Lalla's behalf.[57] Equally important, the basic integrity of these relationships was maintained even as the personnel in them changed. Following Seewoodharry's death, his son and principal heir, Rambelas, joined with Monogilal to purchase three tracts of land, to acquire the right to clear 3,650 arpents of forest in Black River, and to borrow Rs. 24,000 from Jean Baptiste Jourde. Rambelas was also the purchaser of record when Goorachand Lalla decided to divest himself of much of his landed property late in 1881.[58]

These qualities would stand Indian entrepreneurs in good stead as the sugar industry came under increasing financial pressure during the 1870s. Like planters elsewhere, Mauritian estate-owners sought to meet the challenges of the day by beginning to consolidate their holdings to improve efficiency and increase productivity, a strategy epitomized by the steady centralization of sugar manufacturing. Despite the savings produced by such measures, modernizing the industry still required considerable capital expenditure, as did attempts to maintain the financial integrity of these estates. The *petit morcellement* had demonstrated the value of subdividing and selling off undeveloped or more marginal tracts of land. Not only had this process permitted estate-owners to mobilize significant amounts of domestic capital for their own use, but the attendant development of a class of peasant proprietors had also promised to solve many of the problems arising from the need to deal with an expensive and often truculent work force. By the early 1870s, it was evident that the colony housed an Old Immigrant population that was willing and able to participate in such a process. Moreover, a sizable coterie of Old Immigrant entrepreneurs who had access to or control of substantial capital resources, extensive connections within both the

Indian and non-Indian communities, and considerable experience in the local real estate market now resided on the island. These qualities made such entrepreneurs ideal social and economic brokers capable of facilitating their countrymen's purchase of land while helping local estate-owners to minimize the financial and other risks which *morcellement* could entail.[59]

Seewoodharry Bhaguth's career underscores the extent to which these entrepreneurs served as crucial point men in the *morcellement* process, especially in those areas of the countryside being cleared and opened to sugar production for the first time. His involvement with the *terrain* Perrier, for example, began two and a half years before he purchased the property when he and Goorachand Lalla contracted to clear this 312-arpent tract over a two-year period.[60] They presumably did so within the allotted time, because Perrier sold the property to Seewoodharry in mid-1875 who promptly announced his plans to sub-divide the property. As was noted earlier, Perrier concurred subject to two conditions: that the plots had to be sold for not less than $50 an arpent, and that the proceeds of these sales would be turned over to the notary of record to liquidate the $7,020 which Seewoodharry owed on the original purchase price of $9,360. Matapoorsad would agree to similar terms in his dealings with August Blaize.

Perrier and Blaize's willingness to extend substantial lines of credit to Seewoodharry and Matapoorsad is a further indication that, on occasion, these Old Immigrant entrepreneurs functioned as *de facto* agents for local estate-owners. The notarial record contains numerous transactions in which Indians serving in this capacity were required to make little or no down-payment on the properties they were buying, and were allowed to pay off outstanding obligations over a period of several years. August Blaize, for example, required an initial payment of only Rs. 1,500 from Matapoorsad and Dame Ramkalia Beeharry when they bought 325 arpents from him on December 7, 1882, for Rs. 20,000. Blaize agreed furthermore that the new owners had to pay him only Rs. 2,500 on December 7, 1883, and that the outstanding balance could be retired thereafter at the rate of Rs. 4,000 a year, plus 9 percent annual interest.[61]

These new proprietors promptly set out to recoup their investment and retire their outstanding debts, an undertaking facilitated by their insistence that those purchasing *morcellement* lands pay the full purchase price at the time of a sale's formal completion (see table 20, p. 140). Seewoodharry, for one, began to sell off sections of the *terrain* Perrier no later than May, 1876; during the next three and a half years, he sold at least 122 arpents from this property for between $60 and $200 an arpent. He and Monogilal moved as expeditiously following their purchase of

156 arpents from James Currie in November, 1878, as did Matapoorsad after his purchase of portions of "Belle Mare" in 1881. As other Indian entrepreneurs followed in their footsteps during the 1880s and 1890s, they too acted promptly to capitalize upon the willingness and the ability of Old Immigrants to pay hard cash for the privilege of becoming a landowner.

The forces set in motion *circa* 1875 steadily gained momentum as the colony's Indian residents became ever more involved in the *morcellement* process. As early as 1881, the increasing number of transactions involving Indians led the director of the Registration and Mortgage Department to observe that his staff was having difficulty keeping up with the requisite paperwork; two years later, he reported that "the increasing number of transfers of property in which Indians are concerned will render it impossible for the present staff to keep up the work."[62] The notarial record reveals the extent to which this process also facilitated socio-economic mobility within the Indian population. Gardeners and other agriculturalists who presumably owned or otherwise had access to land had been particularly prominent players in the local real estate market during the 1860s. However, with the advent of the *grand morcellement*, increasing numbers of laborers began to join the ranks of the colony's Indian smallholders for the first time (see table 25, p. 153).

Census data confirm these trends. The number of Indian "independent proprietors" in the colony climbed from 314 in 1871 to 701 in 1881 and then to 1,074, or almost one-half of all such persons, by 1891. The ranks of immigrant gardeners also swelled, from 7,513 in 1871 to 10,014 in 1881, and the 1891 census would note that the 8,822 Indian gardeners that had enumerated that year were "very frequently landowners."[63] However, if these data illustrate the growth of a class of Indian landowners during the late nineteenth century, they also underscore the need to keep this process of class formation in perspective. In 1891, despite more than a threefold increase in their numbers since 1871, independent proprietors still accounted for a miniscule 1.1 percent of all Indians reporting an occupation. Although thousands of Old Immigrants also became gardeners during this period, they too comprised only a small percentage of the immigrant population, accounting for just 9 percent of the Indian work force in 1881 and again in 1891.

These figures are a potent reminder that many Old Immigrants and Indo-Mauritians did not, and would not, escape from the bonds of wage labor during the late nineteenth and early twentieth centuries. They are also a reminder that *morcellement* was not the only strategy used to deal with the economic exigencies of the day. In 1887, authorities filed their

Table 26. *Sharecropping and Mauritian sugar estates, 1887–1918*

| | (Annual average) | | | |
|---|---|---|---|---|
| Period | % Estates in métayage | Arpents in métayage | % Cultivated estate area in métayage | % Share-cropped land in sugar |
| 1887–89 | 12.8 | 1,835 | 3.6 | 68.0 |
| 1890–94 | 9.1 | 3,438 | 4.7 | 78.3 |
| 1895–99 | 20.9 | 5,599 | 6.9 | 80.8[a] |
| 1900–04 | 26.9 | 6,645 | 7.7 | — |
| 1905–08 | 21.0 | 5,891 | 5.9 | — |
| 1911–14 | — | 23,509 | 17.0 | 94.1 |
| 1915–18 | — | 34,190 | 22.3 | 85.9 |

*Note:* [a] For 1895 only.
*Sources:* BB 1887–1918.

first reports on *métayage*, or sharecropping, in the colony. Unfortunately, the number of persons who earned their living in this manner was never reported. However, the data at our disposal indicate that even if the incidence of *métayage* initially remained low, the advent of the new century soon found increasing numbers of Indo-Mauritians tied to the land in this particular manner (see table 26).

The existence of a distinct class of Indian small planters by the mid-1890s points not only to important changes in local economic relationships during the late nineteenth century, but also to significant changes in the structure of immigrant and Indo-Mauritian society. As the notarial record demonstrates, these social and economic transformations were inextricably linked to one another. A survey of acts from this period reveals, for instance, that many more Indian families began to purchase land during the 1870s than had been the case during previous decades (see table 24, p. 152). The level of this familial activity increased noticeably as the *grand morcellement* got under way, all the more so if many of the joint purchases made by single men and women are regarded as probably having been made by husbands and wives whose marriage had not been formally acknowledged by the colonial state. Work on Indian society in rural Fiji underscores the linkage that could exist between these series of changes. Chandra Jayawardena, for example, notes that the Colonial Sugar Refining Company's decision in the late 1920s to encourage Indian smallholders to grow cane was predicated upon the explicit belief that the success of such a venture depended upon the existence of stable nuclear families in the Indo-Fijian population.[64]

That a greater degree of social structural stability prevailed within the colony's Indian population by the latter part of the nineteenth century is not surprising. The increasingly settled condition of the contractual labor force during the 1870s is indicative of such a trend, as are the increasingly apparent demographic changes in the Indian population after the late 1860s. Emigration from India began to decline noticeably during the 1860s, and by the early 1880s only a handful of new immigrants reached the island's shores each year. At the same time, fewer Old Immigrants returned to India. The cessation of large-scale population movements between India and Mauritius was matched by an ever greater Indo-Mauritian presence in the colony. The 20,209 locally born Indians enumerated in 1861 comprised only one-tenth of the Indian population; two decades later, the island was home to more than 113,000 Indo-Mauritians who accounted for 45 percent of the island's Indian residents. These individuals, like second-generation immigrants elsewhere, knew no other home or way of life and responded accordingly.

A steady diminution of the early disparity between the sexes also contributed to increasing stability within the larger Indian community. The first wave of indentured laborers to reach the colony had reflected the preference for men to work in the cane fields, and by 1839 the ratio of male to female immigrants stood at a staggering 56 to 1. Disparities of this magnitude became the subject of considerable concern to authorities, who saw a close connection between the shortage of Indian women, the lack of "moral restraint" they discerned within the indentured population as a whole, and the attendant difficulties of maintaining law and order. Imperial officials accordingly mandated in 1857 that at least 35 percent of immigrants arriving in the colony had to be women, a figure subsequently raised to 40 percent in 1858 and to 50 percent from 1859 to 1865.[65] This policy, although imperfectly implemented, soon began to have the desired effect. Despite a steady improvement in the proportion of Indian men and women during the 1860s, witnesses appearing before the 1872 Royal Commission of Inquiry nevertheless continued to dwell upon the evils brought about by a shortage of women in the immigrant community.[66]

While several more decades would pass before the Indian population achieved demographic balance, the increasing number of women reaching the island soon led authorities to pay greater attention to marriage among the immigrant population. The first semi-reliable data on this topic date to 1871 when the colony reportedly housed 13,077 married men and 12,368 married women who accounted for 13 and 35 percent respectively of all adult Indian men and women. The number of such men and women remained relatively constant in subsequent censuses. However, as R.R. Kuczynski points out, these figures do not accurately reflect the number of Indian households actually in the colony. Throughout much of the nineteenth century, the colonial government refused to recognize Indian marriages that had not been conducted before a civil status officer. Even after the government made it easier to register marriages performed according to traditional religious rites, many Indians refused to comply with the alien practices needed to legalize a marriage and were accordingly considered to be living in a state of "concubinage." The extent of this practice was first revealed in 1921, when 44,903 Indian men and women were reported to be living in such a state compared to the 28,242 who had been married according to religious rites and the 34,757 who had been married before civil officials.[67]

Aside from marriage, colonial and imperial authorities paid little attention to the ways in which immigrants sought to order their world. The 1872 Royal Commissioners considered the social, moral, and physical condition of the colony's Indian residents, but the two chapters in their report devoted to these topics contain little substantive information about immigrant social organization. As such, we must turn once again to the notarial record for glimpses of the ways and means by which immigrants began to construct a new social universe.

One way in which many immigrants did so, particularly during the first decades of immigration, is suggested by the agreement Poleechetty Gungachetty, no. 337,593, Rungasamy, no. 337,737, and Nelatchee, Rungasamy's wife, made in 1878 concerning the care of Poleechetty's 2-year-old son, Mardaymootoo.[68] According to the terms of this convention, Rungasamy and Nelatchee agreed to care for Mardaymootoo for a period of five years while Poleechetty, in turn, agreed to pay them Rs. 492 toward defraying the cost of his son's food, clothing, medical care, etc. This arrangement seems somewhat unusual at first glance, since the two male principals were not related by blood or marriage, were not of the same caste, and did not come from the same village or district in southern India. However, Poleechetty's decision to entrust his son to someone other than his own kin becomes comprehensible if it is viewed in light of the fact that he and Rungasamy were shipmates (*jehazis* or *jahajies*) who had arrived together aboard the *Medusa* in 1869. Work on the Indo-Fijian community has revealed that the friendship between *jehazis* was a particularly important non-familial tie linking first generation immigrants to one another.[69] Under such circumstances, Rungasamy and Nelatchee would have been the obvious people to care for Mardaymootoo, especially if no members of Poleechetty's own family were to be found in the colony.

While *jehazi* friendships allowed Indian immigrants to develop and institutionalize long-term social relationships, the demographic tumult which characterized Mauritian life until the late 1860s also meant that these relationships remained highly personalized. The mobility of many agricultural workers before 1870 likewise meant that institutions such as temples and mosques functioned as focal points for community organization only among those immigrants who had settled permanently in a particular locale. Many laborers accordingly structured their social universe on the basis of other criteria until the family and the village began to emerge as the basic units of Indian social structure during the 1870s. As the repeated complaints by planters and colonial officials suggest, the Indian sirdar, or overseer, and job contractor provided the nexus around which many early immigrant social and economic relationships were organized and maintained.[70]

Mauritian planters complained bitterly about sirdars throughout the mid-nineteenth century. In 1847, one group of planters in Pamplemousses readily castigated sirdars as idle, cunning, and dissipated "eastern despots" and observed that "it has become a point of great importance to destroy this abominable system, which has frequently the ruinous effect of disorganizing and dis-peopling the Estates."[71] Only one person who appeared before the 1872 Royal Commission of Inquiry testified in favor of the sirdar system; every other witness concurred with the president of the Chamber of Agriculture that sirdars were nothing less than an "agricultural plague."[72]

These complaints reflected the fact that sirdars and job contractors frequently served as the principal mediating link between planters and laborers, thereby depriving estate-owners of the opportunity to exercise direct control over their work force. Their status as brokers between "masters" and "servants" gave sirdars and job contractors considerable influence over not only the circumstances and conditions under which planters secured the agricultural labor they needed, but also over the workers who relied upon them to secure the work they needed to survive. This influence was heightened still further by the tendency for these individuals to serve as the only visible foci around which agricultural workers seemed to organize themselves for social, as well as economic, purposes.

The Royal Commission of 1872 appreciated the importance of the sirdar system, noting that it was,

so entirely consonant with the habits and customs of India, that we fear there would be great difficulty in breaking through it. Any person acquainted with India must be aware that every village is ruled by its "Patel" or headman, and that every trade and craft has either a "Punchayet" (or guild), or head man

(Mookudum), to rule them, and that even the labourers have their "Moo-kudum," to whom they refer or appeal on all occasions; and, although the immigrants are neither of one village, one caste, nor of one trade, they still naturally seek to find a headman or mentor to whom they should refer when in need.[73]

Various sources attest to the ability of these individuals to serve as the linchpin of extensive social and economic networks. Doolub, a job contractor in Grand Port who came to the Royal Commissioners' attention, had 164 men in his employ, only 72 of whom worked on sugar estates. Of the 92 men not working as estate laborers, 67 performed "job contractor's work," 12 could be found in various yards and shops, 6 worked as hawkers, 2 served as carters, and 5 were jewelers.[74] The inventory made after the death of Joydruth Kisnah, no. 210,883, a former sirdar at Rivière des Créoles in Grand Port, illustrates the extent of such ties in other ways. Joydruth's papers included no fewer than 38 promissory notes ranging in value from Rs. 2 to Rs. 730 from 33 persons, many of whom were other Indian immigrants.[75]

Censuses confirm the increasing prominence of sirdars during the mid-nineteenth century. The number of sirdars employed in agriculture climbed from 349 to 672 between 1846 and 1851, and then to 1,639 in 1861 and to 1,964 by 1871. With the advent of the 1880s, however, the number of sirdars in the colony began to decline, and by 1901 there were one-third fewer than there had been 20 years earlier.

This decline is yet another reflection of the changes which heralded a great degree of Indian social structural stability during the latter part of the nineteenth century. The movement toward a smaller, more stable agricultural work force was matched by greater Indian involvement in other sectors of the local economy, while the *grand morcellement* allowed more and more Old Immigrants and their Indo-Mauritian children to establish themselves as smallholders. Among other things, these trends expanded the parameters of immigrant social structure as the sirdar system, while not yet moribund, was increasingly superseded by other forms of socio-economic organization. The family was one such unit; the village was another.

Information on nineteenth- and early twentieth-century Mauritian villages is scarce. Evidence given before the 1872 Royal Commission indicates that Indian villages, separate and distinct from estate camps, appeared in the countryside by the late 1860s and early 1870s, if not before.[76] Raj Virahsawmy holds that the establishment of these villages was linked closely to the development of a class of small landowners,[77] and many of these communities undoubtedly developed in tandem with the *grand morcellement*. Census data reveal that more than one-third of the Indians living in the island's rural districts already resided in towns and villages by 1871; thirty years later, more than 60 percent would do so.

Contemporary accounts of Mauritian life are generally silent about the socio-cultural dynamics of village formation, a silence which remains largely unbroken to the present day. Only K. Hazareesingh has addressed this issue, arguing that traditional forms of Indian village organization were re-established more completely in Mauritius than in other plantation colonies with large immigrant populations.[78] Indirect references to this process in the archival record suggest, however, that Hazareesingh's assessment is somewhat overstated. Official concern about the purported lack of immigrant "moral restraint" rested in part on the belief that the act of emigration undermined the caste system and its rules of social organization and conduct. Work on other overseas Indian communities likewise emphasizes that traditional forms of social reorganization, and the caste system in particular, did not remain intact in these communities. At the heart of such arguments is the assertion that the circumstances of traveling overseas, especially the necessity of eating together while on board ship, and the common nature of their work shattered the ritual purity and occupational specialization that were crucial to maintaining caste in India.[79]

The shattering of ritually defined and hierarchically organized distinctions between groups did not mean, of course, that caste disappeared entirely from the social and cultural landscape. Adrian Mayer and Chandra Jayawardena note that caste status continued to be a factor of potential importance in delimiting some personal relationships, and especially marriage, in these overseas communities.[80] Despite the survival of highly personalized caste distinctions, the apparent failure of the caste system *per se* to serve as the basis of large-scale immigrant social organization raises the question of just what were the foundations upon which Indian immigrants began to structure new socio-cultural institutions during the latter part of the nineteenth century.

What we know about the 275 men and women who purchased plots during the subdivision of "Belle Mare" estate in Flacq, the *terrains* Currie and Vacher in Plaines Wilhems, and the *terrain* Jacques in Savanne between 1875 and 1891 throw the socio-cultural dynamics of Indian life at the end of the century into sharper relief. In the first instance, these data illustrate the diverse caste status of the immigrants who reached the colony; no fewer than 49 different castes and sub-castes can be identified. A comprehensive survey of caste in nineteenth-century Mauritius remains to be undertaken, but work on Fiji has revealed that hundreds of castes and sub-castes, ranging from the highest to those of the lowest ritual standing, were to be found among overseas Indians.[81] Secondly, these data suggest that it was not un-common for persons of the same or comparable caste status to purchase land near one another in a specific locality. The relatively large number of Chamars and Dosads who participated in the subdivision of "Belle Mare" is one such example. In other cases, religion functioned in lieu of caste as a variable which could influence decisions about purchasing portions of a particular estate; on the *terrain* Vacher, for instance, Muslims accounted for one-third of those who acquired land.

These data suggest that caste status continued to be a somewhat more important factor in shaping early immigrant social organization than previous scholarship on overseas Indian communities has supposed. A survey of sales made jointly to immigrants who were not related either by blood or by marriage lends support to such a conclusion; in 34 of 80 such transactions recorded by three notaries between 1860 and 1889, the partners in question were of the same caste. However, if figures such as these suggest that caste (or religion, in the case of Muslims) helped to shape early Indian society to a greater degree than previously supposed, they also suggest that the depth and extent of caste's impact upon immigrant social structure and organization could vary widely from place to place. On the *terrain* Jacques, for example, caste or religious affiliation were apparently of little or no consequence in decisions to purchase portions of the estate. The fact that a majority of the 80 joint purchases noted above were made by persons of different caste likewise suggests that caste or religion were factors of widely varying importance to the structuring of life in Indian villages during the latter part of the nineteenth century.

A more important factor in the organization of community life seems to have been an immigrant's place of origin. Although the Old Immi-grants who purchased *morcellement* lands came from throughout northern and southern India, the notarial record indicates a certain propensity for immigrants from the same home district in India to settle near one another. Almost one-half of those who bought portions of the *terrain* Currie, for instance, came from one district in Bihar: Arrah. Even when the immigrants who purchased sections of a particular property came from widely separated parts of the sub-continent, there are indica-tions of a tendency for persons from adjoining home districts in India to settle near one another. The largest contingents of new proprietors at "Belle Mare" came from Arrah and its neighboring districts of Gaya in Bihar and Ghazipur in Oudh, with these three districts accounting for more than one-half of all persons purchasing portions of the estate. A similar pattern can be found on the *terrain* Vacher. Implicit in these patterns was the tendency for Old Immigrants to settle near other persons who spoke the same language or dialect, engaged in similar cultural practices, and shared underlying beliefs about the ways in which social relations should be structured.

The transformations in Indian social and economic life that began during the 1870s continued as the nineteenth century gave way to the twentieth. With the exception of a modest surge in immigration from 1900 to 1902 and again in 1904, only several hundred new immigrants reached the island's shores each year, and in 1910 even this influx ceased when the emigration of indentured laborers to Mauritius formally came to an end. Social stability within the Indian community increased as the early disparity between the sexes continued to diminish, the family replaced the sirdar and job contractor as the focal point of social organization, the percentage of Indo-Mauritians increased, and laborers came to live in villages in which certain shared assumptions about how the world should be ordered replaced labor contracts as the foundation upon which social relationships rested.

During this period, growing numbers of Indians also exploited the opportunities presented by the *grand morcellement* to become small land-owners in their own right. Indian smallholders had 27,928 arpents in cane in 1910, or approximately one-fifth of the total area devoted to sugar production. This era also found more direct Indian commercial involvement in sugar production and marketing. *Circa* 1914, for example, the assets of A.G. Hossen & Co. included the 1,500 arpent "Bel Air" sugar estate in Pamplemousses and its factory which was capable of processing from 30 to 40 tons of cane a day.[82] Other Indian merchant houses such as Currimji Jeewanji & Co., Coo-Mootoosamy & Co., and V. Ayassamy also owned or had shares in sugar estates or were heavily involved in the exportation of sugar.[83]

Indian involvement in sugar production continued to expand during World War I and into the early 1920s. The net value of Indian investment in real estate soared 280 percent, to an average of almost Rs. 1,400,000 a year, during the war years, and doubled yet again during the first half of the 1920s (see table 21, p. 142). By 1920, Indian smallholders and estate-owners were farming 54,000 arpents in cane compared to 35,480 arpents just six years earlier. These developments, coupled with the expansion of *métayage*, meant that by 1920 the responsibility for cultivating almost 45 percent of all land devoted to cane rested in Indian hands.

While these trends attest to the growing Indian involvement in the local sugar industry during the first decades of the twentieth century and to the importance of that participation, other data indicate that the significance of this activity to colonial economic life must also be carefully qualified. We may note, for instance, that while the *grand morcellement* facilitated the rise of an Indian small planter class, this class remained comparatively small; in 1921, an Indian population of some 166,000 adults included only 3,036 "planters." An agricultural census in 1930 would subsequently reveal that more than 91 percent of the 14,495 smallholdings planted in sugar encompassed no more than 1.6 acres, and that the average size of Indian holdings off the estates was 2.5 acres compared to 15.1 acres for non-Indians.[84]

These data suggest that immigrant access to land and the establishment of an Indian small planter class during the late nineteenth and early twentieth centuries proved ultimately to be something of a mixed blessing for the Mauritian sugar industry. On the one hand, there can be no doubt that the *grand morcellement* allowed many planters to reduce their operating expenses by shifting some of their labor and other production costs onto the shoulders of Indian small planters. The subdivision of estates also allowed them to meet some of their short-term capital needs by tapping into the significant financial resources at the disposal of the larger Indian population. These benefits to the industry were matched, in turn, by those which accrued to some Old Immigrants and allowed them and their children to escape the confines of wage labor and to become potentially independent landowners in their own right.

However, this independence was often more apparent than real because the great majority of small planters depended more upon the wages they received from temporary employment on the large sugar estates for their livelihood than they did upon the income derived from the sale of their cane.[85] This state of affairs may be traced to the fact that small planters, like large estate-owners, could not escape the consequences of the colony's continuing reliance upon domestic capital. The Royal Commissioners who investigated the colony's financial condition in 1909 noted specifically that the typical small planter "generally sinks all of his money in the purchase of land, and has either to borrow for his working expenses or to leave his land practically uncultivated."[86]

Access to working capital was crucial to small-planter success because, in many instances, the land they had acquired was uncleared or less fertile than that still held by the large estates.[87] Their inability to purchase fertilizer and new canes or to hire the additional labor needed to work their land had a corresponding impact upon sugar production. In 1907, to cite but one example, Indians cultivated 30 percent of the area devoted to sugar but produced only 22 percent of the canes grown.[88] While large estates commonly produced crops of 20 tons or more of cane per arpent, small planters often realized only from 8 to 11 tons per arpent. Figures such as these prompted the 1909 Royal Commissioners to recommend not only that £15,000 of a proposed £115,000 loan to the sugar industry be reserved for small planters, but also that co-operative credit societies be created to provide small planters with ready access to the operating capital they needed.[89]

The Commissioners' recommendations led to the establishment of such societies in 1913, but these co-operatives failed to function as planned, in part because of a lack of governmental support; the colonial administration did not appoint a full-time, trained extension officer to help these societies until 1933. Despite steady growth in their numbers in the years immediately after 1913, many co-operatives soon found themselves in financial straits early in the 1920s because of small and stagnant (or declining) membership rolls and low levels of capitalization. The collapse of world sugar prices in the early 1920s had a pronounced impact upon these societies, reducing their ability to make loans as their capital base shrank and more and more outstanding loans were not repaid on schedule.[90]

The financial constraints under which small planters lived and worked became even more restrictive as the 1920s drew to a close. In his 1929 report on the colony's sugar industry, Sir Francis Watts noted that the great majority of Mauritian smallholders were "for the most part without adequate capital, their cultivation methods are poor, and their yields small, ranging from around 7 to 9 tons per acre."[91] This decline in small-planter productivity compared to earlier in the century was matched by a marked drop in overall Indian cane production; in 1928, Indians produced only one-quarter of the sugar crop despite cultivating 43 percent of the land devoted to cane.

The Great Depression exposed the precarious financial condition of Mauritian small planters in graphic detail. The price of sugar, already low in 1929, plunged still further as the Depression deepened during the early 1930s, with the result that ever-increasing numbers of small planters soon found themselves with their backs against the wall. The area in cane being cultivated by Indians, which had already declined from a high of 83,000 arpents in 1922, dropped precipitously, from some 68,500 arpents in 1928–29 to 52,740 arpents in 1930. The value of the community's real estate holdings began to plummet as well as more and more smallholders were forced to dispose of their property in order to survive. As opportunities for employment declined or disappeared altogether, the number of Indians described as destitute by the colonial government increased, from 11.2 per thousand in 1929, to 17.9 per thousand in 1931, and then to 27.6 per thousand in 1935. Other indices of Indo-Mauritian financial well-being, such as the value of remittances to India, also declined dramatically, from an annual average of Rs. 246,343 between 1921 and 1930 to Rs. 83,835 between 1931 and 1935.

The consequences of Mauritius' dependence upon sugar, a fickle world market, and the limited resources of domestic capital began to manifest themselves in local political life during the mid-1930s. The inability of the colonial or imperial governments to deal with the social and economic distress of the day spurred the establishment in 1936 of the Mauritius Labour Party, the first political organization devoted to protecting the interests of the colony's agricultural workers. The "Uba" cane riots the following year would propel small planters toward greater political activism as they too sought to mitigate the conditions under which they had to live and work.[92] In so doing, the descendants of the men and women once hailed as the regenerators of agricultural prosperity would begin to step firmly beyond the confines of their gardens of sugar and onto the broader stage of Mauritian life.

# Conclusion

Events in Mauritius during the eighteenth and nineteenth centuries had an impact far beyond the shores of this seemingly obscure island in the southwestern Indian Ocean. The local demand for servile labor not only spurred the expansion of the Malagasy and East African slave trades after 1770,[1] but also made the island a center of illegal slave-trading during the 1810s and early 1820s, the repercussions of which reached from London to Antananarivo, Kilwa, Muscat, and Calcutta. The insurrection which followed the appointment in 1832 of the abolitionist John Jeremie as the colony's attorney-general exposed the false premises and defective administrative agencies upon which Britain's policy of slave amelioration rested, and contributed to its abandonment in favor of emancipation by imperial statute.[2] During the 1830s and 1840s, Mauritius became the crucial test case for the use of indentured labor in the colonial plantation world.[3] The success of the Mauritian experiment with Indian immigration in turn encouraged the emigration of hundreds of thousands of African, Chinese, Indian, Japanese, Javanese, and Melanesian workers to the far-flung reaches of the European colonial empires, and beyond, before these labor trades came to an end early in the twentieth century.[4]

Mauritius is important historically, however, for reasons other than its impact upon the Indian Ocean slave trades, British imperial policy-making, and social and economic life in various parts of the colonial world. The introduction notes that, in many respects, our understanding of the colonial plantation experience remains incomplete. At the heart of this problem is the propensity toward compartmentalized studies which obscure both the continuities and differences between the pre- and post-emancipation eras, veil the shared experiences of seemingly separate and distinct groups, and leave important facets of the relationship between capital and local socio-economic institutions unexplored. The consequences of this preoccupation with the particular have been compounded by a reliance upon a limited number of primary source materials, a reluctance to compare plantation systems in different parts of the world, and an aversion to drawing upon the potential insights offered by other disciplines.

The key to understanding the Mauritian experience between 1721 and the mid-1930s, like that of other colonial plantation systems, is to be found in the complex and often nuanced patterns of interaction between labor and capital. The Mauritian case study also illustrates the value of examining the local history of plantation societies as part of the processes of global capitalist development.[5] There can be little doubt that the general outlines of the island's history were framed by forces far beyond local control. From its initial settlement by the Dutch in 1638 until independence in 1968, Mauritius remained a European colonial possession, and metropolitan interests and dicta played a correspondingly important role in shaping the island's history. The decrees which opened Port Louis to free trade during the late eighteenth century are a salient case in point. Eighteenth-century attempts to develop cotton, indigo, and spice plantations likewise point to Mauritius' early incorporation into an expanding capitalist world economy, while developments during the nineteenth century highlight the contradictions inherent in such a process. Sugar, the crop which had rescued colonial fortunes early in the nineteenth century, soon proved to be as much a bane as it was a boon as the Mauritian industry found itself at the mercy of a world market over which it had little control.

If the Mauritian case study illustrates the value of examining the history of plantation systems in light of such global processes, it also demonstrates that it would be a mistake to presume that the course of a colony's social and economic history was in any way pre-ordained. The historical record demonstrates, for example, that Mauritian colonists could and did have a considerable say in their dealings with Paris and London. As their opposition to the suppression of the slave trade during the 1790s and again during the first years of British rule attest, a well-developed sense of class identity, coupled with the tactical advantages conferred by their geographical isolation, allowed the Franco-Mauritian community to co-opt or intimidate imperial officials and to subvert metropolitan directives, often with impunity.

The dynamics of Mauritian history cannot be explained, however, only in terms of the local elite. Compelling research in recent years has documented the various ways and means by which workers in other parts of the colonial plantation world sought to modify the productive process and social relations of production, and Mauritian slaves and indentured laborers were no exception. Their well-documented attempts to evade or subvert the prevailing economic order are the most visible manifestation of their willingness to try to shape their own destiny. Large numbers of slaves fled from their masters each year during the late eighteenth century despite the harsh penalties for doing so, and even larger numbers of bondsmen and apprentices marooned during the early nineteenth century. Equally large percentages of the indentured work force soon followed in their footsteps.

Like their counterparts elsewhere in the colonial world, Mauritian estate-owners and colonial authorities reacted vigorously against the deserters and vagrants in their midst, and thousands of men, women, and children suffered accordingly. The suffering endured by slaves and indentured workers, their resistance to oppression and exploitation, and the ways in which white minority populations sought to maintain their dominance are recurrent themes in colonial plantation historiography. This emphasis upon the violent and coercive nature of these systems is in part a legacy of nineteenth-century abolitionism, its preoccupation with the horrors of slavery, and its concern that the recruitment of indentured labor heralded the advent of a "new system of slavery." The scholarly fascination with these topics also reflects the influence of Weberian ideas about the nature of complex societies. In his theory of social and economic organization, Max Weber held that associative relationships were either voluntarily agreed to or forcibly created, and that even those entered into voluntarily were marked by "a large measure of imposi-tion."[6] Similar interests and concerns pervade Marxian-inspired para-digms in which "master–servant" relations are viewed as having been shaped by the demands of capitalist modes of production.[7]

That coercion and suffering were an integral part of life for many slaves, apprentices, and indentured laborers is undeniable, and colonial plantation labor relations cannot be understood without due considera-tion of these facts of life. However, while the interest in these topics has yielded important insights into the ways in which these systems worked, the end result is also ultimately a rather static and one-dimensional picture of plantation labor relations. Studies of maroonage, to cite a prominent example, have largely ignored the question of the extent to which desertion rates changed through time, much less why they did so. The propensity to view slaves and indentured workers only as laborers trapped in exploitative situations, and not as the consumers, gardeners, landowners, parents, shopkeepers, traders, etc., they also happened to be, or became, has likewise limited our understanding of colonial social and economic relationships in general and the dynamics of local labor relations in particular.

That slaves and indentured workers were much more than just laborers underscores the need to transcend economically deterministic models of colonial labor relations and consider the extent to which social and cultural considerations also shaped these relationships. Anthropologists have long appreciated that power is an integral part of all social relationships, even when it remains latent or unused, that power relationships are always reciprocal, albeit differentially so, and that the use of force is a crude and expensive way of maintaining social order over the long term. They have also noted that an emphasis upon the legal and quasi-legal mechanisms of social control can obscure the extent to which other factors can influence public order.[8] Equally important is the attendant acknowledgment that the perception of what constitutes social order is a variable property in any society, and especially so in plural societies, a point driven home by recent work on colonial Sumatra and Fiji.[9]

The history of desertion and illegal absence in colonial Mauritius underscores the need to take a more holistic view of maroonage and the measures taken to suppress it, and to examine the social relations of production in plantation systems as an interactive process between the various components of colonial society that was continually being conditioned by factors such as changes in technology, local social, economic, and political institutions, or world markets.[10] The fact that the repression generated by fear and racism failed to stem the tide of desertion confirms the importance of doing so. Slave maroonage rates remained constant at about 5 percent a year during the late eighteenth century, and then soared dramatically to more than 11 percent a year by the early 1820s. The substitution of indentured for servile labor did not bring an end to this problem for Mauritian estate-owners. Despite constant tinkering with the local labor laws and regular "maroon" hunts by the colony's police, high rates of illegal absence, desertion, and vagrancy remained an integral part of Mauritian life well into the latter part of the nineteenth century.

These data are of interest on several counts. In the first instance, they illustrate the limited effectiveness of coercive mechanisms of social control over the long term in even the most repressive of plantation systems. Corporal punishment, imprisonment, heavy fines, and even the threat of death did not dissuade large numbers of slaves, apprentices, and indentured laborers from deserting their masters or employers. Accordingly, we would do well to remember, as Ann Stoler and Doug Munro remind us, that persuasion and accommodation, as well as coercion, were integral components of plantation labor relations.[11] Secondly, the high rates of desertion both before and after formal emancipation, the sameness of the complaints about the threat Indian deserters posed to the colony's well-being, and the heritage of the labor ordinances enacted after 1835 point up the structural continuities between the pre- and post-emancipation eras in Mauritius and other plantation colonies. If the mid-nineteenth century did not witness the creation of "new systems of slavery" *per se*, as some historians have argued, it was nevertheless an era during which colonial labor relations continued to be colored by many of the attitudes, beliefs, and traditions associated with slavery.

Such continuities in the fabric of eighteenth- and nineteenth-century Mauritian life do not mean, of course, that the texture of colonial life remained unaltered; the nature of maroon activity during the 1820s demonstrates otherwise. It is tempting to view these changes as being the product of the drive to ameliorate the conditions of slavery, that is, a growing reluctance to sanction the use of the whip and the gun led inevitably to higher desertion rates. However, to attribute these trends largely to modifications of government policy is to ignore the socio-economic context within which desertion flourished, and especially the impact which demographic changes and the restructuring of the colonial economy could have on local labor relations.

Recent work on labor bargaining by slaves in the Americas underlines the need to take such variables into consideration.[12] Census data point not only to significant changes in the size and age and sexual composition of the Mauritian slave population by the 1820s, but also to its increasing creolization. These data also attest to the rapid growth of a native-born free population of color, many of whose members maintained close ties with their enslaved brethren. There can be little doubt that the growth of these creole populations contributed to the changing ideology of maroonage hinted at in the fugitive slave registers of the day, and confirmed by the complaints slaves lodged with the Protector of Slaves after 1829. Slave-owners can hardly have been ignorant of these developments, and it is reasonable to assume that white perceptions of maroon activity changed accordingly. As the case of the slave Azoline suggests, by the 1820s certain kinds of maroon activity were probably perceived, and perhaps were even tolerated to a certain extent, as part of the daily give-and-take between masters and slaves rather than as a threat to the colonial order *per se*.

Similar demographic trends must be taken into account whenever illegal absence, desertion, and vagrancy during the post-emancipation era are discussed. Moreover, as work on British attitudes toward Indian marriage in Fiji demonstrates, attention must also be paid to the ways in which culture shaped the social relations of production.[13] Mauritian planters did not complain incessantly about sirdars and Indian job contractors because they had nothing better to do. Their fulminations against men they described as an "agricultural plague" underscore the important, if not crucial, role these individuals played in organizing and managing the plantation work force during the mid-nineteenth century.

Their importance stemmed from the fact that they functioned in a manner consistent with traditional forms of Indian social and economic organization, and were accordingly well-suited to serve as brokers who could mediate between different social and cultural traditions.[14] As such, sirdars and job contractors could, on the one hand, maintain at least some semblance of what planters thought should be the proper relationship between "masters" and "servants." On the other hand, their standing *vis-à-vis* their countrymen also ensured that sirdars and job contractors were able to limit the control planters exercised over the workers in their employ.

Sirdars and job contractors were not the only such brokers in nineteenth-century Mauritius. The notarial record indicates that some free persons of color clearly functioned in a similar manner during the *petit morcellement*, if not before. Their ability to do so, like that of sirdars and job contractors, was governed by several factors, one of which was the size of the populations in question. *Gens de couleur* comprised one-fifth of the island's total population and two-thirds of its free inhabitants by 1830, while the consequences of Indian immigration were even more profound. Colonial authorities appreciated that the sheer weight of numbers could have a marked impact upon various aspects of the island's social and economic life. The Protector of Immigrants, for one, noted that the massive influx of Indian laborers during the 1850s depressed wages for even the most skilled workmen, thereby consigning many former apprentices once again to the kind of poverty from which they had seemingly begun to escape. In other instances, the impact of these demographic changes was more subtle but no less pronounced. The successful ex-apprentice withdrawal from the sugar estates is a case in point; their ability to do so was clearly facilitated by the presence of a large free colored population willing and able to intercede on their behalf.

The potential power conferred by numbers nevertheless counts for little if the populations in question are fragmented or lack reasonably well-defined and stable institutions capable of mobilizing and managing resources effectively. The marginal status of Mauritian *gens de couleur* prior to the 1820s may be traced in no small measure to the cultural diversity and social anomalies which characterized this population into the early nineteenth century. Similar problems plagued the Indian immigrant population until the end of the century, with similar consequences. However, as these two communities developed better articulated forms of social organization, segments of both populations began to have a greater say in shaping the contours of colonial life. The Commission of Eastern Inquiry appreciated that the existence of a well-developed and institutionalized sense of corporate social identity was behind the free colored attack on the local color bar during the 1820s, and based their recommendation to abolish this bar in part on the fact that such a sense of community existed. A similar trend can be discerned within the immigrant population where the first signs of political awareness coincided with the emergence during the 1870s and 1880s of the family and the village as the foci of Indian social and economic life.

If Mauritian labor relations cannot be understood without due consideration of such socio-demographic changes, neither can they be understood without appropriate reference to the economic realities of the day. The conventional wisdom in plantation studies holds that the hard times sugar and other such colonies experienced because of their dependence upon a single commodity and a fickle world market led to even harsher labor regimes as local proprietors or metropolitan interests acted to cut costs and maximize production in an attempt to remain profitable. The marked changes in the tenor and tone of local labor relations that can be discerned as beginning in the late 1860s indicate, however, that economic distress did not necessarily lead to a deterioration in living and working conditions for agricultural workers. The circumstances surrounding the *petit* and *grand morcellements* suggest, in fact, that financial distress could lead just as easily to a relative improvement in the social relations of production, especially if the laborers in question were themselves persons of some economic consequence.

That *gens de couleur*, ex-apprentices, and Indian immigrants could influence their own destiny as well as that of the larger society of which they were an integral part may be traced to their control of land and capital. More than twenty-five years ago, David Cohen and Jack Greene argued that their exploitation of the opportunities created by the agricultural revolutions of the nineteenth century allowed free populations of color to play a special, if not pivotal, role in the evolution of New World slave plantation societies.[15] The same can be said of Mauritius, where the fortunes of the local sugar industry afforded first *gens de couleur*, then ex-apprentices, and finally Old Immigrants with opportunities to become smallholders, and sometimes even estate-owners, in their own right.

The development of small planter classes or semi-proletarianized peasantries is regarded as one of the more important strategies plantation owners used to ensure their economic survival during the nineteenth and early twentieth centuries.[16] However, if there is a scholarly consensus that the ultimate goal of such endeavors was to allow workers to achieve some degree of economic self-sufficiency, there is considerable debate about the underlying dynamics of this process of class formation. On the one hand there are those who argue that undertakings such as estate *morcellement* were little more than a capitalist ploy to shift production expenses such as the cost of workers' food, clothing, housing, and medical care onto the backs of an emergent peasantry. On the other hand there are those who view these developments as a bid by workers to free themselves from repressive systems of labor control.

As the course of the *petit* and *grand morcellements* demonstrate, the interests of capital and labor were not necessarily mutually exclusive or antithetical to one another. Beginning in 1839 and again in the mid-1870s, Mauritian planters acted in a completely rational manner to protect their way of life. In so doing, their interests coincided with those of many ex-apprentices and Old Immigrants for whom the ownership of even a small plot of land held out the promise of not only escaping the rigors of wage labor, but also improving the quality of their lives and those of their children. At the heart of this mutuality of interests was the colony's dependence upon locally generated and controlled capital.

To argue the importance of domestic capital in shaping the Mauritian experience does not imply that the island remained isolated from or untouched by the rise of the modern capitalist world economy. The Ile de France prospered during the late eighteenth century precisely because it provided European merchants with a convenient venue where they could conduct business with the larger Indian Ocean world. The colony was also no stranger to European financial interests, especially during the 1830s and 1840s when the sugar industry attracted significant British investment. However, as imperial authorities appreciated, metropolitan capital ultimately played a small role in Mauritian agricultural life. Local estate-owners accordingly had to rely upon their own financial resources to survive, and especially upon the income generated by sale of their crop on the world market. When the world market price for sugar was high, the industry flourished, but when falling prices exposed the structural weaknesses in the local system of crop finance, planters were left with few options. While some relied upon tactics such as sharecropping to deal with the problems created by an imperfect capital market,[17] others sought to tap into the financial resources in the hands of the very people upon whose labor their fortunes already depended.

That Mauritian *gens de couleur*, ex-apprentices, and Old Immigrants controlled significant economic resources comes as no real surprise. Studies of plantation colonies in the New World have, after all, occasionally noted the large sums of cash in slave hands and discussed how some bondsmen even managed to acquire what passed locally for small fortunes. Despite such evidence, there nevertheless continues to be a widespread sense of incredulity among historians that agricultural and other workers, whether servile or indentured, could amass significant capital resources, much less use them in ways that had potentially profound implications for local economies. The attendant failure to explore how such resources were accumulated may be traced to the assertion that colonial plantation economies were driven by metropolitan capital. An unwillingness to probe the dynamics of local social and economic relationships more deeply is also to blame, as is the already noted reluctance to regard slaves, freedmen, and indentured laborers as playing any other substantive role in economic life than that of fieldhand or household servant.

The archival record reveals that large numbers of Mauritian *gens de couleur*, ex-apprentices, and Old Immigrants possessed significant financial resources, and that these resources permitted them to exploit the opportunities created by the economic crises of the nineteenth century and to become players of some consequence on the local scene. By 1830, the free population of color controlled perhaps one-fifth, if not more, of the island's agricultural wealth. The ability of 9,000 apprentices to purchase their freedom before March 31, 1839, at a cost of at least $1,800,000, together with the high rates of payment-in-full made during the *petit morcellement*, indicates that many of these former slaves had sizable sums at their disposal. Indian immigrants soon flexed their financial muscles as well, investing more than Rs. 24,000,000 in real estate between 1864 and 1900 and accounting for one-third of the value of all property changing hands by the beginning of the new century.

Control of capital resources was not the only factor, however, which dictated the extent to which *gens de couleur*, former apprentices, and Indian immigrants shaped the contours of nineteenth-century Mauritian economic life. Of equal, if not greater, importance was the ability of these new proprietors to consolidate their position in the wake of the *petit* and *grand morcellements*. As the census of 1851 and the notarial record reveal, many of the ex-apprentice smallholders enumerated in 1846 returned to the ranks of the colony's landless proletariat soon after the *petit morcellement* came to an end. The Indian small planter class that took shape after 1875, on the other hand, continued to increase in size and prominence well into the twentieth century.

Contemporary accounts are silent about the reasons why one community of smallholders failed to consolidate its position while another did so successfully. To those observers who were aware of them, these developments served only to confirm their belief that the local Creole (i.e., of African or Malagasy descent) population was one in which the forces of ignorance, indolence, and insubordination ran riot, while the emergence of an Indian small-planter class proved that immigration had indeed allowed many men and women to escape the grinding poverty in which they would otherwise have languished. Modern historians have likewise said little about these developments, partly because of their tendency to ignore Creole populations after 1839, and partly because the scholarship on overseas Indian communities has been driven by the same issues and concerns that preoccupied nineteenth-century imperial apologists of indentured labor.

The argument could be made that the fortunes of these two communities depended ultimately upon their size, demographic structure, or the extent of their involvement in the plantation sector of the colonial economy: for example, the small size of the Creole population relative to the number of Indian immigrants in the colony, together with the decision by ex-apprentices to withdraw from plantation labor, placed this community at a distinct disadvantage in the struggle to accumulate capital resources. As the preceding pages have demonstrated, reconstructing the social and economic history of Mauritius and other plantation colonies must take these factors into consideration. A closer reading of the archival record indicates, however, that the failure of Creole smallholders to hold their own after the *petit morcellement* cannot be explained only in terms of these variables. Due attention must also be paid to the structural constraints which limited the ability of these individuals to acquire the operating and developmental capital that was crucial to their long-term survival.

Mauritian authorities noted throughout the mid-nineteenth century that while many of the island's Creole residents possessed or had access to the money needed to purchase a small plot of land, they often lacked the fiscal resources needed to develop their property. Implicit in these remarks is an acknowledgment that the colony's credit institutions remained poorly developed. One of the striking features of economic life at this time is the absence of a Creole commercial community capable of mobilizing and extending the credit needed by many of the island's small proprietors. Censuses reveal, for example, that relatively few *gens de couleur* engaged in commerce and trade during the first decades of the nineteenth century, and that most of these who did so were individuals of modest means whose ability to extend lines of credit was correspondingly limited. Furthermore, the notarial record indicates that the interests of these free colored businessmen who could be found on the island were centered largely upon Port Louis and its immediate environs, a fact of economic life which further restricted smallholder access to the credit they needed to survive, much less prosper.

On the eve of the *grand morcellement* some twenty-five years later, by comparison, there is every indication that this situation had changed radically. The presence of thousands of Indian hawkers, peddlers, and shopkeepers in the colony provided the foundation for a network of credit services which reached from Port Louis into the smallest hamlet in the most remote part of the island. Equally important, as the careers of Goorachand Lalla, Seewoodharry Bhaguth, and their associates demonstrate, and work on Indian entrepreneurs elsewhere in the Indian Ocean basin confirms,[18] the presence of wealthy Indian merchants and established Indian merchant houses in Port Louis held out the prospect that, should the need arise, small planters might even be able to tap, albeit indirectly, into the capital reserves of the great commercial networks based in Gujerat, Calcutta, and Madras.

If the history of Mauritian slaves, freedmen, and indentured laborers attests to the ability of such populations to put their stamp upon the colonial plantation experience, the Mauritian case study also reminds us of the need to keep these accomplishments in perspective. We must remember, for example, that while many of the island's Creole and Indian residents secured some measure of control over their own destinies during the nineteenth and early twentieth centuries, many more did not. While high rates of illegal absence and desertion confirm the willingness of slaves and indentured laborers to resist oppression and expand their own social and economic horizons, maroon activity did not, in and of itself, lead to slavery's demise or to a noticeable improvement in post-emancipation labor relations. While the *petit* and *grand morcellements* permitted many men, women, and children to escape from the immediate confines of wage labor, land-ownership proved to be no guarantee of social or economic mobility. As the course of events would demonstrate time and again, to become a gardener of sugar was one thing, to become master of the garden was something else.

# Notes

## INTRODUCTION

1 *MRC*, para. 61.
2 AR 1868, para. 69. PP 1870 XLIX [C. 151], p. 34.
3 AR 1886, para. 4. PP 1888 LXXII [C. 5249], No. 2.
4 AR 1896, p. 22. PP 1898 LIX [C. 8650–13].
5 Bowman 1991, pp. 112–22.
6 Adamson 1972; Sheridan 1973, especially chap. 12; Eisenberg 1974.
7 Deerr 1950, pp. 490–91.
8 Galloway 1989, chap. 6.
9 Wolf and Mintz 1957; Best 1968.
10 Beckford 1970, 1972.
11 Mandle 1972; Benn 1974; Bernstein and Pitt 1974.
12 Cooper 1977, 1980; Lovejoy 1978, 1979.
13 Van Zwanenberg 1975; Knapman 1987.
14 Silverman 1987; Stern 1988.
15 Lobdell 1972.
16 Graves and Richardson 1980; Richardson 1982.
17 Schnakenbourg 1984; Zahedieh 1986; Menard 1994.
18 Higman 1984; Watts 1987.
19 Handler 1974.
20 A noteworthy step toward correcting this deficiency is Look Lai 1993.
21 Watson 1980; Lal, Munro, and Beechert 1993; M. Klein 1993.
22 Allen 1995; Munro 1995a, 1995b.
23 Carter 1994, 1995, 1996.
24 Glassman 1991, p. 287.
25 Besson 1992, p. 209.
26 Sakarai 1980, 1981; Clarence-Smith 1988.

## 1 CREATING A GARDEN OF SUGAR: LAND, LABOR, AND CAPITAL, 1721–1936

1 CL: Orig. Ms., Maximillien Wiklinsky, "Voyage aux îles de France et de Bourbon et dans l'Inde (1769–70)," p. 76. Wiklinsky first arrived in the Ile de France in August, 1769 (*DBM*, p. 446).
2 A. North-Coombes 1979.
3 de Nettancourt 1979.

4  Lagesse 1978; Ly-Tio-Fane Pineo 1993.
5  Ly-Tio-Fane 1958, 1970.
6  Ly-Tio-Fane 1995. See also Toussaint 1954.
7  Toussaint 1977, p. 21, and 1974, p. 53, respectively.
8  Toussaint 1982, p. 124.
9  A. North-Coombes 1937, 1938–39.
10  Toussaint 1977, pp. 102ff.
11  On the quality of Mauritian slaves' lives during the early nineteenth century, see Belrose-Huyghues 1985; Reddi 1989a, pp. 108–14; Barker 1996, especially chap. 7.
12  Noël 1954, pp. 304–05.
13  CO 167/79 – Despatch No. 48, Sir Lowry Cole to Earl Bathurst, September 12, 1825.
14  Alpers 1970.
15  Filliot 1974, p. 96.
16  Filliot 1974, pp. 55, 67–68. On the development of the Mascarene slave trade after 1769, see also Freeman-Grenville 1965; Akinola 1970.
17  CO 172/38 – Three Years Administration of the Isle de France ... p. 344; Gerbeau 1979a, p. 292; Nwulia 1981, p. 46; Reddi 1989a, p. 108.
18  Barker 1996, especially chap. 10.
19  *Report of the Commissioners of Inquiry upon the Slave Trade at Mauritius* (hereafter Slave Trade Inquiry), pp. 14–15. PP 1829 XXV [292].
20  Ly-Tio-Fane Pineo 1992, pp. 649–51; MA: B1B – Statement shewing the Compensation granted by the Imperial Government for the slaves emancipated in Mauritius and its Dependencies.
21  C. Anderson, Esq., to Lord John Russell, May 1, 1840. PP 1840 XXXVII [331], pp. 194–96.
22  Kuczynski 1949, pp. 767, 797; CO 167/24 – Appendix 23: Return of the number of Indian Convicts at Mauritius 30th October 1828 ...
23  Allen 1991.
24  Slave Trade Inquiry, especially pp. 1, 14–15, 19, 36; Burroughs 1976.
25  On the factors contributing to Indian emigration, see Kondapi 1951; Cumpston 1953; Saha 1970; Tinker 1974; Northrup 1995.
26  Lamusse 1964a, 1964b, 1964c, 1965.
27  UCJRL: Ms. f-1051, Vol. 2, Doc. 1 (Culture Des Isles de France et de Bourbon), fol. 1; Walter 1910, pp. 4–5; A. North-Coombes 1937, pp. 7–9; Haudrère 1989, pp. 925–29.
28  BL: Add. Ms. 33765, fol. 8 verso and 12 recto.
29  CAOM: G$^1$ 505, no. 2 – Tableau Général de l'Etat de Population et de Culture ou étoit L'Isle de France, L'Année 1766.
30  IOL: Home Miscellaneous Series, Vol. 111, p. 132 – Copy of the Remarks made by Mr. Colpoys at the Mauritius, June 1772. See also Ly-Tio-Fane 1968.
31  BL: Add. Ms. 29210, fol. 274 recto and verso.
32  IOL: Home Miscellaneous Series, Vol. 153, p. 612 – Letter from Mr. John Buncle to the Court of Directors, dated Cape of Good Hope, 20th December 1780.
33  IOL: Home Miscellaneous Series, Vol. 153, p. 611 – Letter from Mr. John Buncle ... 20th December 1780.

34  MA: A 11/5–8 – Etats de situation de la caisse de l'Etat, 1791–1802; A 108/1
    – Extrait du Compte d'Ordre des Recettes et Dépenses des Isles de France et
    de Bourbon, Ex$^{ce}$ 1783 ...; A 108/4 – Tableau Général des Dépenses faites par
    le Trésor National à L'Isle de France pendant les années 1789, 1790, 1791,
    1792, 1793, 8.1$^{er}$ mois à 21 1$^{er}$ Jours de 7$^{bre}$ 1794 ...; OA 114/3 – Tableau des
    Grains nourriciers remis dans les Magasins du Roi par les habitans de L'Isle
    de France; OA 119/2 – Etat des dépenses à faire pour le Service du Roi aux
    Isles de France et de Bourbon (29 mars 1784).
35  IOL: Home Miscellaneous Series, Vol. 102, p. 524 – Col. Call's Observa-
    tions and Reflections on the State of the Island of Mauritius in April 1770
    ... Call visited the Ile de France from March 22 to April 15, 1770 (*DBM*,
    p. 604).
36  UCJRL: Ms. f-1051, Vol. 2, Doc. 1 (Culture Des Isles de France et de
    Bourbon), fol. 10.
37  Milburn 1813, Vol. II, p. 568.
38  Raynal 1781, Releve général du produit net, escompte à dix pour cent déduit,
    des Marchandises des Indes, de la Chine, & des Isles de France et de Bourbon
    ... Milburn reports comparable figures on the sale at Lorient of merchandise
    imported from the Mascarenes, India, and China during the same period
    (1813, Vol. I, p. 399).
39  Raynal 1781, p. 341.
40  CL: Wiklinsky, ms. p. 78.
41  Pitot Frères et C$^{ie}$ à M. de Courcy à Bourbon, 14 janvier 1781, in *The
    Commercial Gazette* (Mauritius), August 16, 1870.
42  Pitot Frères et C$^{ie}$ à M. de Maurville, au Port-Louis, 27 juin 1781, in *The
    Commercial Gazette* (Mauritius), August 27, 1870.
43  UCJRL: Ms. f-1051, Vol. 2, Doc. 15, fol. 1.
44  Haudrère 1989, p. 938.
45  Pitot Frères et C$^{ie}$ à M. le Comte de St. Maurice, Gouverneur de Bourbon, 26
    mars 1781, in *The Commercial Gazette* (Mauritius), August 20, 1870.
46  Pitot Frères et C$^{ie}$ à M. de Murville à Paris, 11 août 1781, in *The Commercial
    Gazette* (Mauritius), September 3, 1870.
47  Pitot Frères et C$^{ie}$ à MM. Frin et C$^{ie}$, Banquiers à Paris, 14 septembre 1781,
    in *The Commercial Gazette* (Mauritius), September 3, 1870.
48  Milburn 1813, Vol. II, p. 566, citing a gentleman at Madras.
49  Toussaint 1979, pp. 273–74. Toussaint notes that a lack of documentation
    precludes estimating the value of the prizes taken by French frigates between
    1793 and 1802.
50  Keber n.d., chap. 6.
51  MA: OB 18/6 – 12 octobre 1780.
52  MA: OB 18/8 – 28 septembre 1782.
53  MA: OB 18/4 – 31 juillet 1780.
54  Martha Turner Keber, personal communication, February 28, 1994.
55  Toussaint 1967, pp. 84–88.
56  Toussaint 1975, pp. 43–44.
57  G.C.O. 1812.
58  Rouillard 1979, pp. 7–8.
59  Lamusse 1964c, p. 354.

60 Toussaint 1953, p. 9.
61 Toussaint 1953, p. 10.
62 MCA 1902, in a resolution adopted 4 décembre 1902.
63 Memorandum by Sir Cavendish Boyle, March 11, 1909. PP 1910 XXVII [Cmd. 5194], p. 97.
64 *MRC*, para. 56.
65 *MRC*, paras. 56–59. See Eisenberg 1974, pp. 63ff., on *correspondentes* and Tomich 1990, pp. 116–23, on *commissionnaires*.
66 Lamusse 1964c, p. 355.
67 MCA 1902, in a resolution adopted 4 décembre 1902.
68 *MRC*, para. 55.
69 *FSM*, pp. 226–27.
70 CO 167/29 – Despatch No. 41, Sir Robert Farquhar to Earl Bathurst, October 11, 1816; CO 167/107 – Despatch No. 37, Sir Charles Colville to the Rt. Hon. Sir George Murray, June 1, 1829; CO 167/148 – Despatch No. 31, Sir Charles Colville to the Rt. Hon. Sir George Murray, May 31, 1830.
71 *MRC*, paras. 270, 273–75.
72 *FSM*, p. 233.
73 *MRC*, paras. 295–96.
74 AR 1845. PP 1846 XXIX [728], p. 14; Lamusse 1964c, pp. 356ff. Edward Chapman characterized British investment from 1834–37 as a "very considerable outlay" (*Second Report of the Select Committee on Sugar and Coffee Planting* [hereafter Sugar and Coffee Committee], para. 3518). PP 1847–48 XXIII [137].
75 Sugar and Coffee Committee, para. 3518.
76 AR 1849. PP 1850 XXXVI [1287], p. 374.
77 *MRC*. Part III, Appendix C, pp. 31–39. PP 1910 XLII [Cd. 5187].
78 *FSM*, p. 13.
79 Sugar and Coffee Committee, para. 3755.
80 Successful Caribbean planters probably realized a minimum of 4 percent and an average of between 7 and 10 percent on their crop each year during the late eighteenth and early nineteenth centuries (Pitman 1931; Courtenay 1965, p. 18; Aufhauser 1974–75; Ward 1978).
81 CO 167/144 – Appendix No. 1: Questions addressed by the Commissioners of Inquiry to the respective Civil Commissaries in the Island of Mauritius with the Replies of the latter upon the present state of agriculture in Mauritius, the Employment and condition of the Slave Population, and the Employment of Free Laborers. Question 25.
82 Sugar and Coffee Committee, para. 3985.
83 Sugar and Coffee Committee, para. 3471.
84 Sugar and Coffee Committee, para. 3983.
85 Walter 1910, p. 22; Deerr 1949–50, Vol. II, p. 531. Profit margins in Fiji, by comparison, averaged 3 percent between 1887 and 1898 and 9 percent between 1901 and 1911 (Knapman 1987, pp. 14, 16).
86 *MRC*. Part III, Appendix C, p. 7.
87 While these four estates realized a substantial profit in 1906, the industry as a whole apparently operated at a loss that year.
88 Sornay 1920, p. 627; A. North-Coombes 1937, p. 165; Deerr 1949–50, Vol. I,

p. 185; Rouillard 1979, pp. 8, 136, 201, 243, 344, 402, 462. For similar developments in the Caribbean, see Schnakenbourg 1984.
89 MCA 1927–28, section iv of a resolution adopted March 1928.
90 MCA 1932–33, in a resolution adopted August 28, 1933.
91 Simmons 1982; Storey 1995.

## 2 A STATE OF CONTINUAL DISQUIETUDE AND HOSTILITY: MAROONAGE AND SLAVE LABOR, 1721–1835

1 Delaleu 1777, No. 174.
2 Barnwell 1948, p. 143.
3 Kuczynski 1949, p. 752.
4 La Bourdonnais 1827, pp. 15–16.
5 Cited in Grant 1801, pp. 77–78. According to P.J. Barnwell, this account is actually the work of C.F. Noble who visited the Ile de France in 1755 (*DBM*, pp. 919, 950).
6 SPG: Africa-Madagascar, Mauritius & Seychelles, 1821–1960/pamphlet by Henry Shepherd, Senior Presidency Chaplain, Bengal Establishment, dated December 1, 1821, entitled "Suggestions as to the Best Means of Propagating Christianity in Madagascar, and of Benefitting the Condition of the Planter and Slave in the Mauritius."
7 MA: HA 103/letter dated 19 août 1832.
8 Grant 1801, p. 297.
9 BL: Add. Ms. 33765, p. 10 verso.
10 Milbert 1812, Vol. II, p. 177.
11 Carroll 1977; Flory 1979; Price 1979, especially chaps. 11–13; de Groot 1985a, 1985b; McFarlane 1985; Schwartz 1992, chap. 4.
12 Kopytoff 1973, 1976a, 1976b.
13 MA: OA 90 – Registre de jugements, ordonnances et sentences de police, 21 juillet 1767–11 mai 1769.
14 Grant 1801, p. 297.
15 Milbert 1812, Vol. II, p. 177.
16 Grant 1801, p. 297; Milbert 1812, Vol. II, pp. 176–77.
17 G. Hall 1971, p. 81; Genovese 1976, p. 658.
18 *RCETI*, paras. 803–04, 3180.
19 Geggus 1985; Heuman 1985; Kay and Cary 1985; Morgan 1985.
20 For a summary of maroonage rates in Bahia, Guadeloupe, Jamaica, and Saint Domingue, see Geggus 1985, p. 117.
21 Kuczynski 1949, p. 750; Lagesse 1978, p. 23; Baker and Corne 1982, p. 144.
22 Lagesse 1978, p. 23.
23 Barassin 1979, p. 359.
24 Poivre 1797, p. 222.
25 IOL: Home Miscellaneous Series, Vol. 111, p. 135 – Copy of the Remarks made by Mr. Colpoys at the Mauritius, June 1772; Bompar, cited in Kuczynski 1949, p. 758.
26 MA: OA 54 – Receveur de la Commune, Livre pour servir à porter jour par jour les captures de noirs fugitifs dans tous quartiers (15 décembre 1772–31 décembre 1775). The estimate that these captures may represent from 40 to

50 percent of all reported escapes is based upon figures from 1823–26, when slightly more than 48 percent of the maroon slaves returned to their masters were recorded as having been captured (MA: IB 6/No. 9 – Return of slaves and prize negroes declared marrons between 1 January 1820 and 15 December 1826 and of those captured and declared entered within the same period ...).

27  MA: OA 70 – Registre pour l'enregistrement des déclarations de noirs fugitifs envoyées du quartier de la Rivière Basse du Rempart (14 novembre 1772–31 mai 1794). The district housed 1,741 slaves in 1776 (CAOM: G$^1$ 473 – Recensement général de l'Isle de France, 1776).

28  A 76 – Municipalité des Plaines Wilhems, Registre de déclarations de marronage, 16 germinal An VII–30 brumaire An XIV (5 avril 1799–1 novembre 1805).

29  The district housed 7,356 slaves in 1806 (Milbert 1812, Vol. II, p. 233 bis).

30  MA: IB 6/No. 9 – Return of slaves and prize negroes declared marrons between 1 January 1820 and 15 December 1826 ...; Kuczynski 1949, p. 770.

31  MA: IA 40 – Registre des marronages, Moka (1 janvier 1825–15 mai 1833).

32  B.H. de Froberville, *Ephémérides mauriciennes*, p. 93, cited in Kuczynski 1949, p. 764.

33  The birth and death rates among government slaves, for example, averaged 26.1 and 51.5 per thousand respectively from 1814 through 1832 (Kuczynski 1949, p. 852).

34  Lovejoy 1983, pp. 62, 138; Geggus 1989.

35  Female maroons were identified on the basis of common women's names and/ or the use of the feminine case in their ethnic description. Where a fugitive's gender could not be established clearly, the slave was assumed to be male. N.B. some of the women listed as maroons were reported as having been "taken by maroon blacks" rather than fleeing on their own accord.

36  Males accounted for 80 percent or more of maroons in Saint Domingue and the Carolinas (Geggus 1985, p. 117; Kay and Cary 1985, p. 41; Morgan 1985, p. 70), but for only 63.5 percent of Barbadian fugitives (Heuman 1985, p. 98).

37  See Ly-Tio-Fane Pineo 1992 on the cultural and ethnic diversity of the Mauritian slave population *circa* 1823.

38  BL: Add. Ms. 33765, p. 10 recto and verso; Grant 1801, pp. 74–77, 297–98; Milbert 1812, Vol. I, p. 218, and Vol. II, pp. 162–74; Bernardin de St. Pierre 1834, pp. 120–22; d'Unienville 1885–86, Vol. I, pp. 255–58.

39  CWM: Mauritius, Incoming Letters From: Box 1, Folder 1, Jacket B – J. Le Brun to Rev. Father Burder, January 7, 1817.

40  Similar findings are reported for colonial North and South Carolina (Kay and Cary 1985, pp. 42–43; Morgan 1985, pp. 67–68).

41  MA: B1B – Statement shewing the Compensation granted by the Imperial Government for the slaves emancipated in Mauritius and its Dependencies. "Effective" slaves were defined as those not under six years old, aged, diseased, or otherwise infirm.

42  Geggus 1985, p. 123; Heuman 1985, pp. 102–03; Kay and Cary 1985, p. 47.

43  MA: IB 7/pp. 38–39 – Evidence of John Finniss, Chief Commissary of Police at Mauritius given before the Commissioners of Enquiry between 31 March and 17 May 1828.

44 MA: IB 6 – Return of Marroons [*sic*] captured by the Chiefs of Detachments during the Year 1826. See also Allen 1983, p. 223.

45 MA: Z2B/9 – Journal de police, 1$^{er}$ floréal An VIII (21 avril 1800) au 9 pluviôse An IX (29 janvier 1801), entry no. 262, 26 brumaire An VIII. Camille declared that she had passed as a free person of color throughout her three weeks at liberty.

46 MA: OA 90/entry dated 29 juillet 1767.

47 MA: A 58 – Registre du Bureau du Marronage 3 germinal An VII (23 March 1799) – 20 novembre 1812/entry dated 6 fructidor An XII.

48 MA: A 58/entry dated 18 ventôse An XIII.

49 MA: IB 7/pp. 48–49 – Evidence of John Finniss . . .

50 BL: Add. Ms. 33765, p. 10 verso.

51 CL: Wiklinsky ms., pp. 88–89.

52 Ramdoyal 1979, pp. 1–8.

53 Payet 1990, pp. 60–62.

54 MA: A 58/entry dated 18 vendémiaire An IX.

55 MA: HA 103/letter dated 19 août 1832.

56 MA: IB 6/No. 9 – Return of slaves and prize negroes declared marrons between 1 January 1820 and 15 December 1826 . . .

57 Grant 1801, p. 297.

58 Payet 1990, pp. 61, 73–74.

59 MA: IB 6 – Return of Marroons captured by the Chiefs of Detachments during the Year 1826.

60 This population was also increasingly locally born; by 1827, slightly more than one-half of the colony's slaves were Creoles (MA: ID 14 – Return of the slave population of Mauritius [1827]).

61 MA: IB 6/No. 9 – Correspondence and returns relating to the marron branch of the Police Department at Mauritius. Return of maroons killed by the detachments or others since the 23rd January 1813 to 17th June 1828; A 58.

62 A Lady 1830, pp. 154–56; Backhouse 1844, p. 17.

63 See n. 45.

64 MA: Z2B/6 – Journal de police, 1$^{er}$ juillet 1790 au 28 janvier 1791, fols. 57 verso–60 verso – three entries dated 6 septembre 1790.

65 Bernard 1889, p. 552.

66 BL: Add. Ms. 33765, p. 10 verso; Grant 1801, p. 77; Bernardin de St. Pierre 1834, p. 124; Gerbeau 1979b.

67 Poivre 1797, p. 222; A Lady 1830, p. 151; Bernardin de St. Pierre 1834, pp. 122–23; Bennett and Brooks 1965, p. 7. See Fuma 1992, pp. 77–102, on early nineteenth-century slave life on the Ile de Bourbon.

68 MA: IB 6/No. 9 – J. Finniss to G.A. Barry, February 24, 1825.

69 Beginning in 1829, the Protector of Slaves kept detailed records of the complaints Mauritian slaves filed against their masters. For an analysis of the complaints lodged between 1832 and 1835, see Teelock 1995, pp. 56–89.

70 McFarlane 1985, pp. 147ff.; Barker 1996, p. 125.

71 MA: A 76/entry dated 17 floréal An XIII.

72 MA: IA 40. Azoline was declared maroon three times in 1825 and 1828, four times in 1826 and 1831, twice in 1827, 1829, and 1832, and once in 1830.

73 Stinchcombe 1994.

74  MA: ID 14 – Return of the Slave Population of Mauritius (1827).

75  CO 167/209 – Report of John Finniss, Chief Commissary of Police, August 20, 1838 (Increase of the Police Force), Statement No. 6, enclosed in Despatch No. 40, Sir William Nicolay to Lord Glenelg, March 25, 1839.

76  CO 167/209 – Report of John Finniss . . . August 20, 1838, para. 12.

## 3 INDENTURED LABOR AND THE LEGACY OF MAROONAGE: ILLEGAL ABSENCE, DESERTION, AND VAGRANCY, 1835–1900

1  MA: HA 108/circular from Geo. Dick, Colonial Secretary, to Civil Commissioners, March 15, 1837.

2  See the reports of the commissions of inquiry based in Mauritius (PP 1840 XXXVII [58], pp. 18–35, 45–68, and PP 1840 XXXVII [331], pp. 12–94, 107–83), and Calcutta (PP 1841 XVI [45], pp. 4–12) on early immigrant living and working conditions.

3  See Northrup 1995, chaps. 5 and 6, for an overview of government regulation of the Indian indentured labor trade.

4  AR 1851, para. 23. PP 1852 XXXI [1539], p. 247.

5  AR 1845. PP 1846 XXIX [728], p. 142.

6  AR 1854. PP 1856 XLII [2050], p. 178.

7  AIR 1860, para. 76.

8  RCETI, para. 3180.

9  Lal, Munro, and Beechert 1993.

10  Barnwell and Toussaint 1949; Toussaint 1972; Hazareesingh 1975; M.D. North-Coombes 1984; Ly-Tio-Fane Pineo 1984.

11  Gillion 1962; Mayer 1963; Jain 1970; Tayal 1977; Shlomowitz 1981, 1982; Graves 1983; Breman 1989.

12  Tinker 1974; Hazareesingh 1975; Tayal 1977; Mannick 1979; Jain 1984; M.D. North-Coombes 1984; Behal and Mohapatra 1992; Ramasamy 1992.

13  Munro 1993a, p. 6.

14  RCETI, paras. 2826ff.; Carter 1995, pp. 88–98.

15  Kuczynski 1949, pp. 821, 832. The number of married Indian men was actually higher, but how much so is difficult to determine because Mauritian authorities did not recognize marriages contracted in India until 1856, and colonial civil law made no specific provision for immigrant marriages until 1853 (RCETI, paras. 2785ff.; Kuczynski 1949, p. 828).

16  Bernardin de St. Pierre 1834, pp. 120–21; Milbert 1812, Vol. I, p. 218, and Vol. II, p. 170; d'Unienville 1885–86, Vol. I, p. 256.

17  RCETI, para. 1960.

18  RCETI, para. 664.

19  RCETI, para. 480.

20  Sugar and Coffee Committee, para. 3755.

21  1846 Census, p. 197.

22  On the factors shaping the indentured labor trades, see Kondapi 1951; Saha 1970; Tinker 1974; Newbury 1974–75; Marks and Richardson 1984, especially pp. 1–18, 186–232; Emmer 1986, especially pp. 3–15, 125–61, 263–94; Look Lai 1993, especially pp. 19–37; Munro 1993b.

23  *RCETI*, paras. 237, 1960; Carter 1992, and 1995, pp. 154–59.

24  AIR 1860, para. 53.

25  AIR 1860–63, Appendix M; AIR 1864, Appendix N.

26  AIR 1865, para. 43.

27  CO 167/284/A3 – Address to Sir Wm. Gomm by W.W. West, M. Baudot, Ed. Rouillard, Pamplemousses, April 20, 1847, enclosed in Despatch No. 141, Sir William Gomm to Earl Grey, July 3, 1847; CO 167/284/C1 – Report of the Proceedings of the Immigration Committee at their Meeting on the 7$^{th}$ June 1847, para. 6, enclosed in Despatch No. 152, Sir William Gomm to Earl Grey, July 12, 1847.

28  *RCETI*, p. 10 (para. 17).

29  AIR 1881, para. 39.

30  See the accounts of immigrant life published as part of the Old Immigrant petition of June 6, 1871 (*RCETI*, pp. 3–7); Carter 1995, pp. 159–82, and 1996, pp. 102–16.

31  AIR 1862, para. 39.

32  AIR 1864, para. 57.

33  AIR 1875, para. 55.

34  *RCETI*, para. 2026.

35  *RCETI*, para. 2040.

36  PP 1840 XXXVII [58], pp. 18–35, 45–68, and PP 1840 XXXVII [331], pp. 12–94, 107–83.

37  *RCETI*, para. 236. Other sources indicate that 6.8 percent of sugar estate laborers deserted that year, while another 5.1 percent were absent from work and 5.4 percent were ill (Carter 1995, p. 225).

38  Messrs. Gobarz, J. Currie, P.N. Truquez & E. Dupont to David Barclay, Esq., M.P., & John Irving, Esq., Agents for Mauritius, July 22, 1846. PP 1847–48 XLIV [61], pp. 2–3.

39  Carter 1995, p. 225.

40  Colony of Mauritius, *Report of the Prison Committee on the Prison Establishment, 1857*, Appendix B; AR 1856, Sub-Enclosure 5. PP 1857–58 XL [2403], p. 154; AR 1857, para. 172. PP 1859 XXI Sess. 2 [2567], p. 173; AR 1858, para. 175. PP 1860 XLIV [2711], p. 122; AR 1859, Appendix C, para. 8. PP 1861 XL [2841], p. 113.

41  *RCETI*, paras. 554, 2247.

42  AR 1860, para. 135. PP 1862 XXXVI [2955], p. 123; AR 1861, para. 96. PP 1863 XXXIX [3165], p. 104; AR 1863, Procureur General's Report. PP 1865 XXXVII [3423], p. 119.

43  AIR 1866, paras. 61–62; AIR 1867, paras. 31–32; AIR 1868, paras. 33–34; AIR 1869, paras. 40–41; AIR 1870, paras. 31–32; AIR 1871, para. 22.

44  Unlawful absence accounted for one-half of all complaints lodged against indentured laborers in Fiji between 1885 and 1906 (Lal 1993, p. 209).

45  More than 16 percent of the laborers employed by one company in Samoa during 1889–90 became runaways (Munro and Firth 1993, p. 117). This number fluctuated from 10.6 to 12.6 percent between 1891 and 1894 before falling to about 4 percent a year between 1895 and 1898. The incidence of desertion and refusing service ranged from 17.3 to 33.7 percent of the Hawaiian work force during the 1880s and 1890s (Beechert 1993a, p. 53).

Tayal (1977, pp. 543–44) reports that 4 percent of Natal's indentured Indian population was convicted of desertion between 1900 and 1910, a figure which she notes understates the local desertion rate.

46  AIR 1862, para. 39; *RCETI-A*, Appendix G (No. 44).
47  *RCETI*, para. 704.
48  AIR 1891, para. 50; AIR 1892, para. 54; AIR 1893, para. 51.
49  *RCETI-A*, Appendix B.
50  AIR 1873, para. 41.
51  AIR 1875, para. 65.
52  AIR 1884, para. 53.
53  AIR 1881, para. 40.
54  AR 1856, para. 49. PP 1857–58 XL [2403], pp. 144–45.
55  AIR 1866, para. 44.
56  AIR 1881, para. 57.
57  AIR 1898, para. 25.
58  AIR 1864, para. 60; AIR 1865, para. 63.
59  AIR 1869, para. 55.
60  Pike 1873, p. 474.
61  *RCETI*, paras. 879–82.
62  *RCETI*, para. 883.
63  Beechert 1993b, p. 319.
64  AIR 1860, para. 49.
65  *RCETI*, paras. 2934–47.
66  AIR 1881, para. 60.
67  Brereton 1994; Carter 1995, chap. 1.
68  Lal, Munro, and Beechert 1993, especially pp. 129–85, 241–96.

## 4  BECOMING AN APPROPRIATED PEOPLE: THE RISE OF THE FREE POPULATION OF COLOR, 1729–1830

1  CO 415/19/Q3 – "Exposé" of Mr. Marcenay relative to the Cultivation of Land by Free Persons of Colour as the means of assisting that Class, and at the same time increasing the Public Revenue (October 12, 1827).
2  Piggott, Thibaud, and Herchenroder 1896, Vol. I, pp. 98–99.
3  CO 167/143 – Report of the Commissioners of Inquiry upon the condition of the Free People of Colour at Mauritius (July 15, 1828).
4  Patterson 1982, pp. 209ff.; Sio 1987.
5  Goveia 1965; Hayot 1969; Foner 1969–70; Brathwaite 1971, especially pp. 167–75; Cohen and Greene 1972; H. Klein 1973; Berlin 1974; Campbell 1976; Sio 1976; Heuman 1981; B. Marshall 1982; Cox 1984; Gaspar 1985, especially pp. 162–68; N. Hall 1992, especially chaps. 8–10.
6  Mintz and Price 1976.
7  Ragatz 1928, especially pp. 286–330; Williams 1966, pp. 126–53; Green 1976, pp. 35–64; Drescher 1977, pp. 38–54; Watts 1987, chaps. 6, 7, 9; Ward 1988, pp. 38–60.
8  CO 172/42 – Tableau No. 17 – Mouvements de la Population Esclave depuis 1767 Jusqu'en 1825.
9  Jumeer 1979, p. 26.

10  PP 1823 XVIII [89], p. 125 – Return of all Manumissions effected by Purchase, Bequest or otherwise, since the 1st of January 1808 ...
11  This rate also applied to the Ile de Bourbon where only 0.17 percent of the slave population was manumitted between 1787 and 1793 (Wanquet 1977, p. 133).
12  Jumeer 1979, pp. 17, 26.
13  Jumeer 1979, p. 26.
14  PP 1823 XVIII [89], p. 125 – Return of all Manumissions ... since the 1st of January 1808; PP 1828 XXV [204], pp. 58–75 – Return of the Number of Manumissions effected by Purchase, Bequest or otherwise ... from 1st January 1821 to 1st June 1826, respectively.
15  MA: OA 39B/2; Baker and Corne 1982, p. 195.
16  MA: OA 39B/4 and LC 16/83, respectively.
17  CO 172/42 – Tableau No. 14 – Rapports des Naissances, décès, Mariages aux Populations blanche et libre dans les différents Quartiers, Etablis sur les relevés des Régistres de l'Etat Civil de 21 Années, 1$^{er}$ Janv$^r$ 1804 au 1$^{er}$ Janvier 1825.
18  MA: KK 3 – Recensement des populations blanche et libre, Port Louis (1805–06).
19  *DBM*, pp. 1022–24; Mantaux and Adolphe 1972.
20  MA: LC 5/47 and LC 5/52, respectively.
21  Comparable figures are reported for Barbadian freedmen (Handler 1974, pp. 118–19).
22  MA: NA 15/1B/70 – 28 décembre 1763.
23  MA: NA 15/2D/141 – 20 décembre 1764.
24  MA: NA 12/11A/25 – 1 avril 1763.
25  MA: NA 18/5A/3 – 2 avril 1770.
26  MA: NA 22/21/24 – 24 août 1790; NA 22/21/27 – 28 août 1790; NA 22/21/43 – 14 décembre 1790.
27  MA: NA 18/4E/134 – 8 janvier 1770.
28  MA: NA 22/1/63 – 6 avril 1774.
29  MA: NA 33/2/10 – 28 janvier 1786.
30  MA: NA 33/6/64 – 15 janvier 1788.
31  MA: NA 12/1A/54 – 12 mai 1755.
32  CAOM: G$^1$ 473 – Recensement général de l'Ile de France, 1776.
33  MA: KK 46 – Recensement de l'Ile de France, 1788.
34  Milbert 1812, Vol. II, p. 233 bis; CAOM: G$^1$ 505, No. 9 – Relevé du cadastre général de l'Isle de France fait pour l'année 1809 d'après les Recensemens fournis par les habitans.
35  CAOM: G$^1$ 473; MA: KK 3.
36  Allen 1989, p. 134.
37  Contemporary sources are silent about the reason for this difference. However, it is likely that the lower rate applied to women and children, while the higher rate applied to men.
38  MA: KK 7 – Recensement des populations blanche et libre, Plaines Wilhems (1810–12).
39  In table 13, the values for 1806 were calculated using Milbert's figures on free colored land, livestock, and slave-ownership that year (1812, Vol. II, p. 233

bis), the average price of land and commodities between 1812 and 1816, and slave and livestock prices in 1817. Since free colored production figures do not exist for 1806, these were estimated on the basis of the 1829 production figures reported by d'Unienville (1885–86, Vol. I, pp. 52–228, as corrected). The values for 1829–30 are based upon d'Unienville's census and production figures for that year and the price of land, livestock, slaves, and commodities in 1824. Prices were determined on the basis of information recorded by d'Unienville in CO 172/42 – Tableaux Nos. 24, 25, 27, 30 31, 33, 34.

40 MA: LC 8/79.

41 Goveia (1965, p. 224) notes similar limitations on free colored opportunities in the Leeward Islands.

42 Based upon figures reported in d'Unienville 1885–86, Vol. I, pp. 52–228, as corrected.

43 MA: NA 43/14 – 18 août 1811, 12 octobre 1811, 29 janvier 1812; NA 33/112A – 30 octobre 1815, 19 décembre 1815 (2 acts); NA 43/16B – 6 juin 1816 (2 acts), 11 décembre 1816.

44 MA: KK 8 – Recensement des populations blanche et libre, Plaines Wilhems, 1819, and KK 13 – Recensement des populations blanche et libre, Plaines Wilhems, 1825, respectively.

45 MA: KK 7; KK 8; KK 13.

46 MA: NA 43/5/31 – 21 thermidor An VIII.

47 MA: NA 43/5/38 – 29 fructidor An VIII; NA 43/7/24 – 21 ventôse An XIII; NA 43/14 – 17 août 1811 (3 acts).

48 MA: NA 43/8/75 – 5 mai 1808; NA 43/16A – 29 novembre 1813.

49 MA: NA 43/16B – 17 février 1817.

50 Milbert 1812, Vol. I, p. 233 bis; MA: ID 14 – Return of the slave population of Mauritius (1827).

51 The number of households owning six or more slaves increased from approximately 13 percent *circa* 1805 to more than 23 percent in 1827 (MA: KK 3; ID 14).

52 MA: KK 5 – Registre des impositions de l'an XII, populations blanche et libre (25 mars 1805); KK 20 – Recensement des populations blanche et libre, Port Louis (1828–29).

53 MA: NA 33/110A – 11 octobre 1811.

54 MA: NA 33/51/13 – 21 mars 1809.

55 MA: NA 33/51/135 – 5 janvier 1810.

56 Allen 1991, pp. 356–57.

57 For comparable developments in the Americas, see Kinsbruner 1990.

58 Kuczynski 1949, p. 827.

59 For comparable developments in the Caribbean, see Garrigus 1993.


5 THE GENERAL DESIRE TO POSSESS LAND: EX-APPRENTICES AND THE POST-EMANCIPATION ERA, 1839–1851

1 CO 167/331 – Despatch No. 166, Governor Higginon to Earl Grey, October 14, 1851, para. 7.

2  CO 167/209 – Despatch No. 40, Sir William Nicolay to Lord Glenelg, March 25, 1839.
3  CO 167/209 – Report of John Finniss ... August 20, 1838, para. 38.
4  Backhouse 1844, p. 20.
5  CO 167/209 – Report of John Finniss ... August 20, 1838, Statement No. 6.
6  CWM/Mauritius, Incoming Letters From/Box 2, Folder 3, Jacket C – Edward Baker to Rev. William Ellis, April 12, 1839.
7  Despatch No. 57, Sir William Nicolay to Lord Glenelg, May 4, 1839. PP 1840 XXXVII [58], p. 5.
8  Baker to Ellis, April 12, 1839.
9  MA: HA 108 – Th. Cordouan à Monsieur A. Hugnin, Commissaire Civil & de Police (Plaines Wilhems), 29 avril 1839; Vᵉ Senneville à Hugnin, 30 avril 1839.
10  Nicolay to Glenelg, May 4, 1839.
11  Petition of the Planters, Merchants, Traders and other Inhabitants of Mauritius, May 18, 1839, enclosed in a despatch from Sir William Nicolay to Lord Glenelg, May 21, 1839. PP 1840 XXXVII [58], p. 8.
12  C. Anderson, Esq., to Lord John Russell, May 1, 1840. PP 1840 XXXVII [331], p. 195.
13  1851 Census, p. 8.
14  CO 167/272 – Despatch No. 174, Sir William Gomm to W.E. Gladstone, September 7, 1846.
15  Howell 1951; Toussaint 1972, 1977; Mannick 1979; Paturau 1988; Carter 1993.
16  Nwulia 1978, 1981; Benoît 1985. An exception is Teelock 1990.
17  Nwulia 1981, p. 232.
18  More recent studies include Rivière 1972; D. Hall 1978; Mintz 1979; Beckford 1985; H. Klein and Engerman 1985; W. Marshall 1985; Craton 1988, 1992; Trouillot 1988; Emmer 1992, 1993; Holt 1992; Olwig 1995. See also Fuma 1979 on the post-emancipation era on Réunion.
19  Smith 1995, pp. 102–03, 108–09.
20  Smith 1995, p. 126.
21  E.g., Engerman 1984, 1992.
22  See Bolland 1981, 1984 and Green 1984 for the debate on this issue.
23  Recent work on slave provision grounds includes Beckles 1991; W. Marshall 1991; Tomich 1991; Mullin 1992, especially chap. 6; Sheridan 1993; Barickman 1994.
24  An exception is Scott 1988, p. 412.
25  Only Besson (1992) has made at least passing references to the role of domestic or peasant capital in shaping the post-emancipation world.
26  An exception is Butler 1995.
27  Howell 1951, p. 185.
28  CO 167/284 – Report of the Committee appointed by the Council on the 20th April ... on the subject of the Emancipated Population in the Colony (4 June 1847), para. 2, enclosed in Despatch No. 153, Sir William Gomm to Earl Grey, July 12, 1847.
29  Anderson to Russell, May 1, 1840.
30  1846 Census, para. 17.

31  1851 Census, para. 20.
32  CO 167/267 – Despatch No. 5, Sir William Gomm to Lord Stanley, 7 January 1846.
33  1846 Census, para. 19.
34  AR 1856, para. 10. PP 1857–58 XL [2403], p. 139.
35  Kuczynski 1949, pp. 873–74.
36  AR 1854. PP 1856 XLII [205], pp. 176–77.
37  Gomm to Stanley, January 7, 1846.
38  1851 Census, para. 20.
39  1846 Census, para. 19; 1851 Census, para. 23.
40  BB 1835, pp. 322–23; BB 1838, pp. 147–48.
41  Cordouan à Hugnin, 29 avril 1839.
42  MA: HA 108 – Mr. Fortenay à Hugnin, n.d.
43  MA: HA 108 – William S. Saunders à A. Hugnin, May 15, 1839.
44  MA: HA 108 – A. Hugnin à Mr. Finniss, May 3, 1839.
45  CO 167/226 – Capt. J.A. Lloyd to John Irving, April 4, 1840.
46  1851 Census, para. 17.
47  Lloyd to Irving, April 4, 1840.
48  CO 167/284 – Address to Earl Grey by certain planters of Pamplemousses & Rivière du Rempart, June 30, 1847, enclosed in Despatch No. 141, Sir William Gomm to Earl Grey, July 3, 1847.
49  CO 167/272 – Report of Peter Aug$^s$ Heyliger, Stipendiary Magistrate (South Pamplemousses), December 24, 1845, enclosed in Despatch No. 174, Sir William Gomm to W.E. Gladstone, September 7, 1846.
50  Saunders à Hugnin, May 15, 1839.
51  Cordouan à Hugnin, 29 avril 1839.
52  Senneville à Hugnin, 30 avril 1839.
53  MA: HA 108 – George Dick to A. Hugnin, May 10, 1839; A. Hugnin à George Dick, May 15, 1839.
54  Lloyd to Irving, April 4, 1840. The *pas géometriques* was a narrow strip of land along the coast, originally reserved by the Crown for defensive purposes.
55  Lloyd to Irving, April 4, 1840.
56  CO 167/267 – Report of J. Davidson, Stipendiary Magistrate (Grand Port), December 20, 1845, enclosed in Despatch No. 5, Sir William Gomm to Lord Stanley, January 7, 1846.
57  Report of the Committee . . . on the subject of the Emancipated Population in the Colony (June 4, 1847), para. 4.
58  SPG/J.9/pp. 229–30 – Rev. A. Denny to the Secretary, Society for the Propagation of the Faith in Foreign Parts, July 30, 1845.
59  Gomm to Gladstone, September 7, 1846.
60  MA: NA 85/5 – 26 novembre 1839; NA 85/9 – 11 novembre 1841.
61  Report of Peter Aug$^s$ Heyliger, December 24, 1845.
62  MA: HA 103 – Report on the State of the Population of African origin, emancipated from Slavery, in the District of Moka, by D$^{is}$ Beaugendre, Civil Commissary, December 19, 1845.
63  MA: HA 111 – Report on the state of the African population, emancipated from Slavery, in the District of Savanne, by F. Giblot Ducray, Civil Commissioner, November 26, 1845.

64 Report of J. Davidson, December 20, 1845.
65 MA: NA 76/10/109 – 10 décembre 1836; NA 76/10/114 – 14 décembre 1836.
66 MA: NA 84/3/PM311 – 16 octobre 1838.
67 MA: NA 83/1/PM28 – 30 novembre 1838.
68 MA: NA 84/3/PM373 – 18 décembre 1838.
69 D. Hall 1978, pp. 16ff.; Trouillot 1988, pp. 84ff.; Sheridan 1993, pp. 25ff.
70 Billiard 1822, p. 40.
71 CO 167/272 – Report of James Hervey, Stipendiary Magistrate (Black River), November 20, 1845, enclosed in Despatch No. 174, Sir William Gomm to W.E. Gladstone, September 7, 1846.
72 Lloyd to Irving, April 4, 1840. For comparable developments in the Caribbean, see Trouillot 1988, p. 78.
73 d'Unienville 1885–86, Vol. I, pp. 52–230.
74 MA: HA 101 – Report on the state of the African population ... by Civil Commissioner Montocchio, Flacq, December 12, 1845; CO 167/272 – Report of Henry Maxwell Self, Stipendiary Magistrate (Rivière du Rempart), November 29, 1845, enclosed in Despatch No. 174, Sir William Gomm to W.E. Gladstone, September 7, 1846.
75 A Lady 1830, pp. 154–56; Backhouse 1844, pp. 17, 26.
76 Bernard 1889, p. 552.
77 Fortenay à Hugnin, n.d.; CO 167/262 – Report of Armand Hugnin, Civil Commissioner (Plaines Wilhems), December 1, 1845, enclosed in Despatch No. 174, Sir William Gomm to W.E. Gladstone, September 7, 1846.
78 Senneville à Hugnin, 30 avril 1839.
79 Lloyd to Irving, April 1, 1840.
80 Report of Peter Aug[s] Heyliger, December 24, 1845; Report of Armand Hugnin, December 1, 1845.
81 Despatch No. 28, Sir William Gomm to Lord Stanley, February 17, 1843. PP 1844 XXXV [530], p. 191.
82 Despatch No. 56, Sir William Gomm to Lord Stanley, March 9, 1846. PP 1846 XXIX [728], pp. 142, 144.
83 AR 1846, para. 10. PP 1847 XXXVII [869], p. 197.
84 Virts 1991.
85 MA: NA 76/9/98 – 22 avril 1836; NA 76/11/135 – 5 juin 1837.
86 Turner 1988, p. 28.
87 Berlin and Morgan 1991, p. 14.
88 MA: NA 83/2/120 – 25 mai 1841.
89 MA: NA 83/3/18 – janvier 1842.
90 MA: NA 83/3/44 – 6 avril 1842; NA 83/3/46 – 6 avril 1842.
91 1846 Census, para. 12.
92 Gomm to Stanley, January 7, 1846.
93 Gomm to Gladstone, September 7, 1846.
94 CO 167/272 – Report of Ed. Kelly, Stipendiary Magistrate (Port Louis), November 25, 1845, Despatch No. 28, enclosed in Despatch No. 174, Sir William Gomm to W.E. Gladstone, September 7, 1846.
95 CO 167/267 – Report of J. Regnard, Stipendiary Magistrate (Flacq), December 19, 1845, enclosed in Despatch No. 5, Sir William Gomm to Lord Stanley, January 7, 1846.

96  AR 1846, para. 3. PP 1847 XXXVII [869], p. 192.
97  Denny to Society for the Propagation of the Gospel in Foreign Parts, July 30, 1845.
98  Mouat 1852, p. 33.
99  Ryan 1864, p. 20.
100 Despatch from Governor Sir Henry Barkly to the Rt. Hon. Edward Cardwell, M.P., July 26, 1866, para. 137. PP 1867 XLVIII [3812], p. 118.
101 Rudolph and Rudolph 1967, pp. 36–64; Srinivas 1968, pp. 94–100.
102 1846 Census, para. 24; 1851 Census, p. 8.
103 Lloyd to Irving, April 4, 1840.
104 CO 167/272 – Report of Severin Seignette, Stipendiary Magistrate (Plaines Wilhems), December 3, 1845, enclosed in Despatch No. 174, Sir William Gomm to W.E. Gladstone, September 7, 1846.
105 CO 167/272 – Report of Emile Magon, Civil Commissioner (South Pample-mousses), December 20, 1845, enclosed in Despatch No. 174, Sir William Gomm to W.E. Gladstone, September 7, 1846.
106 Report ... by F. Giblot Ducray, November 26, 1845.
107 Report ... by D$^{is}$ Beaugendre, December 19, 1845.
108 Report of Armand Hugnin, December 1, 1845.
109 Report of Ed. Kelly, November 25, 1845.
110 Barkly to Cardwell, July 26, 1866, para. 134.
111 1861 Census, para. 2.
112 Barkly to Cardwell, July 26, 1866, para. 146.

## 6 THE REGENERATORS OF AGRICULTURAL PROSPERITY: INDIAN IMMIGRANTS AND THEIR DESCENDANTS, 1834–1936

1  CO 167/184 – enclosed in Despatch No. 141, Sir William Gomm to Earl Grey, July 3, 1847.
2  MGI: PC 635/3; PE 50.
3  MA: NA 83/18/2564 – 27 août 1858.
4  AR 1851, para. 23. PP 1852 XXXI [1539], p. 247.
5  AR 1857, para. 213. PP 1859 XXI, Sess. 2 [2567], p. 176; AR 1865, para. 128. PP 1867 XLVIII [3812], p. 117.
6  RCETI, para. 4087.
7  Munro 1993b, pp. 4–6; Carter 1994, pp. 1–5.
8  E.g., Beejadhur 1935; Hazareesingh 1975; Ly-Tio-Fane Pineo 1984. The same holds true for much of the literature on Indian immigration in general and the Indian experience in specific colonies: Kondapi 1951; Cumpston 1953; Gillion 1962; Mayer 1963; Jain 1970; Saha 1970; Tinker 1974; Look Lai 1993; Laurence 1994.
9  Toussaint 1972, pp. 238ff.
10 Virahsawmy 1979.
11 M.D. North-Coombes 1984, 1987.
12 MA: NA 84/8/PM1280 – 19 juin 1841.
13 MA: NA 83/4/103 – 12 août 1843 (2 acts).
14 A. North-Coombes 1937, p. 36.

15  MA: NA 102/99 – 30 juin & 22 juillet 1875.
16  MA: NA 102/138 – 21 juin 1881; NA 102/141 – 28 septembre 1881; NA 102/ 156 – 7 décembre 1882.
17  AR 1895, p. 17. PP 1897 LIX [C. 8279-7].
18  AR 1896, p. 23. PP 1898 LIX [C. 8650-13].
19  AR 1897, para. 63. PP 1899 LXII [C. 9046-18]; AIR 1895, Ann. 22 & 23; AIR 1896, Ann. 21.
20  MA: NA 83/8/906 – 19 août 1850.
21  MA: NA 83/19/2753 – 21 avril 1859.
22  *RCETI*, para. 2947.
23  MA: RA 790/Immigration Report No. 16 – Report of the Immigration Committee, at a Meeting held at Government House the 10th, 16th, and 26th July 1844.
24  See n. 1.
25  Report of the Proceedings of the Immigration Committee at their Meeting on the 7th June 1847. PP 1847–48 XLIV [61], p. 191.
26  AIR 1860, Appendix O; AIR 1861, Appendix K; AIR 1871, Appendix F.
27  MA: HA 110 – Report on the state of the African population ... by Civil Commissioner Ravel, Rivière du Rempart, 4 décembre 1845, para. 2.
28  Mouat 1852, p. 33.
29  GSB 1837.
30  GSB 1851–53, 1855, Appendix No. 5.
31  MA: NA 84/19/PM200 – 15 avril 1847.
32  MA: NA 84/21 – 19 février 1848.
33  MA: NA 84/25/204–205 (PM5660–61) – 22 novembre 1852.
34  MA: NA 83/13/1604 – 25 juin 1855.
35  MA: NA 83/9/970 – 12 mars 1851.
36  MA: NA 83/19/2768–2770 – 5 mai 1859.
37  Carter 1994, especially chaps. 3, 5, and Conclusion.
38  Kalla 1984.
39  MA: NA 33/117 – 6 septembre 1823.
40  MA: NA 67/25 – 24 juillet 1835.
41  Kalla 1987.
42  MA: NA 112/12 – 15 juin 1875.
43  MA: NA 83/19/SM2684–86 – 31 janvier 1859; NA 83/19/SM2707–08 – 21 février 1859; NA 83/20/SM2835 – 19 juillet 1859; NA 83/20/SM2917 – 21 octobre 1859; NA 83/20/SM2925 – 28 octobre 1859; NA 83/20/SM2926 – 29 october 1859.
44  MA: NA 83/36/SM5671 – 14 septembre 1867.
45  MA: NA 83/7/700 – 14 décembre 1848.
46  MA: NA 83/11/1272 – 8 juin 1853.
47  MA: NA 83/21/2991 – 9 février 1860; NA 83/22/3235 – 24 décembre 1860.
48  MA: NA 102/138 – 21 juin 1881.
49  MA: NA 102/116 – 18 novembre 1878; NA 102/125 – 10 & 15 décembre 1879.
50  MA: NA 119/7 – 9 janvier 1877.
51  MA: NA 102/174 – 22 septembre 1884.
52  MA: NA 102/179 – 8 mai 1885.
53  MA: NA 102/97 – 26 février 1875.

54  MA: NA 102/84 – 13 janvier 1873; NA 102/84 – 2 janvier 1873; NA 102/90 – 29 décembre 1873.
55  MA: NA 84/24/205 (PM5401) – 11 novembre 1851.
56  MA: NA 102/112 – 3 avril 1878; NA 102/117 – 30 décembre 1878.
57  MA: NA 102/111 – 25 février 1878; NA 102/117 – 30 décembre 1878.
58  MA: NA 102/143 – 22 novembre 1881; NA 102/144 – 9 décembre 1881; NA 112/35 – 17 février 1882; NA 102/149 – 19 mai 1882; NA 102/166 – 6 novembre 1883; NA 102/165 – 23 octobre 1883.
59  See Adams 1970, 1975 on social and economic brokers in complex societies.
60  MA: NA 102/84 – 20 janvier 1873.
61  MA: NA 102/156 – 7 décembre 1882.
62  RMD 1881, para. 6; RMD 1883, para. 10.
63  1891 Census, para. 38.
64  Jayawardena 1983, pp. 143–44.
65  Carter 1992, p. 8, and 1994, pp. 29–34.
66  *RCETI*, para. 581.
67  Kuczynski 1949, p. 833 (Table 44).
68  MA: NA 102/114 – 9 août 1878.
69  Gillion 1962, p. 126; Jayawardena 1971, p. 92.
70  Sirdars received higher wages and extra rations for supervising fellow-laborers. Job contractors, many of whom were ex-sirdars, employed their own bands of laborers to complete specific tasks at a predetermined price; upon completion of the contract, planters paid the job contractor who, in turn, was responsible for paying the workers in his band.
71  CO 167/284 – Address to Sir Wm. Gomm by certain planters of Pamplemousses, 30 June 1847. Enclosed in Despatch No. 142, Sir William Gomm to Earl Grey, July 3, 1847.
72  *RCETI*, paras. 2301–05.
73  *RCETI*, para. 2333.
74  *RCETI*, para. 2414.
75  MA: NA 102/173 – 7 & 13 février & 1 août 1884.
76  *RCETI*, para. 2766.
77  Virahsawmy 1979, p. 144.
78  Hazareesingh 1966, p. 257.
79  Gillion 1962, p. 123; Mayer 1963, p. 28 and 1967, pp. 1–19; Jayawardena 1971, pp. 89–91, 115–17; Lal 1977–78, p. 70; Kelly 1988, p. 41. See also Brown 1981.
80  Mayer 1967, p. 17; Jayawardena 1971, p. 108. See Hollup 1994 for the most recent account of caste in Mauritius.
81  Lal 1980, p. 60.
82  Macmillan 1914, p. 380.
83  Macmillan 1914, pp. 362, 401–02.
84  Koenig 1931, No. 56, p. 70, and No. 57, p. 115.
85  M.D. North-Coombes 1987, p. 9.
86  *MRC*, para. 70.
87  Sir Francis Watts, *Report on the Mauritius Sugar Industry* (hereafter Watts Report), para. 44. PP 1929–30 VIII [Cmd. 3518].
88  *MRC*, para. 52.

89  *MRC*, paras. 270, 298.
90  Burrenchobay 1944, pp. 15–20, 27–28; Saxena 1979, pp. 5–7.
91  Watts Report, para. 43.
92  Simmons 1982, pp. 52ff.; Storey 1995. See also Reddi 1989b.

## CONCLUSION

1  Alpers 1970, pp. 82–84, 123.
 2  Burroughs 1976, p. 243.
 3  Cumpston 1953, p. 85.
 4  Northrup 1995, pp. 156–60.
 5  Tomich 1990, p. 6.
 6  Weber 1964, p. 148.
 7  Munro 1993a, p. 18; Emmer 1997, pp. 13–14.
 8  Swartz, Turner, and Tuden 1966, pp. 9–10; Adams 1975; Pospisil 1978, pp. 14–15; Roberts 1979, p. 13.
 9  Stoler 1985a and 1985b, pp. 5ff.; Kelly 1989; Kaplan and Kelly 1994.
10  Adas 1986; Beechert 1993b, p. 319.
11  Stoler 1985b, p. 8; Munro 1993a, pp. 6ff.
12  Turner 1995, especially pp. 1–14.
13  Kelly 1989, pp. 388–89.
14  Adams 1970.
15  Cohen and Greene 1972, pp. 3, 9.
16  Stoler 1985b, p. 6.
17  Huff 1992.
18  Adas 1974; Evers 1988.

# Bibliography

ARCHIVAL SOURCES

Archives Nationales, Centre des Archives d'Outre-Mer, Aix-en-Provence: Série G$^1$, nos. 473, 474, 505.

Archives of the Council for World Mission, School of Oriental and African Studies, London: File: Mauritius, Incoming Letters.

Archives of the United Society for the Propagation of the Gospel, London: File: Africa – Madagascar, Mauritius & Seychelles, 1821–1960.

British Library, London: Add. Ms. 33765, 294210.

Carnegie Library, Curepipe, Mauritius: Orig. Ms., Maximillien Wiklinsky, "Voyage aux îles de France et de Bourbon et dans l'Inde (1769–70)."

India Office Library, London: Home Miscellaneous Series: Vols. 99, 102, 111, 153.

Mahatma Gandhi Institute, Moka, Mauritius: Series PC – Indian Emigration Certificates.

    Series PE – Indian Immigration Registers.

    Series PH – Vagrant Registers.

Mauritius Archives, Coromandel:

    Series A – Gouvernement Républicain: Divers.

    Series B – Gouvernement Républicain: Assemblées Coloniales: Procès Verbaux.

    Series GA – Gouvernement Impérial: Divers.

    Series HA – British Government: Early Years: Miscellaneous.

    Series IA – Miscellaneous.

    Series IB – Commission of Eastern Enquiry.

    Series ID – Statistics.

    Series KK – Census Returns.

    Series LC – Land Registry: Grants of Land (Originals).

    Series LH – Land Registry: Petitions for Grants of Land (Originals).

    Series LL – Land Registry: Miscellaneous.

    Series NA – Original Deeds.

    Series OA – Gouvernement Royal: Divers.

    Series OC – Gouvernement Royal: Guerre et Marine.

    Series RA – General Correspondence: In-Letters.

    Series Z2B – Police Department: Declaration and Occurrence Books (1770–1828).

Public Record Office, Kew: Colonial Office:

Series 167 – Original correspondence; letters received by the Secretary of State.
Series 170 – Sessional papers.
Series 172 – Miscellanea: newspapers, reports of Protectors of Slaves, Blue Books of statistics, etc.
Series 415 – Papers of the Commission of Eastern Enquiry.
University of Chicago, Joseph Regenstein Library, Chicago, Illinois: Ms. f-1051, Vol. 2 – Ministère de la marine. Mémoirs, rapports, lettres, etc. Manuscrits provenant de Louis de Curt, commissaire du roi. Etablissemens à l'est du Cap de Bonne Espérance.


## COLONY OF MAURITIUS PRINTED DOCUMENTS

Annual Reports:
  On the colony's condition, 1845–97.
  Government Savings Bank, 1837, 1851–53, 1881–85, 1889–1906/07.
  Protector of Immigrants/Immigration Department, 1859–1937.
  Registration and Mortgage Department, 1904–31.
Blue Books: 1825–26, 1834–43, 1846–51, 1864–74, 1887–1918, 1920.
Censuses:
  *Report of the Committee appointed to conduct and complete the census of the colony (1846).* PP 1849 XXXVII (280–II).
  *Report of the Commissioners Appointed to Take a Census of the Island of Mauritius and Its Dependencies, November 1851.*
  *Report of the Commissioners Appointed to Take a Census of the Island of Mauritius and Its Dependencies, April 1861.*
  *Census of Mauritius & Its Dependencies Taken on the 11th April 1871.*
  *Census of Mauritius & Its Dependencies Taken on the 4th April 1881.*
  *Census of Mauritius & Its Dependencies Taken on the 6th April 1891.*
  *Census of Mauritius & Its Dependencies Taken on the 1st April 1901.*
  *Report of the Census Enumeration Made in the Colony of Mauritius and Its Dependencies on the Night of the 31st March, 1911.*
  *Final Report of the Census Enumeration Made in the Colony of Mauritius and Its Dependencies on the Night of the 21st of May, 1921.*
  *Final Report of the Census Enumeration Made in the Colony of Mauritius and Its Dependencies on the April 26th, 1931.*


## WORKS CITED

Adams, Richard N. 1970. "Brokers and Career Mobility Systems in the Structure of Complex Societies," *Southwestern Journal of Anthropology*, 26, pp. 315–27.
  1975. *Energy and Structure: A Theory of Social Power* (Austin and London).
Adamson, Alan H. 1972. *Sugar Without Slaves: The Political Economy of British Guiana, 1838–1904* (New Haven and London).
Adas, Michael. 1974. "Immigrant Asians and the Economic Impact of European Imperialism: The Role of the South Indian Chettiars in British Burma," *Journal of Asian Studies*, 33, pp. 385–401.
  1986. "From Footdragging to Flight: The Evasive History of Peasant

Avoidance Protest in South and South-east Asia," *Journal of Peasant Studies*, 13/2, pp. 64–86.

Akinola, G.A. 1970. "The French on the Lindi Coast, 1785–1789," *Tanzania Notes and Records*, No. 70, pp. 13–20.

Allen, Richard B. 1983. "Marronage and the Maintenance of Public Order in Mauritius, 1721–1835," *Slavery and Abolition*, 4, pp. 214–31.

1989. "Economic Marginality and the Rise of the Free Population of Colour in Mauritius, 1767–1830," *Slavery and Abolition*, 10, pp. 126–50.

1991. "Lives of Neither Luxury Nor Misery: Indians and Free Colored Marginality on the Ile de France, 1728–1810," *Revue française d'histoire d'outre-mer*, 78, pp. 337–58.

1995. "The Intellectual Complacency of Contemporary Plantation Studies," *The Historian*, 57/3, pp. 582–86.

Alpers, Edward A. 1970. "The French Slave Trade in East Africa (1721–1810)," *Cahiers d'études africaines*, No. 37, pp. 80–124.

Aufhauser, R.K. 1974–75. "Profitability of Slavery in the British Caribbean," *Journal of Interdisciplinary History*, 5, pp. 45–67.

Backhouse, James. 1844. *A Narrative of a Visit to the Mauritius and South Africa* (London).

Baker, Philip, and Chris Corne. 1982. *Isle de France Creole: Affinities and Origins* (Karoma Publishers).

Barassin, Jean. 1979. "La révolte des esclaves à l'Ile Bourbon (Réunion) au XVIIIᵉ siècle," in *Mouvements de populations dans l'océan indien* (Paris), pp. 357–91.

Barickman, B.J. 1994. "'A Bit of Land, Which They Call *Roça*': Slave Provision Grounds in the Bahian Recôncavo, 1780–1860," *Hispanic American Historical Review*, 74, pp. 649–87.

Barker, Anthony J. 1996. *Slavery and Antislavery in Mauritius, 1810–33* (Basingstoke and New York).

Barnwell, P.J. 1948. *Visits and Despatches (Mauritius, 1598–1948)* (Port Louis).

Barnwell, P.J. and A. Toussaint. 1949. *A Short History of Mauritius* (London).

Beckford, George L. 1970. "The Dynamics of Growth and the Nature of Metropolitan Plantation Enterprise," *Social and Economic Studies* (Jamaica), 19, pp. 435–65.

1972. *Persistent Poverty: Underdevelopment in Plantation Economies of the Third World* (New York).

1985. "Caribbean Peasantry in the Confines of the Plantation Mode of Production," *International Social Science Journal*, 37, pp. 401–14.

Beckles, Hilary. 1991. "An Economic Life of Their Own: Slaves as Commodity Producers and Distributors in Barbados," *Slavery and Abolition*, 12, pp. 31–47.

Beechert, Edward D. 1993a. "Patterns of Resistance and the Social Relations of Production in Hawaii," in *Plantation Workers: Resistance and Accommodation*, eds. Brij V. Lal, Doug Munro and Edward D. Beechert (Honolulu), pp. 45–67.

1993b. "Reflections," in *Plantation Workers: Resistance and Accommodation*, eds. Brij V. Lal, Doug Munro and Edward D. Beechert (Honolulu), pp. 317–22.

Beejadhur, Aunauth. 1935. *Les indiens à l'Ile Maurice* (Port Louis).

Behal, Rana P. and Prabhu P. Mohapatra. 1992. "'Tea and Money versus Human Life': The Rise and Fall of the Indenture System in the Assam Tea Plantations, 1840–1908," *Journal of Peasant Studies*, 19/3–4, pp. 142–72.

Belrose-Huyghues, V. 1985. "Religion et esclavage aux Mascareignes sous le gouvernement de Farquhar," in *Le mouvement des idées dans l'océan indien occidental* (St. Denis), pp. 317–30.

Benn, D.M. 1974. "The Theory of Plantation Economy and Society: A Methodological Critique," *Journal of Commonwealth and Comparative Politics*, 12, pp. 249–60.

Bennett, Norman R. and George E. Brooks, Jr., eds. 1965. *New England Merchants in Africa: A History Through Documents, 1802 to 1865* (Boston).

Benoît, Gaëtan. 1985. *The Afro-Mauritians: An Essay* (Moka, Mauritius).

Berlin, Ira. 1974. *Slaves Without Masters: The Free Negro in the Antebellum South* (New York).

Berlin, Ira and Philip D. Morgan, eds. *The Slaves' Economy: Independent Production by Slaves in the Americas* (London).

Bernard, Eugène. 1889. "Essai sur les nouveaux affranchis de l'Ile Maurice," (originally published as "Les Africains de l'Ile Maurice" in 1834 in *Le Mauricien*), *Revue historique et littéraire de l'île Maurice*, 2/40–3/9.

Bernardin de St. Pierre, J.H. 1834. *Voyage à l'Ile de France* (Paris).

Bernstein, H. and M. Pitt. 1974. "Plantations and Modes of Exploitation," *Journal of Peasant Studies*, 1, pp. 514–26.

Besson, Jean. 1992. "Freedom and Community: The British West Indies," in *The Meaning of Freedom: Economics, Politics and Culture After Slavery*, eds. Frank McGlynn and Seymour Drescher (Pittsburgh and London), pp. 183–219.

Best, Lloyd. 1968. "Outlines of a Model of Pure Plantation Economy," *Social and Economic Studies* (Jamaica), 17, pp. 283–326.

Billiard, Aug^te. 1822. *Voyage aux colonies orientales, ou lettres écrites des îles de France et de Bourbon pendant les années 1817, 1818, 1819 et 1820, à M. le C^te de Montalivet, pair de France, ancien ministre de l'Interieur, etc.* (Paris).

Bolland, O. Nigel. 1981. "Systems of Domination after Slavery: The Control of Land and Labor in the British West Indies after 1838," *Comparative Studies in Society and History*, 23, pp. 591–619.

     1984. "Reply to William A. Green's 'The Perils of Comparative History'," *Comparative Studies in Society and History*, 26, pp. 120–25.

Bowman, Larry W. 1991. *Mauritius: Democracy and Development in the Indian Ocean* (Boulder, San Francisco, and London).

Brathwaite, Edward. 1971. *The Development of Creole Society in Jamaica, 1770–1820* (Oxford).

Breman, Jan. 1989. *Taming the Coolie Beast: Plantation Society and the Colonial Order in Southeast Asia* (Delhi).

Brereton, Bridget. 1994. "The Other Crossing: Asian Migrants in the Caribbean, A Review Essay," *Journal of Caribbean History*, 28/1, pp. 99–122.

Brown, Carolyn Henning. 1981. "Demographic Constraints on Caste: A Fiji Indian Example," *American Ethnologist*, 8, pp. 314–28.

Burrenchobay, M. 1944. *A Short Account of the Co-operative Credit Societies Movement in Mauritius* (Port Louis).

Burroughs, Peter. 1976. "The Mauritius Rebellion of 1832 and the Abolition of British Colonial Slavery," *Journal of Imperial and Commonwealth History*, 4/3, pp. 243–65.

Butler, Kathleen Mary. 1995. *The Economics of Emancipation: Jamaica and Barbados, 1823–1843* (Chapel Hill and London).

Campbell, Mavis C. 1976. *The Dynamics of Change in a Slave Society: A Sociopolitical History of the Free Coloreds of Jamaica, 1800–1865* (Rutherford, NJ).

Carroll, Patrick J. 1977. "Mandinga: The Evolution of a Mexican Runaway Slave Community," *Comparative Studies in Society and History*, 19, pp. 488–505.

Carter, Marina. 1992. "The Family Under Indenture: A Mauritian Case Study," *Journal of Mauritian Studies*, 4/1, pp. 1–21.

1993. "The Transition from Slave to Indentured Labour in Mauritius," *Slavery and Abolition*, 14/1, pp. 114–30.

1994. *Lakshmi's Legacy: The Testimonies of Indian Women in 19th Century Mauritius* (Stanley, Rose Hill, Mauritius).

1995. *Servants, Sirdars and Settlers: Indians in Mauritius, 1834–1874* (Delhi).

1996. *Voices From Indenture: Experiences of Indian Migrants in the British Empire* (London and New York).

Clarence-Smith, William Gervase. 1988. "The Economics of the Indian Ocean and Red Sea Slave Trades in the 19th Century: An Overview," *Slavery and Abolition*, 9/3, pp. 1–20.

Cohen, David W. and Jack P. Greene, eds. 1972. *Neither Slave Nor Free – The Freedmen of African Descent in the Slave Societies of the New World* (Baltimore).

Cooper, Frederick. 1977. *Plantation Slavery on the East Coast of Africa* (New Haven).

1980. *From Slaves to Squatters: Plantation Labor and Agriculture in Zanzibar and Coastal Kenya, 1890–1925* (New Haven).

Courtenay, P.P. 1965. *Plantation Agriculture* (London).

Cox, Edward L. 1984. *Free Coloreds in the Slave Societies of St. Kitts and Grenada, 1763–1833* (Knoxville).

Craton, Michael. 1988. "Continuity Not Change: The Incidence of Unrest Among Ex-Slaves in the British West Indies, 1838–1876," *Slavery and Abolition*, 9, pp. 144–70.

1992. "The Transition from Slavery to Free Wage Labour in the Caribbean, 1780–1890: A Survey with Particular Reference to Recent Scholarship," *Slavery and Abolition*, 13/2, pp. 37–67.

Cumpston, I.M. 1953. *Indians Overseas in British Territories, 1834–1854* (London).

Deerr, Noël. 1949–50. *The History of Sugar*, 2 vols. (London).

de Groot, Silvia W. 1985a. "A Comparison between the History of Maroon Communities in Surinam and Jamaica," *Slavery and Abolition*, 6/3, pp. 173–84.

1985b. "The Maroons of Surinam: Agents of Their Own Emancipation," in

*Abolition and Its Aftermath: The Historical Context, 1790–1916*, ed. David Richardson (London), pp. 55–79.

Delaleu, Jean Baptiste Etienne. 1777. *Code des Isles de France et de Bourbon* (L'Isle de France; 2nd ed., Port Louis, 1826).

de Nettancourt, Gabrielle. 1979. "Le peuplement neerlandais à l'Ile Maurice (1598–1710)," in *Mouvements de populations dans l'océan indien* (Paris), pp. 219–29.

Drescher, Seymour. 1977. *Econocide: British Slavery in the Era of Abolition* (Pittsburgh, 1977).

d'Unienville, Baron. 1885–86. *Statistiques de l'île Maurice et ses dépendances suivie d'une notice historique sur cette colonie et d'un essai sur l'île de Madagascar*, 2nd ed., 3 Vols. (Maurice).

Eisenberg, Peter L. 1974. *The Sugar Industry of Pernambuco: Modernization Without Change, 1840–1910* (Berkeley).

Emmer, Pieter C., ed. 1986. *Colonialism and Migration; Indentured Labour Before and After Slavery* (Dordrecht).

1992. "The Price of Freedom: The Constraints of Change in Postemancipation America," in *The Meaning of Freedom: Economics, Politics, and Culture After Slavery*, eds. Frank McGlynn and Seymour Drescher (Pittsburgh and London), pp. 23–47.

1993. "Between Slavery and Freedom: The Period of Apprenticeship in Suriname (Dutch Guiana), 1863–73," *Slavery and Abolition*, 14/1, pp. 87–113.

1997. "European Expansion and Unfree Labour: An Introduction," *Itinerario*, 21/1, pp. 9–14.

Engerman, Stanley L. 1984. "Economic Change and Contract Labor in the British Caribbean: The End of Slavery and the Adjustment to Emancipation," *Explorations in Economic History*, 21, pp. 133–50.

1992. "The Economic Response to Emancipation and Some Economic Aspects of the Meaning of Freedom," in *The Meaning of Freedom: Economics, Politics, and Culture After Slavery*, eds. Frank McGlynn and Seymour Drescher (Pittsburgh and London), pp. 49–68.

Evers, Hans-Dieter. 1988. "Chettiar Moneylenders in Southeast Asia," in *Marchands et hommes d'affaires asiatiques dans l'océan indien et la mer de Chine, 13e–20e siècles*, eds. Denys Lombard and Jean Aubin (Paris), pp. 199–219.

Filliot, J.-M. 1974. *La traite des esclaves vers les Mascareignes au XVIIIe siècle* (Paris).

Flory, Thomas. 1979. "Fugitive Slaves and Free Society: The Case of Brazil," *Journal of Negro History*, 54/2, pp. 116–30.

Foner, Laura. 1969–70. "The Free People of Color in Louisiana and St. Domingue: A Comparative Portrait of Two–Three Caste Slave Societies," *Journal of Social History*, 3, pp. 406–30.

Freeman-Grenville, G.S.P. 1965. *The French at Kilwa Island* (Oxford).

Fuma, Sudel. 1979. *Esclaves et citoyens, le destin de 62.000 Réunionnais. Histoire de l'insertion des affranchis de 1848 dans la société réunionnaise* (St. Denis, Réunion).

1992. *L'Esclavagisme à La Réunion* (Paris, St. Denis).

Galloway, J.H. 1989. *The Sugar Cane Industry: An Historical Geography from Its Origins to 1914* (Cambridge).

Garrigus, John. 1993. "Blue and Brown: Contraband Indigo and the Rise of a Free Colored Planter Class in French Saint-Domingue," *The Americas*, 50, pp. 233–63.

Gaspar, David Barry. 1985. *Bondmen and Rebels: A Study of Master-Slave Relations in Antigua, With Implications for Colonial British America* (Baltimore and London).

G.C.O. 1939–44. "A Brief Sketch of the Present State of the Isle of France" (originally published in the *Courier*, October 21, 1812), ed. Auguste Toussaint, *Bulletin de la société de l'histoire de l'île Maurice*, 2, pp. 48–50.

Geggus, David. 1985. "On the Eve of the Haitian Revolution: Slave Runaways in Saint Domingue in the Year 1790," *Slavery and Abolition*, 6/3, pp. 112–28.

   1989. "Sex Ratio, Age and Ethnicity in the Atlantic Slave Trade: Data from French Shipping and Plantation Records," *Journal of African History*, 30, pp. 23–44.

Genovese, Eugene. 1976. *Roll, Jordan, Roll: The World the Slaves Made* (New York).

Gerbeau, Hubert. 1979a. "Quelques aspects de la traite illegale des esclaves à l'Ile Bourbon au XIXᵉ siècle," in *Mouvements de populations dans l'océan indien* (Paris), pp. 273–308.

   1979b. "Les esclaves et la mer à Bourbon au XIXᵉ siècle," *Minorités et gens de mer en océan indien, XIXᵉ–XXᵉ siècles*, I.H.P.O.M. Etudes et Documents No. 12 (Aix-en-Provence), pp. 10–51.

Gillion, K.L. 1962. *Fiji's Indian Migrants* (Melbourne).

Glassman, Jonathon. 1991. "The Bondsman's New Clothes: The Contradictory Consciousness of Slave Resistance on the Swahili Coast," *Journal of African History*, 32, pp. 277–312.

Goveia, Elsa V. 1965. *Slave Society in the British Leeward Islands at the End of the Eighteenth Century* (New Haven).

(Grant, Baron). 1801. *The History of Mauritius, or the Isle of France, and the Neighboring Islands; From Their First Discovery to the Present Time; Composed Principally from the Papers and Memoirs of Baron Grant, Who Resided Twenty Years in the Island, By His Son, Charles Grant, Viscount de Vaux* (London).

Graves, Adrian. 1983. "Truck and Gifts: Melanesian Immigrants and the Trade Box System in Colonial Queensland," *Past and Present*, No. 101, pp. 87–124.

Graves, Adrian and Peter Richardson. 1980. "Plantations in the Political Economy of Colonial Sugar Production: Natal and Queensland, 1860–1914," *Journal of Southern African Studies*, 6, pp. 214–29.

Green, William A. 1976. *British Slave Emancipation: The Sugar Colonies and the Great Experiment, 1830–1865* (Oxford).

   1984. "The Perils of Comparative History: Belize and the British Sugar Colonies after Slavery," *Comparative Studies in Society and History*, 26, pp. 112–19.

Hall, D. 1978. "The Flight from the Estates Reconsidered: The British West Indies, 1838–42," *Journal of Caribbean History*, 10 & 11, pp. 7–24.

Hall, Gwendolyn. 1971. *Social Control in Slave Plantation Societies: A Comparison of St. Domingue and Cuba* (Baltimore).

Hall, Neville A.T. 1992. *Slave Society in the Danish West Indies* (Baltimore and London).

Handler, Jerome S. 1974. *The Unappropriated People: Freedmen in the Slave Society of Barbados* (Baltimore and London).

Haudrère, Philippe. 1989. *La Compagnie française des Indes au XVIII^e siècle* (Paris).

Hayot, E. 1969. "Les gens de couleur libre du Fort-Royal, 1679–1823," *Revue française d'histoire d'outre-mer*, 56, pp. 5–163.

Hazareesingh, K. 1966. "The Religion and Culture of Indian Immigrants in Mauritius and the Effect of Social Change," *Comparative Studies in Society and History*, 8/2, pp. 241–57.

1975. *History of Indians in Mauritius*, 2nd ed. (London).

Heuman, Gad. 1981. *Between Black and White: Race, Politics, and the Free Coloreds of Jamaica, 1792–1865* (Westport, CT).

1985. "Runaway Slaves in Nineteenth-Century Barbados," *Slavery and Abolition*, 6/3, pp. 95–111.

Higman, B.W. 1984. *Slave Populations in the British Caribbean, 1807–1834* (Baltimore and London).

Hollup, Oddvar. 1994. "The Disintegration of Caste and Changing Concepts of Indian Ethnic Identity in Mauritius," *Ethnology*, 33/4, pp. 297–316.

Holt, Thomas C. 1992. *The Problem of Slavery: Race, Labor, and Politics in Jamaica and Britain, 1832–1938* (Baltimore and London).

Howel, Brenda M. 1951. "Mauritius, 1832–1849: A Study of a Sugar Colony," Dissertation, University of London.

Huff, W.G. 1992. "Sharecroppers, Risk, Management, and Chinese Estate Rubber Development in Interwar British Malaya," *Economic Development and Cultural Change*, 40/2, pp. 743–73.

Jain, Ravindra K. 1970. *South Indians on the Plantation Frontier in Malaya* (New Haven and London).

1984. "South Indian Labour in Malaya, 1840–1920: Asylum Stability and Involution," in *Indentured Labour in the British Empire, 1834–1920*, ed. Kay Saunders (London and Canberra), pp. 158–82.

Jayawardena, Chandra. 1971. "The Disintegration of Caste in Fiji Indian Rural Society," in *Anthropology in Oceania: Essays Presented to Ian Hogbin*, ed. L.R. Hiatt and Chandra Jayawardena (Sydney), pp. 89–119.

1983. "Farm, Household and Family in Fiji Indian Rural Society," in *Overseas Indians: A Study in Adaptation*, eds. George Kurian and Ram P. Srivastava (New Delhi), pp. 141–79.

Jumeer, Musleem. 1979. "Les affranchisements et les libres à l'île de France à la fin de l'ancien régime (1768–1789)," MA thesis, Faculté des Sciences Humaines, Université de Poitiers.

Kalla, Abdool Cader. 1984. "Runtongee Bickagee: premier négoçiant parsi à Maurice," *La Gazette des Iles de la Mer des Indes*, No. 4 (April), pp. 27–29.

1987. "The Gujarati Merchants in Mauritius, c. 1850–1900," *Journal of Mauritian Studies*, 2/1, pp. 45–65.

Kaplan, Martha and John D. Kelly. 1994. "Rethinking Resistance: Dialogics of 'Disaffection' in Colonial Fiji," *American Ethnologist*, 21, pp. 123–51.

Kay, Marvin L. Michael and Lorin Lee Cary. 1985. "'They are Indeed the Constant Plague of Their Tyrants': Slave Defence of a Moral Economy in Colonial North Carolina, 1748–1772," *Slavery and Abolition*, 6/3, pp. 37–56.

Keber, Martha Turner. n.d. "Crossing the Line: The Intersecting Worlds of Christophe Poulain DuBignon" (unpublished manuscript).

Kelly, John D. 1988. "From Holi to Diwali in Fiji: An Essay on Ritual and History," *Man*, New Ser., 23, pp. 40–55.

1989. "Fear of Culture: British Regulation of Indian Marriage in Post-Indenture Fiji, *Ethnohistory*, 36, pp. 372–91.

Kinsbruner, Jay. 1990. "Caste and Capitalism in the Caribbean: Residential Patterns and House Ownership among the Free People of Color of San Juan, Puerto Rico, 1823–46," *Hispanic American Historical Review*, 70, pp. 433–61.

Klein, Herbert S. 1973. "Neither Slave Nor Free: The *Emancipados* of Brazil, 1818–1868," *Hispanic American Historical Review*, 53, pp. 50–70.

Klein, Herbert S. and Stanley L. Engerman. 1985. "The Transition to Free Labor: Notes on a Comparative Economic Model," in *Between Slavery and Free Labor: The Spanish-Speaking Caribbean in the Nineteenth Century*, eds. Manuel Moreno Fraginals, Frank Maya Pons and Stanley L. Engerman (Baltimore and London), pp. 255–69.

Klein, Martin, ed. 1993. *Breaking the Chains: Slavery, Bondage, and Emancipation in Modern Africa and Asia* (Madison).

Knapman, Bruce. 1987. *Fiji's Economic History, 1874–1939: Studies of Capitalist Colonial Development* (Canberra).

Koenig, M. 1931. "Agricultural Census in Mauritius, 1930," *Revue agricole de l'Ile Maurice*, No. 56, pp. 67–74; No. 57, pp. 114–19; No. 58, pp. 158–70.

Kondapi, C. 1951. *Indians Overseas, 1838–1949* (New Delhi).

Kopytoff, Barbara S. 1973. "The Maroons of Jamaica: An Ethnohistorical Study of Incomplete Polities, 1655–1905," Diss., University of Pennsylvania.

1976a. "The Development of Jamaican Maroon Ethnicity," *Caribbean Quarterly*, 22/2 & 3, pp. 33–50.

1976b. "Jamaican Maroon Political Organization: The Effects of the Treaties," *Social and Economic Studies* (Jamaica), 25/2, pp. 87–105.

Kuczynski, R.R. 1949. *Demographic Survey of the British Colonial Empire*, Vol. II (London).

(La Bourdonnais, B.F. Mahé de). 1827. *Mémoires historiques de B.F. Mahé de la Bourdonnais, gouverneur des îles de France et de Bourbon; recueillis et publiés par son petit-fils* (Paris).

Lady, A (Lady Robert Bertram). 1830. *Recollections of Seven Years Residence at the Mauritius, or Isle of France* (London).

Lagesse, Marcelle. 1978. *L'Ile de France avant La Bourdonnais* (Port Louis).

Lal, Brij V. 1977–78. "Exhaustion and Persistence: Aspects of Rural Indian Society of Fiji," *Quarterly Review of Historical Studies*, 17, pp. 69–79.

1980. "Approaches to the Study of Indian Indentured Emigration with Special Reference to Fiji," *Journal of Pacific History*, 15, pp. 52–70.

1993. "'Nonresistance' on Fiji Plantations: The Fiji Indian Experience, 1879–1920," in *Plantation Workers: Resistance and Accommodation*, eds. Brij V. Lal, Doug Munro and Edward D. Beechert (Honolulu), pp. 187–216.

Lal, Brij V., Doug Munro and Edward D. Beechert, eds. 1993. *Plantation Workers: Resistance and Accommodation* (Honolulu).

Lamusse, Roland. 1964a. "The Economic Development of the Mauritius Sugar Industry. I. Development in Field and Factory," *Revue agricole et sucrière de l'île Maurice*, 43, pp. 22–38.

1964b. "The Economic Development of the Mauritius Sugar Industry. II. Labour Problems," *Revue agricole et sucrière de l'île Maurice*, 43, pp. 113–27.

1964c. "The Economic Development of the Mauritius Sugar Industry. III. The Sources of Capital and System of Crop Finance," *Revue agricole et sucrière de l'île Maurice*, 43, pp. 354–72.

1965. "The Economic Development of the Mauritius Sugar Industry. IV. Mauritius Sugar in World Trade," *Revue agricole et sucrière de l'île Maurice*, 44, pp. 11–36.

Laurence, K.O. 1994. *A Question of Labour: Indentured Immigration into Trinidad and British Guiana, 1875–1917* (New York).

Lobdell, Richard A. 1972. "Patterns of Investment and Sources of Credit in the British West Indian Sugar Industry, 1838–97," *Journal of Caribbean History*, 4, pp. 31–53.

Look Lai, Walton. 1993. *Indentured Labor, Caribbean Sugar: Chinese and Indian Migrants to the British West Indies, 1838–1918* (Baltimore and London).

Lovejoy, Paul E. 1978. "Plantations in the Economy of the Sokoto Caliphate," *Journal of African History*, 19, pp. 341–68.

1979. "The Characteristics of Plantations in the Nineteenth-Century Sokoto Caliphate (Islamic West Africa)," *American Historical Review*, 84, pp. 1267–91.

1983. *Transformations in Slavery: A History of Slavery in Africa* (Cambridge).

Ly-Tio-Fane, Madeleine. 1958. *Mauritius and the Spice Trade: The Odyssey of Pierre Poivre* (Port Louis).

1968. "Problèmes d'approvisionnement de l'Ile de France au temps de l'intendant Poivre," *Proceedings of the Royal Society of Arts and Sciences of Mauritius*, 3/1, pp. 101–15.

1970. *The Triumph of Jean Nicolas Céré and His Isle Bourbon Collaborators* (Paris and The Hague).

1995. "The Americans and the Franchise of Port Louis, Ile de France," *The Indian Ocean Review* (June–September), pp. 19–22.

Ly-Tio-Fane Pineo, Huguette. 1984. *Lured Away: The Life History of Indian Cane Workers in Mauritius* (Moka, Mauritius).

1992. "Les esclaves 'de plantation' de l'Ile Maurice à la veille de l'abolition, d'après le recensement de 1823," in *Histoires d'outre-mer: Mélanges en l'honneur de Jean-Louis Miège*, Vol. II (Aix-en-Provence), pp. 635–55.

1993. *Ile de France, 1715–1746: L'Emergence de Port Louis* (Moka, Mauritius).

McFarlane, Anthony. 1985. "*Cimarrones* and *Palenques*: Runaways and Resistance in Colonial Colombia," *Slavery and Abolition*, 6/3, pp. 131–51.

Macmillan, Allister, ed. 1914. *Mauritius Illustrated. Historical and Descriptive, Commercial and Industrial Facts, Figures & Resources* (London).

Mandle, Jay R. 1972. "The Plantation Economy: An Essay in Definition," *Science and Society*, 36, pp. 49–62.

Mannick, A.R. 1979. *Mauritius: The Development of a Plural Society* (Nottingham).

Mantaux, Christian G. and Harold Adolphe. 1972. "Documents officiels inédits sur Elisabeth Marie Sobobie Betia," *Bulletin de l'Académie Malgache*, 50/1, pp. 65–113.

Marks, Shula and Peter Richardson, eds. 1984. *International Labour Migration: Historical Perspectives* (Hounslow).

Marshall, Bernard A. 1982. "Social Stratification and the Free Coloured in the Slave Society of the British Windward Islands," *Social and Economic Studies* (Jamaica), 31/1, pp. 1–39.

Marshall, W.K. 1985. "Apprenticeship and Labour Relations in Four Windward Islands," in *Abolition and Its Aftermath: The Historical Context, 1790–1916*, ed. David Richardson (London), pp. 203–24.

    1991. "Provision Ground and Plantation Labour in Four Windward Islands: Competition for Resources during Slavery," *Slavery and Abolition*, 13/2, pp. 48–67.

Mayer, Adrian C. 1963. *Indians in Fiji* (London).

    1967. "Introduction," in *Caste in Overseas Indian Communities*, ed. Barton M. Schwartz (San Francisco), pp. 1–19.

Menard, Russell R. 1994. "Financing the Lowcountry Export Boom: Capital and Growth in Early South Carolina," *The William and Mary Quarterly*, 3rd Ser., 51/4, pp. 659–76.

Milbert, M.J. 1812. *Voyage pittoresque à l'Ile de France, au Cap de Bonne-Espérance et à l'Ile de Ténériffe*, 2 vols. (Paris).

Milburn, William, Esq. 1813. *Oriental Commerce*, 2 vols. (London).

Mintz, Sidney W. 1979. "Slavery and the Rise of Peasantries," *Historical Reflections/Réflexions historiques*, 6, pp. 213–42.

Mintz, Sidney W. and Richard Price. 1976. "An Anthropological Approach to the Afro-American Past: A Caribbean Perspective," *I.S.H.I. Occasional Papers in Social Change*, No. 2 (Philadelphia).

Morgan, Philip D. 1985. "Colonial South Carolina Runaways: Their Significance for Slave Culture," *Slavery and Abolition*, 6/3, pp. 57–78.

Mouat, Frederic J., M.D. 1852. *Rough Notes of a Trip to Reunion, Mauritius and Ceylon* (rpt., New Delhi, 1984).

Mullin, Michael. 1992. *Africa in America: Slave Acculturation and Resistance in the American South and the British Caribbean, 1736–1831* (Urbana and Chicago).

Munro, Doug. 1993a. "Patterns of Resistance and Accommodation," in *Plantation Workers: Resistance and Accommodation*, eds. Brij V. Lal, Doug Munro and Edward D. Beechert (Honolulu), pp. 1–43.

    1993b. "The Pacific Islands Labour Trade: Approaches, Methodologies, Debates, *Slavery and Abolition*, 14/2, pp. 87–108.

    1995a. "Revisionism and Its Enemies: Debating the Queensland Labour Trade," *Journal of Pacific History*, 30/2, pp. 240–49.

1995b. "The Labor Trade in Melanesians to Queensland: An Historiographical Essay," *Journal of Social History*, 28/3, pp. 609–27.

Munro, Doug and Stewart Firth. 1993. "Samoan Plantations: The Gilbertese Laborers' Experience, 1867–1896," in *Plantation Workers: Resistance and Accommodation*, eds. Brij V. Lal, Doug Munro and Edward D. Beechert (Honolulu), pp. 101–27.

Newbury, Colin. 1974–75. "Labour Migration in the Imperial Phase: An Essay in Interpretation," *Journal of Imperial and Commonwealth History*, 3, pp. 234–56.

Noël, Karl. 1954. "La condition matérielle des esclaves à l'Ile de France, période française (1715–1810)," *Revue d'histoire des colonies françaises*, 56, pp. 303–13.

North-Coombes, Alfred. 1937. *The Evolution of Sugarcane in Mauritius* (Port Louis).

1938–39. "The First Hundred Years of the Mauritian Sugar Industry (1650–1750)," *Bulletin annuel de la société de l'histoire de l'île Maurice*, 1, pp. 48–54.

1979. *La découverte des Mascareignes par les arabes et les portugais* (Port Louis).

North-Coombes, M.D. 1984. "From Slavery to Indenture: Forced Labour in the Political Economy of Mauritius, 1834–1867," in *Indentured Labour in the British Empire, 1834–1920*, ed. Kay Saunders (London and Canberra), pp. 78–125.

1987. "Struggles in the Cane Fields: Small Cane Growers, Millers and the Colonial State in Mauritius, 1921–1937," *Journal of Mauritian Studies*, 2/1, pp. 1–44.

Northrup, David. 1995. *Indentured Labor in the Age of Imperialism, 1834–1922* (Cambridge, New York and Melbourne).

Nwulia, Moses D.E. 1978. "The 'Apprenticeship' System in Mauritius: Its Character and Its Impact on Race Relations in the Immediate Post-Emancipation Period, 1839–1879," *African Studies Review*, 21/1, pp. 89–101.

1981. *The History of Slavery in Mauritius and the Seychelles, 1810–1875* (London and Toronto).

Olwig, Karen Fog, ed. 1995. *Small Islands, Large Questions: Society, Culture and Resistance in the Post-Emancipation Caribbean* (London).

Patterson, Orlando. 1982. *Slavery and Social Death: A Comparative Study* (Cambridge, MA).

Paturau, J. Maurice. 1988. *Histoire économique de l'Ile Maurice* (Les Pailles, Mauritius).

Payet, J.V. 1990. *Histoire de l'esclavage à l'Ile Bourbon* (Paris).

Piggott, Francis Taylor, Louis Arthur Thibaud and Furcy Alfred Herchenroder. 1896. *The Laws of Mauritius*, Vol. I (Port Louis).

Pike, Nicholas. 1873. *Sub-tropical Rambles in the Land of the Aphanapteryx* (New York).

Pitman, F.W. 1931. "The Settlement and Financing of British West India Plantations in the Eighteenth Century," in *Essays in Colonial History*

*Presented to Charles McLean Andrews by His Students* (New Haven), pp. 252–83.

(Poivre, Pierre). 1797. *Œuvres complettes de P. Poivre, Intendant des Isles de France et de Bourbon, correspondant de l'académie des sciences, etc.; Précédées de sa vie, et accompagnées de notes* (Paris).

Pospisil, Leopold J. 1978. *The Ethnology of Law*, 2nd ed. (Menlo Park, NJ).

Price, Richard, ed. 1979. *Maroon Societies: Rebel Slave Communities in the Americas*, 2nd ed. (Garden City, NY).

Ragatz, Lowell Joseph. 1928. *The Fall of the Planter Class in the British Caribbean, 1763–1833* (New York).

Ramasamy, P. 1992. "Labour Control and Labour Resistance in the Plantations of Colonial Malaya," *Journal of Peasant Studies*, 19/3–4, pp. 87–105.

Ramdoyal, Ramesh. 1979. *Tales From Mauritius* (Moka, Mauritius).

Raynal, Guillaume-Thomas. 1781. *Histoire philosophique et politique des établissemens et du commerce des européens dans les deux indes* (Geneva).

Reddi, Sadasivam J. 1989a. "Aspects of Slavery During the British Administration," in *Slavery in South West Indian Ocean*, eds. U. Bissoondoyal and S.B.C. Servansing (Moka, Mauritius), pp. 106–23.

1989b. "The Development of Political Awareness among Indians, 1870–1930," *Journal of Mauritian Studies*, 3/1, pp. 1–15.

Richardson, Peter. 1982. "The Natal Sugar Industry, 1849–1905: An Interpretive Essay," *Journal of African History*, 23, pp. 515–27.

Rivière, W.E. 1972. "Labour Shortage in the British West Indies After Emancipation," *Journal of Caribbean History* (Barbados), 4, pp. 1–30.

Roberts, Simon. 1979. *Order and Dispute: An Introduction to Legal Anthropology* (Harmondsworth).

Rouillard, Guy. 1979. *Histoire des domaines sucriers de l'Ile Maurice* (Les Pailles, Mauritius).

Rudolph, Lloyd I. and Susanne Hoeber Rudolph. 1967. *The Modernity of Tradition: Political Development in India* (Chicago and London).

Ryan, Vincent W. 1864. *Mauritius and Madagascar: Journals of An Eight Years' Residence in the Diocese of Mauritius, and of a Visit to Madagascar* (London).

Saha, Panchanan. 1970. *Emigration of Indian Labour, 1834–1900* (Delhi).

Sakarai, Lawrence J. 1980. "Indian Merchants in East Africa. Part I: The Triangular Trade and the Slave Economy," *Slavery and Abolition*, 1, pp. 292–338.

1981. "Indian Merchants in East Africa. Part II: British Imperialism and the Transformation of the Slave Economy," *Slavery and Abolition*, 2, pp. 2–30.

Saxena, M.P. 1979. *Survey of Agricultural Cooperative Credit Societies in Mauritius* (New Delhi).

Schnakenbourg, Christian. 1984. "From Sugar Estate to Central Factory: The Industrial Revolution in the Caribbean (1840–1905)," in *Crisis and Change in the International Sugar Economy*, eds. Bill Albert and Adrian Graves (Norwich and Edinburgh), pp. 83–93.

Schwartz, Stuart B. 1992. *Slaves, Peasants, and Rebels: Reconsidering Brazilian Slavery* (Urbana and Chicago).

Scott, Rebecca J. 1988. "Exploring the Meaning of Freedom: Postemancipation

Societies in Comparative Perspective," *Hispanic American Historical Review*, 68, pp. 407–28.

Sheridan, Richard B. 1973. *Sugar and Slavery: An Economic History of the British West Indies, 1623–1775* (Baltimore).

1993. "From Chattel to Wage Slavery in Jamaica, 1740–1860," *Slavery and Abolition*, 14/1, pp. 13–40.

Shlomowitz, Ralph. 1981. "Markets for Indentured and Time-expired Melanesian Labour in Queensland, 1863–1906," *Journal of Pacific History*, 16, pp. 70–91.

1982. "Melanesian Labor and the Development of the Queensland Sugar Industry, 1863–1906," *Research in Economic History*, 7, pp. 327–61.

Silverman, Marilyn. 1987. "Agrarian Processes within 'Plantation Economies': Cases from Guyana and Coastal Ecuador," *Canadian Review of Sociology and Anthropology*, 24, pp. 550–70.

Simmons, Adele Smith. 1982. *Modern Mauritius: The Politics of Decolonization* (Bloomington, IN).

Sio, Arnold A. 1976. "Race, Colour, and Miscegenation: The Free Coloured of Jamaica and Barbados," *Caribbean Studies*, 16 (April), pp. 5–21.

Smith, Kevin D. 1995. "A Fragmented Freedom: The Historiography of Emancipation and its Aftermath in the British West Indies," *Slavery and Abolition*, 16/1, pp. 101–30.

Sornay, Pierre. 1920. *La canna à sucre à l'Ile Maurice* (Paris).

Srinivas, M.N. 1968. *Social Change in Modern India* (Berkeley and Los Angeles).

Stern, Steve J. 1988. "Feudalism, Capitalism, and the World-System in the Perspective of Latin America and the Caribbean," *American Historical Review*, 93, pp. 829–72.

Stinchcombe, Arthur L. 1994. "Freedom and Oppression of Slaves in the Eighteenth Century Caribbean," *American Sociological Review*, 59, pp. 911–29.

Stoler, Ann Laura. 1985a. "Perceptions of Protest: Defining the Dangerous in Colonial Sumatra," *American Ethnologist*, 12, pp. 642–58.

1985b. *Capitalism and Confrontation in Sumatra's Plantation Belt, 1870–1979* (New Haven and London).

Storey, William Kelleher. 1995. "Small-Scale Sugar Cane Farmers and Biotechnology in Mauritius: The 'Uba' Riots of 1937," *Agricultural History*, 69/2, pp. 163–76.

Swartz, Marc J., Victor Turner and Arthur Tuden. 1966. *Political Anthropology* (Chicago).

Tayal, Maureen. 1977. "Indian Indentured Labor in Natal, 1890–1911," *The Indian Economic and Social History Review*, 14, pp. 519–47.

Teelock, Vijaya. 1990. "Breaking the Wall of Silence: The History of Afro-Malagasy Mauritians in the Nineteenth Century," *Journal of Mauritian Studies*, 3/2, pp. 1–20.

1995. *A Select Guide to Sources on Slavery in Mauritius and Slaves Speak Out: The Testimony of Slaves in the Era of Sugar* (Bell Village, Mauritius).

Tinker, Hugh. 1974. *A New System of Slavery: The Export of Indian Labour Overseas, 1830–1920* (London).

Tomich, Dale W. 1990. *Slavery in the Circuit of Sugar: Martinique and the World Economy, 1830–1848* (Baltimore and London).

1991. "*Une Petite Guinée*: Provision Ground and Plantation in Martinique, 1830–1848," *Slavery and Abolition*, 12/1, pp. 68–91.

Toussaint, Auguste. 1953. *Historique de la Chambre d'Agriculture, Ile Maurice* (Mauritius Chamber of Agriculture).

1954. *Early American Trade with Mauritius* (Port Louis).

1967. "Le domaine de Bénarès et les débuts du sucre à l'Ile Maurice," *Annales de l'Université de Madagascar*, Série Lettres et Sciences Humaines, 6, pp. 35–89.

1972. *Histoire des îles Mascareignes* (Paris).

1974. *Histoire de l'Ile Maurice* (Paris).

1975. "Les Lyonnais à l'île de France (île Maurice), 1721–1810," *Cahiers d'histoire*, 20/1, pp. 39–58.

1977. *Le mirage des îles: Le négoce français aux Mascareignes au XVIIIᵉ siècle* (Aix-en-Provence).

1979. *Les frères Surcouf* (Paris).

1982. "Le Port-Louis de l'Ile Maurice," in *Les ports de l'océan indien, XIXᵉ– XXᵉ siècles*, I.H.P.O.M. Etudes et Documents No. 15 (Aix-en-Provence), pp. 120–35.

Trouillot, Michel-Rolph. 1988. *Peasants and Capital: Dominica in the World Economy* (Baltimore and London).

Turner, Mary. 1988. "Chattel Slaves Into Wage Slaves: A Jamaican Case Study," in *Labour in the Caribbean*, eds. Malcolm Cross and Gad Heuman (London and Basingstoke), pp. 14–31.

Turner, Mary, ed. 1995. *From Chattel Slaves to Wage Slaves: The Dynamics of Labour Bargaining in the Americas* (Kingston, Bloomington and Indianapolis, London).

Van Zwanenberg, R.M.A. 1975. *Colonial Capitalism and Labour in Kenya, 1919–1939* (Nairobi).

Virahsawmy, Raj. 1979. "Le développement du capitalisme agraire et l'émergence de petits planteurs à l'Ile Maurice," *African Development*, 4/2–3, pp. 136–48.

Virts, Nancy. 1991. "The Efficiency of Southern Tenant Plantations, 1900–1945," *Journal of Economic History*, 51, pp. 385–95.

Walters, A. 1910. *The Sugar Industry of Mauritius: A Study in Correlation* (London).

Wanquet, Claude. 1977. "Aperçu sur l'affranchissement des esclaves à Bourbon à la fin du XVIIIᵉ siècle," *Annuaire des pays de l'océan indien*, 4, pp. 131–49.

Ward, J.R. 1978. "The Profitability of Sugar Planting in the British West Indies, 1650–1834," *Economic History Review*, Ser. 2, 31, pp. 197–213.

1988. *British West Indian Slavery, 1750–1834: The Process of Amelioration* (Oxford).

Watson, James L., ed. 1980. *Asian and African Systems of Slavery* (Berkeley and Los Angeles).

Watts, David. 1987. *The West Indies: Patterns of Development, Culture and Environmental Change Since 1492* (Cambridge, New York and Melbourne).

Weber, Max. 1964. *The Theory of Social and Economic Organization*, trans. A.M. Henderson and Talcott Parsons, ed. Talcott Parsons (New York).

Williams, Eric. 1966. *Capitalism and Slavery* (Chapel Hill, 1944; rpt., New York).

Wolf, Eric R. and Sidney W. Mintz. 1957. "Haciendas and Plantations in Middle America and the Antilles," *Social and Economic Studies* (Jamaica), 6, pp. 380–412.

Zahedieh, Nuala. 1986. "Trade, Plunder, and Economic Development in Early English Jamaica, 1655–89," *Economic History Review*, Ser. 2, 39, pp. 205–22.

# Index

# Other books in the series